AGE ASSURANCE IN PRACTICE

The Challenges of Applying It in the Real World

A Practical Guide to Understanding, Governing and Applying Age Assurance in Complex Multi-Layered Systems.

TONY ALLEN

Grosvenor House
Publishing Limited

This book is published by
Grosvenor House Publishing Ltd
Link House
140 The Broadway, Tolworth, Surrey, KT6 7HT.
www.grosvenorhousepublishing.co.uk

A CIP record for this book
is available from the British Library

Paperback ISBN 978-1-83615-750-2
eBook ISBN 978-1-83615-674-1

Foreword

In international and most national laws a child's actual and evolving capacities are at the heart of how we determine what is in the best interests of an individual child when it comes to their readiness or ability to engage with particular activities, engage in particular environments or consume or use particular goods and services.

Age is the best available proxy we have to help us determine a child's capacities and this explains why in so many countries around the world age assurance has become central to the debate about how we regulate the internet to make it both a better and a safer place for minors.

Yet, in its different forms, age assurance is still one of the most contested and misunderstood areas of digital policy and systems design.

It sits at the intersection of child protection, privacy, design, freedom of expression, access, technology and trust. As a result, it is too often framed as a question of restriction: what children should be kept away from or what must be prohibited in order to manage risk.

This framing is incomplete. The real challenge is not whether children and young people should participate in digital life (they already do) but how digital environments can be designed so that participation is more appropriate to their age and therefore their likely capacities.

Age assurance, when used well, is not a tool for exclusion. It is a foundational capability for age-appropriate design.

Tony Allen is uniquely well placed to explore this challenge. As Technical Editor of the ISO/IEC 27566 family of international standards on age assurance and through years of practical engagement with policymakers, regulators, system designers and assurance bodies across multiple jurisdictions, he has seen first-hand how age assurance works (and sometimes doesn't) in real systems. Few people have had comparable exposure to both the intentions behind age-based protections and their operational consequences. This book reflects that experience. It does not present age assurance as a simple solution, but neither does it treat it as inherently dangerous. Instead, it explains why age assurance has become unavoidable, even essential, in modern digital systems, why it can be difficult to do well, and why familiar debates framed around technology, regulation or rights in isolation often obscure the real design choices that have to and ought to be made.

Crucially, it shows how age assurance can support differentiated experiences enabling services to meet children and young people where they are on their journey to adulthood rather than forcing a single, lowest-common-denominator outcome.

The book's value lies in its refusal to offer comfort through certainty. It treats trade-offs as real, systems as dynamic and governance as an ongoing responsibility. It recognises that age assurance only earns legitimacy when it supports appropriate forms of participation, respects privacy and is accountable.

For anyone involved in shaping digital environments for children and young people, whether through policy, regulation, design, procurement or certification, this book provides a way to think clearly about age assurance as an enabling infrastructure for age-appropriate design, not as a barrier to digital life. At a time when the stakes could not be higher, that perspective is badly needed.

John Carr OBE

Contents

Foreword iii
Preface xiii
Introduction xv
Chapter 1 – Why Age Assurance Became Inevitable 1
 1.1 We encounter it every day 1
 1.2 From local judgement to global systems 2
 1.3 Societies protect children while they are becoming adults 3
 1.4 Age is not identity 5
 1.5 Privacy mischiefs before age assurance 7
 1.6 Acceptability as a condition for effectiveness 10
 1.7 Configuration as invisible policy 14
 1.8 What we mean by "age assurance" 18
Chapter 2 – Age Assurance Is a System, Not a Check 20
 2.1 The temptation of the "age check" 20
 2.2 Beyond the single check 20
 2.3 Age assurance as decision support, not truth discovery 22
 2.4 What we mean by a "system" in age assurance 23
 2.5 Components, interactions and emergent behaviour 25
 2.6 Actors, roles and invisible labour 27
 2.7 Practices, not just design 29
 2.8 Why system thinking changes everything that follows 31
Chapter 3 – What Is Age Assurance For? 33
 3.1 Outcomes first: what are we really trying to decide? 33
 3.2 Age as a proxy for risk and capacity 34
 3.3 The cost of over-precision 36

3.4 Classes of age-based decisions 37
Protection decisions 37
Eligibility decisions 38
Participation decisions 39
Exposure decisions 40
3.5 Why different classes imply different tolerances 41
3.6 Why regulation matters and where its limits lie 42
3.7 Thresholds, categories and grey areas 43
3.8 Binding: why correct attachment is a functional requirement, not a detail 45
3.9 Why pass/fail oversimplifies reality 47
3.10 Why ambiguity is unavoidable 48
3.11 Having confidence in age assurance results 49
3.12 Why accuracy alone is an unreliable guide 50
3.13 Error is inherent, not exceptional 53
Chapter 4 – Understanding ISO/IEC 27566 as a Framework, Not a Rulebook 56
4.1 Why age assurance resists simple rules 56
4.2 From prescription to characteristics 58
4.3 The mischiefs the framework is trying to contain 61
4.4 Why trade-offs are central, not accidental 63
4.5 Context as the unifying thread 65
4.6 Why configuration and practice matter more than architecture 67
4.7 What a framework can (and cannot) do 69
4.8 Reading the framework as a guide to judgement 71
Chapter 5 – Methods In The Real World: Verification, Estimation And Inference 73
5.1 Why methods are not solutions 73

5.2 What age assurance methods are actually doing 74
5.3 Behaviour changes everything 77
5.4 Privacy harms as method side-effects 83
5.5 Acceptability is what keeps methods alive 86
5.6 Why methods are combined in practice 89
5.7 Configuration determines method behaviour 91
5.8 Why method debates distract from the real work 93
Chapter 6 – From Methods to Systems: Components, Flows and Dependencies 96
6.1 Why systems matter more than components 96
6.2 Drawing the system boundary (and why it's hard) 98
6.3 Components, interfaces and the spaces between 101
6.4 Data flows are not decision flows 104
6.5 Dependencies, assumptions and fragility 106
6.6 Where confidence is gained, lost and misplaced 108
6.7 Configuration as system behaviour, not tuning 112
6.8 Why system thinking changes what "good" looks like 114
Chapter 7 – Context of Use: The Variable That Changes Everything 117
7.1 Why context is the first question, not the last 117
7.2 What we mean by "context of use" 119
7.3 How the same system behaves differently in different contexts 122
7.4 Context, risk and proportionality 125
7.5 When context assumptions break down over time 128
7.6 Why context breaks comparisons and benchmarks 130
7.7 Context as a governance responsibility 132
7.8 Why context forces judgement 136

Chapter 8 – The Trade-offs You Cannot Eliminate 138
8.1 What do we mean by trade-offs? 138
8.2 Why trade-offs are structural, not accidental 138
8.3 Functionality: when "working" is not the same as working well 141
8.4 Performance: The pressure that quietly distorts everything else 144
8.5 Security: When defensiveness becomes fragility 148
8.6 Privacy: Not a constraint, but a trade-off made visible 150
8.7 Demographic consistency: When performance depends on who is using the system 154
8.8 Acceptability: The characteristic that decides whether anything else matters 156
8.9 Where trade-offs actually live: Configuration, practice and drift 159
8.10 Owning trade-offs as a governance obligation 161
Chapter 9 – Failure Is Normal: Breakdown, Fallback and Appeal 164
9.1 Why age assurance must be designed for breakdown, not perfection 164
9.2 Contra-indicators: When evidence conflicts instead of fails 166
9.3 What breakdown looks like in practice 168
9.4 Fail-Safe behaviour: What responsible systems do when assurance breaks down 171
9.5 Functional breakdown: When the system cannot decide 172
9.6 Performance breakdown: When the system cannot keep up 175
9.7 Security breakdown: When the system is used against itself 177

9.8 Acceptability breakdown: When people stop cooperating 179
9.9 Fallback as a design choice, not a last resort 182
9.10 Appeal, contestability and legitimacy 184
9.11 What breakdown teaches us about responsibility 187
Chapter 10 – Trust And Confidence in Age Assurance 189
10.1 Why trust cannot simply be engineered 189
10.2 Accountability: The question that never goes away 192
10.3 Practice statements: Making systems, claims and responsibility legible 195
10.4 Purpose limitation and retention: When data outlives its justification 197
10.5 Transparency and auditability: Making system behaviour observable over time 199
10.6 Governance happens even when no one names it 202
10.7 Transparency as infrastructure, not disclosure 205
10.8 Change is the core governance problem 208
10.9 Monitoring, feedback and learning 211
10.10 When governance fails (and how it looks) 214
10.11 Governance as an ongoing commitment 217
Chapter 11 – Procurement, Markets and the Problem of Who is Actually Involved 220
11.1 Approaching procurement 220
11.2 Why age assurance is rarely bought as a single thing 221
11.3 The expanding cast of actors 223
11.4 Delegated and inherited assurance 226
11.5 Power asymmetry in layered ecosystems 228
11.6 How assurance is framed when there are many actors 230
11.7 Procurement with limits (and how choice is shaped) 232

11.8 When things go wrong: Who is answerable? 234
11.9 What procurement decisions really lock in 236
11.10 Rethinking "buying" in an ecosystem world 238
Chapter 12 – Certification, Testing and Assurance: Building Trust in Age Assurance Systems 241
12.1 Getting checked 241
12.2 Why age assurance needs independent assurance 241
12.3 What certification actually contributes 244
12.4 Certification, regulation and earned recognition 247
12.5 Testing, assessment and assurance as complementary activities 249
12.6 The central role of declared scope and context 252
12.7 Components, systems and layered confidence 255
12.8 Evidence as a foundation for confidence 257
12.9 Ongoing assurance and the maintenance of trust 259
12.10 Certification in multi-actor and platform ecosystems 262
12.11 Using certification well 264
Chapter 13 – Change, Monitoring and Learning Over Time 267
13.1 Why age assurance systems never stand still 267
13.2 What changes in practice (and why it matters) 269
13.3 Monitoring as the maintenance of confidence 272
13.4 Learning from use, not just design 274
13.5 Change control as a governance activity 276
13.6 Assurance over time 278
13.7 When change goes wrong 280
13.8 Maturity as the capacity to learn 282
Chapter 14 – The Future of Age Assurance (and Why It Will Never Be Finished) 285
14.1 Why age assurance has no final form 285

14.2 Why there will be no "end state" for age assurance 287
14.3 What actually changes over time 290
14.4 Convergence, fragmentation and coexistence 293
14.5 The ongoing role of standards and certification 295
14.6 Why confidence will always be contextual 297
14.7 Risks of overconfidence and premature lock-in 299
14.8 What Progress Really Looks Like in Age Assurance 302
14.9 Looking forward without predicting 304
14.10 Will we ever solve age assurance? 305

Preface

This book was written in response to a recurring problem. As age assurance has moved from a niche technical concern to a mainstream policy and operational issue, many people have found themselves required to make decisions about it without having chosen to specialise in the field. Policymakers, regulators, engineers, architects, product owners, procurement professionals, auditors and trust-and-safety teams are increasingly expected to assess age assurance claims, select approaches and defend outcomes, often under time pressure and public scrutiny.

For those readers, existing materials are frequently unsatisfying. Technical documentation tends to focus on individual methods or products. Standards provide necessary structure and shared terminology but are written for specialist audiences and are not designed to explain how age assurance systems behave in practice. Public debate often compresses age assurance into simplified narratives that obscure the real trade-offs involved. The result is a gap between formal frameworks and practical understanding.

This book exists to help close that gap.

It does so by focusing on explanation rather than instruction. Rather than prescribing designs, recommending technologies or offering compliance guidance, it examines age assurance as a system-level activity shaped by context, incentives, behaviour and governance. It explores why certain approaches have emerged, how systems behave once deployed, and what predictable challenges arise over time. The emphasis throughout is on understanding and judgement, not on providing definitive answers.

Throughout the book, the ISO/IEC 27566 family of standards is used as a reference framework for orientation and discussion.

The book does not reproduce, restate or interpret the standards' requirements, nor should it be used as a substitute for them. Readers responsible for implementation, certification or regulation must always consult the relevant standards and applicable law directly. The purpose here is to support more informed and critical engagement with those materials, not to replace them.

This is not a manual, checklist or design guide. It does not offer a single "right" way to do age assurance, nor does it attempt to resolve the underlying trade-offs that shape age-related decisions. Those trade-offs are unavoidable. They differ by context, risk, population and purpose and they evolve over time. What this book aims to provide is a way of thinking that makes those trade-offs visible, discussable and governable.

The chapters are arranged to build progressively. Early chapters establish shared concepts and mental models. Later chapters examine system behaviour, failure modes, governance, markets and assurance. The final chapters step back to consider change over time and the role of standards, evidence and judgement together. Readers may choose to read the book sequentially or selectively, depending on their needs.

Disagreement is expected. Age assurance sits at the intersection of law, technology, human behaviour and trust and reasonable people will differ in how they weigh risks and priorities. The value of this book lies not in offering final answers, but in helping readers ask better questions, recognise limitations earlier and make more defensible decisions in practice.

Age assurance is not simple and it is not static. But it can be approached responsibly. This book is written for those who need to do so without illusions and without pretending that complexity can be avoided.

Introduction

Age assurance can be done. It's not easy and whilst it is increasingly treated as a necessary feature of modern digital and physical services, it remains widely misunderstood. Public debate often frames age assurance as a question of tools or technologies or as a compliance obligation imposed by regulation. In practice, age assurance is neither a single mechanism nor a straightforward rule to be applied. It is a system-level activity that requires judgement, trade-offs and ongoing governance.

At its core, age assurance exists to support age-related eligibility decisions: whether a person should be permitted to access a service, view content, enter a space or complete a transaction for age restricted goods. These decisions are shaped by policy goals such as child protection, harm reduction, fairness, inclusion and privacy. Translating those goals into operational systems is difficult. Different contexts demand different approaches and choices that improve outcomes in one dimension often introduce risk or cost in another.

This complexity is not accidental. It involves children and young people, whose rights and vulnerabilities require particular care. It touches on identity, privacy and autonomy. It is deployed in environments that evolve rapidly, where incentives, threats and expectations change over time. As a result, there is no universal solution and no configuration that can be considered correct in all circumstances.

Much of the public discourse around age assurance is dominated by arguments about risk. Concerns are raised about privacy erosion, the chilling of lawful speech, state surveillance, the mandatory use of digital identity systems or the creation of large, attractive targets for data breach. These risks are real and deserve serious attention. But in public debate they are often treated not as challenges to be managed, but as reasons to conclude that age assurance itself is fundamentally flawed, constitutionally unsound, inherently unsafe or incompatible with a free and open society.

This framing encourages a familiar response: the search for cloaking arguments that prevent deployment altogether. Free expression is invoked as an absolute barrier. Digital identity is treated as the inevitable and unacceptable end state. Privacy risk is assumed to imply pervasive tracking. From this perspective, the safest option appears to be inaction, to declare the problem too hard, the risks too great and the trade-offs unacceptable.

This book takes a different starting point. Age assurance *is* hard. It involves trade-offs that cannot be eliminated, only governed. Poorly designed systems can and do create new harms. But the conclusion that age assurance cannot be done responsibly does not follow. Nor do policy responses that rely on blanket denial, mandatory identity infrastructures or the suspension of privacy expectations, offer credible solutions. These approaches collapse distinct questions about access, identity, surveillance and speech into a single, paralysing objection.

The central argument of this book is simple but demanding. Age assurance can be done, but only if it is approached as a system-level, context-dependent activity, governed with humility and care. The real challenge is not choosing between deployment and prohibition but understanding how age assurance systems actually behave in practice, how they fail, how they drift, how they interact with people and how confidence can be earned without overreach. Refusing to engage with those realities does not preserve rights; it merely leaves age-related decisions to be made implicitly, inconsistently and without accountability exposing children and young people to unacceptable risk and harm.

International standards such as ISO/IEC 27566 provide a shared framework for reasoning about this complexity. They establish common language and structure, helping different actors engage with age assurance in a more consistent and transparent way. At the same time, standards deliberately stop short of resolving the underlying tensions. They describe what should be considered, not what should be chosen.

Age assurance will continue to evolve. Technologies will change, regulations will diverge and converge and social expectations will shift. The purpose of this book is not to freeze that evolution, but to help readers navigate it with greater confidence, clarity and responsibility.

Chapter 1 – Why Age Assurance Became Inevitable

1.1 We encounter it every day

Every day, decisions are made about people because of their age.

Some of these decisions are visible and familiar. Buying alcohol. Entering a venue. Watching a particular film. Applying for certain jobs or services. Others are less obvious. What content is shown by default. Which features are enabled. What data may be collected. How much protection is assumed to be needed. In many cases, the individual affected may not even realise that an age-based eligibility decision has been made at all.

Most of the time, these decisions feel unremarkable. They are woven into everyday life. They reflect long-standing legal rules and social expectations about maturity, vulnerability, responsibility and protection, particularly where children and young people are concerned. For generations, societies have relied on age as a simple, widely understood proxy for capability and risk.

Because these decisions are so familiar, it is easy to assume that the mechanisms supporting them are also settled.

They are not.

What has changed is not *whether* age matters, but how age-based decisions are made and what now depends on them.

For most of history, age decisions were made locally, by people, in context. A shopkeeper exercised judgement. A teacher knew their students. A staff member checked identification when it mattered. These processes were imperfect, but their limitations were visible.

Errors were usually isolated. Accountability was personal. When judgement failed, it failed in ways that were understandable and contained.

In these environments, age-based safeguards were not systems. They were practices.

They relied on social cues, shared expectations, human discretion and physical separation. Crucially, they were embedded in environments where the consequences of error were limited by scale and proximity. Today, many age-based decisions are no longer made by people at all. They are made by systems.

Digital services, online platforms, automated kiosks, self-checkout, remote access controls and algorithmic moderation now apply age rules continuously, across borders and often without human intervention. A single design choice can affect millions of users instantly. A single configuration setting can alter outcomes globally. A single misunderstanding can persist unnoticed for years.

In this environment, age-based decisions are no longer occasional or situational. They are infrastructural.

They determine who can participate, what is visible and which risks are accepted by default. They shape experiences at scale, often invisibly. And if they fail, they fail in ways that are amplified, persistent and difficult to unwind.

It is in this context, not because of a sudden moral shift, nor because of new discoveries about childhood that age assurance systems became unavoidable.

1.2 From local judgement to global systems

The change that forced age assurance onto the agenda was not a change in social values. It was a change in operational reality.

As age-based decisions migrated into these environments, familiar controls failed to translate.

Age gates that relied on self-assertion became symbolic rather than protective. Where incentives to misrepresent age existed, misrepresentation became routine. Visual judgement disappeared entirely in online settings. Parental consent mechanisms proved uneven and easy to bypass, particularly when they were bolted onto systems that were never designed to accommodate them.

At the same time, the nature of failure changed. When an age-based safeguard fails in a physical setting, the impact is usually local and bounded. A mistake may affect one transaction, one interaction, one consumer. When the same safeguard fails in a digital or automated system, harm can be systemic, persistent and difficult to detect. Errors repeat at speed. Weaknesses can be exploited deliberately. The same design flaw can affect thousands or millions of people before it is recognised.

Operational teams experienced this shift first. What once looked like a manageable exception rate became a constant background condition. What once felt like rare misuse became routine behaviour. The gap between how a policy was written and how a system behaved in practice grew steadily wider.

Age assurance did not arise because policymakers suddenly demanded stricter controls. It arose because existing mechanisms and protections no longer functioned in the digitally enabled and technology driven environments where age-based decisions were now being made.

1.3 Societies protect children while they are becoming adults

The instinct to protect children and young people from certain forms of harm is not new.

Every society recognises that development happens over time and that experiences encountered during that development can shape future behaviour in lasting ways. Childhood and adolescence are periods in which judgement, empathy, self-restraint and responsibility are still forming. This process is uneven and individual, but its significance is widely understood.

Once these internal frameworks (sometimes described as a moral or ethical compass) are established, they tend to be relatively stable. Adults may encounter violent, explicit or disturbing material without it fundamentally altering how they behave or understand the world. Change is still possible, but it usually requires significant disruption: trauma, sustained pressure or major life events.

Earlier exposure is different. When boundaries are still being learned, repeated or unmediated exposure to harmful material can influence what feels normal, acceptable or expected. It can shape attitudes before the individual has the tools to contextualise, critique or resist what they are seeing. Timing matters, not just content. Age-based protection is a way societies try to manage that timing.

This logic long predates the digital era. For more than a century, laws have restricted children's access to alcohol, tobacco, gambling, certain workplaces, films and venues. These rules were never based on the assumption that such things are inherently corrupting. They reflect a measured belief: that exposure during development carries different risks than exposure after it.

What has changed is not the principle, but the environment in which it must be applied. Historically, age-based protections were supported by physical separation, social norms and human judgement. Certain spaces were clearly adult. Certain materials were difficult to access accidentally or at scale. Exposure usually required proximity, effort or intent.

In contemporary systems, those buffers have weakened or disappeared. Content, services and interactions that were once clearly bounded are now accessible instantly, privately and repeatedly. The distinction between adult and child spaces is no longer enforced by walls, staff or shared expectations, but by design choices embedded in systems.

As a result, long-standing social expectations have increasingly been expressed through law, regulation and policy aimed at large-scale services. Political attention has followed public concern not because something fundamentally new has been discovered about childhood, but because the mechanisms that once supported age-based protections no longer work reliably on their own.

Age assurance emerged at this intersection: between an enduring social expectation and a radically altered operational context.

1.4 Age is not identity

As age-based decisions moved into automated systems, a second problem became increasingly visible: age and identity were being treated as the same thing or at least age as a simple subset of identity.

In many traditional settings, age was established through identity. A document included a date of birth and presenting that document answered the question. In physical environments, this shortcut was often acceptable. In large-scale systems, it proved problematic.

Many age-based decisions do not require knowing who someone is. They require only confidence that an age requirement is met. Yet organisations repeatedly defaulted to identity-heavy approaches because those were familiar, auditable and already available.

Alongside this technical conflation sat a political and commercial temptation. For governments seeking to increase uptake of digital identity and for providers invested in digital ID infrastructure, age assurance appeared to offer a compelling, everyday use case: widely applicable, socially defensible and easy to explain. Proving age was presented as a simple, low-controversy entry point through which digital identity could become familiar, trusted and normalised.

Over time, this framing hardened into expectation. Age checks were no longer seen as one possible use of digital identity, but as an obvious and universal one. Mandatory requirements to use digital identity to prove age followed naturally, not always because age decisions demanded identity, but because identity systems were already available and needed justification at scale. In this way, age assurance was quietly recast from an eligibility question into an adoption strategy, further entrenching the assumption that proving age necessarily meant proving who you are.

Operationally, this created friction. Users were asked to provide documents or credentials that felt disproportionate to the activity. Support teams dealt with exclusion cases that had little to do with age and everything to do with documentation, access or circumstance. Systems designed to answer a narrow eligibility question became gateways to far broader identity processes.

This conflation also shaped system behaviour over time. Once identity data was collected, it tended to persist. Once stored, it tended to be reused. Age checks quietly became identity checks, not because policy demanded it, but because systems drifted in that direction.

Age assurance began to emerge as a way of reframing the problem: treating age-based eligibility as its own decision, rather than as a side-effect of proving who someone was.

1.5 Privacy mischiefs before age assurance

If a system needed to know whether someone was old enough, proving who that person was and extracting a date of birth seemed like a straightforward solution. Identity documents existed. ID verification vendors were available. Audit trails could be produced. From a distance, the problem appeared solved. But this approach quietly reshaped the problem it was meant to address.

A low-risk interaction inherited the same data collection practices as a high-risk one. A one-off eligibility check became the trigger for persistent records. Systems built to answer a simple question became gateways to far broader data processing.

This was not accidental.

It arose from a conceptual shortcut: treating age as a property that could only be established by proving identity. Once that assumption was made, intrusive data collection followed naturally, even where it was disproportionate to the risk being managed.

In practice, this produced a range of privacy mischiefs that were often invisible at the design stage but very visible in operation.

In practice, many of these mischiefs arose because systems were designed with data collection as the default, rather than with avoiding data collection as an objective in its own right. Teams rarely set out to minimise the data a system would ever see, instead they focused on how data would be stored, secured, justified and explained once collected. Privacy was treated as a constraint on processing, not as a design goal in itself. This inverted the problem.

The most reliable way to reduce privacy risk is not to manage data well, but to avoid collecting it at all. When non-collection is treated as a primary design objective, entire classes of risk disappear where there is nothing to retain, nothing to repurpose, nothing to breach and nothing to explain years later. Where systems fail to start from that premise, they tend to accumulate data simply because it is technically easy and organisationally familiar to do so.

One common pattern was reuse through convenience. Identity data collected to answer an age question was already present, already verified and already trusted. It became tempting to reuse it for other purposes: account recovery, fraud detection, marketing segmentation, advertising or future eligibility checks. Each reuse felt minor in isolation. Together, they transformed a narrowly justified age check into a persistent digital identity footprint.

Another pattern was normalisation through repetition. Users encountered identity-heavy age checks in contexts where they felt unnecessary or excessive. Over time, intrusive checks became the expected price of participation, even for low-risk activities. This did not increase trust; it eroded it. Users complied because they had little choice, not because the process felt legitimate.

Operational teams felt the consequences directly. Support channels filled with questions about why so much data was required. Data access and deletion requests increased. Complaints were not about age decisions themselves, but about how information was handled once collected. The system may have reduced one category of harm, but it created another that demanded constant management.

In some cases, the privacy harm was more subtle. Data retention policies designed for compliance rather than necessity meant that age-related information persisted long after its relevance had expired. Systems accumulated historical records that no longer reflected current eligibility but still carried sensitivity and risk. The risk of major data breaches materialised and the cost of managing, securing and explaining that data grew over time.

These outcomes were rarely the result of malicious intent. They emerged from operational momentum.

Once identity infrastructure was in place, it became the default answer to new problems. New services copied existing flows. New teams reused existing components. Decisions that should have prompted fresh thinking about proportionality instead inherited legacy assumptions about what was "normal".

Crucially, many of these systems *did* reduce some forms of age-related harm. That success made the secondary harms harder to challenge. Privacy issues were framed as acceptable side effects rather than as failures of design. The question became "is this allowed?" rather than "is this necessary?"

Over time, this led to a deeper misalignment between policy intent and system behaviour. Policies often spoke about protecting children while respecting rights and minimising intrusion. Systems, however, optimised for certainty and auditability, not proportionality. The result was a widening gap between what organisations believed they were doing and what users experienced in practice.

Age assurance reflects a growing recognition that privacy harm was not simply a compliance issue to be managed downstream, but a design failure upstream. Collecting more data than necessary did not just increase risk; it undermined the legitimacy of the entire age-based decision. Users who felt watched were less likely to engage honestly. Trust eroded and with it the reliability of outcomes.

Importantly, this shift did not arise because privacy suddenly became more important. It arose because privacy mischiefs made age controls less effective over time.

Systems that over-collected data became brittle. They attracted scrutiny. They required constant justification. They invited resistance, avoidance and workaround behaviour. In trying to reduce one form of harm, they created conditions that undermined the system as a whole.

Age assurance emerged, in part, as a way to reset that balance. By separating the question of age from the question of identity, it created space to ask a simpler, more disciplined question: *what is the minimum information needed to support this decision, in this context, for this risk?*

That question was largely absent from early age controls. Its absence explains why privacy became a central concern later, not as an add-on, but as a necessary condition for systems that could function sustainably at scale.

1.6 Acceptability as a condition for effectiveness

A second major reason early age controls failed was not technical at all. They failed because people did not use them in the way designers expected.

Many age-related systems appeared effective on paper. They produced results. They logged decisions. They generated metrics that suggested compliance. Yet once deployed, their real behaviour diverged sharply from their intended purpose because the systems themselves were unacceptable to those required to interact with them.

Acceptability, in this context, is not about whether people *liked* a system. It is about whether they were willing and able to use it consistently, honestly and as intended over time.

When that condition was not met, failure followed, often quietly. In operational environments, acceptability problems rarely announced themselves as outright rejection. Instead, they appeared as patterns of behaviour that gradually undermined system reliability.

These dynamics were particularly pronounced where the intended users were children and young people. Developmentally, adolescence is a period marked by boundary-testing, experimentation and a heightened sensitivity to exclusion and unfairness. Prohibition does not simply block behaviour; it often becomes part of the behaviour being negotiated.

When systems imposed blunt or poorly explained age restrictions, they did not merely deny access, they created incentives to evade, explore and share methods of circumvention. Workarounds spread socially. Techniques were learned and normalised. What might have begun as individual curiosity or frustration quickly became collective adaptation. In this context, resistance was not necessarily defiant or malicious; it was a predictable response to controls that felt arbitrary, inconsistent or misaligned with lived experience. Systems that failed to account for this behavioural reality consistently underestimated how quickly and creatively young users would adapt to them.

Some users abandoned processes entirely. Faced with friction that felt disproportionate or confusing, they simply disengaged. This exclusion was often invisible: a user who never completed a flow did not appear in failure metrics, yet the system's reach narrowed and skewed.

Other users persisted but misrepresented themselves. When the cost of honesty felt too high, false declarations became routine. This did not always look like deliberate evasion; it often appeared as resigned compliance with what the system seemed to demand. The system continued to function, but the meaning of its outputs degraded. Users were left with a persistent false age or persona degrading their online experiences.

In still other cases, users learned how to game the system. They retried repeatedly until they succeeded. They adjusted inputs incrementally. They shared tips informally. Over time, what looked like individual behaviour became collective adaptation. The system's apparent accuracy masked a growing gap between intended and actual outcomes.

In physical or semi-supervised settings, a different pattern emerged. Staff overrides became normal.

Frontline staff were rarely hostile to safeguards. More often, they were under pressure to keep queues moving, avoid confrontation or deal compassionately with edge cases the system did not handle well. When automated age decisions felt wrong or impractical, staff intervened.

These interventions were rarely documented as policy decisions. They appeared as informal workarounds: "just this once", "use your judgement", "we know this regular". Over time, such exceptions accumulated into parallel systems of human discretion that quietly replaced the automated control.

Mystery shopping exercises and tests descended into an analysis of whether the particular counter clerk or bar staff were awake and concentrating rather than any useful systemic analysis.

From the outside, the system still appeared to be in place. From the inside, it was being selectively bypassed to make daily operations workable.

Crucially, many of these behaviours did not register as failure in conventional reporting. Completion rates, where measured, often lacked context. Error rates reflected only what the system saw, not what users avoided. Overrides were invisible unless explicitly tracked.

This created a dangerous illusion of effectiveness. A system could appear compliant while producing unreliable outcomes. Metrics suggested success, while lived experience told a different story. Risk was not eliminated; it was displaced-often onto frontline staff or onto users least able to navigate the system.

Acceptability failures also distorted data in subtler ways. When users disengaged or misrepresented themselves, the remaining data skewed toward those most willing or able to comply. Systems began to "learn" from a non-representative population. Decisions that appeared consistent were consistent only within a narrowed, self-selecting group.

Over time, this created feedback loops. Designers adjusted systems based on distorted signals. Controls were tightened or loosened in response to behaviour that was itself shaped by earlier design choices. The system drifted further from its original intent, even as confidence in its operation increased.

Operational teams often recognised these patterns intuitively. They saw where friction caused drop-off. They noticed which checks triggered complaints. They understood which controls were routinely ignored. Yet without a shared language for describing acceptability as a structural concern, these observations were often dismissed as user behaviour rather than system failure.

Acceptability was treated as a "soft" issue, something to be addressed after effectiveness, if at all.

This proved to be a mistake.

A system that users refuse to engage with cannot reduce risk. A system that staff routinely ignore or override cannot reliably enforce policy. A system that encourages misrepresentation cannot produce trustworthy outcomes. In each case, the failure is not peripheral; it strikes at the system's core function.

Age assurance emerged alongside a growing recognition that acceptability is not a secondary consideration, but a precondition for effectiveness.

This did not mean that systems had to be frictionless or universally liked. It meant they had to be *usable in context*. They had to align with real human behaviour, real operational pressures and real social norms. Where they did not, they failed in predictable, repeatable ways.

Importantly, acceptability failures often interacted with privacy failures. Systems that felt intrusive were more likely to be resisted. Systems that demanded disproportionate effort were more likely to be bypassed. Each failure amplified the other.

By the time age assurance began to be articulated as a distinct approach, these lessons were widely understood in practice, even if they were rarely stated explicitly. The problem was no longer how to make age checks stronger, but how to make them *work at all* in real environments.

This shift-from asking whether a control was theoretically effective to asking whether it could function sustainably was a critical step toward the inevitability of age assurance.

1.7 Configuration as invisible policy

Many of the failures attributed to age-checking "methods" were not, in practice, failures of method at all, they were failures of configuration.

Thresholds, defaults, retry limits, fallbacks and escalation paths quietly shaped how age-related systems behaved day to day. These settings determined who was challenged, who was excluded, who was waved through and how often decisions were revisited. Yet they were rarely treated as policy choices. More often, they were treated as technical details.

Operationally, configuration choices were usually made for sensible, short-term reasons.

Defaults were adopted because they were already in use elsewhere. Thresholds were set conservatively “to be safe”. Retry limits were introduced to prevent abuse or manage load. Fallbacks were added to keep systems functioning when components failed. Escalation paths were created to handle complaints or edge cases without halting operations. Each of these decisions made sense in isolation. The problem was that, taken together, they *became the system’s real policy*.

In practice, configuration determined how strictly age rules were applied, how much uncertainty was tolerated and where risk ultimately landed. Yet these outcomes were rarely visible to those responsible for setting policy intent. The system appeared to be doing what it was told, even as its behaviour drifted.

One common pattern was conservative configuration at launch. When organisations first deployed age controls, they often configured them cautiously. The aim was to demonstrate seriousness and reduce legal exposure. Operational teams then encountered the consequences.

Legitimate users were excluded. Complaints increased. Staff faced pressure to intervene. In response, configurations were adjusted incrementally: an extra retry here, a broader fallback there, a slightly lower threshold to reduce friction. None of these changes were framed as policy revisions. They were framed as operational tuning.

Over time, the cumulative effect was significant. What began as a strict control became more permissive. Or, in some cases, the opposite occurred: repeated attempts to close perceived loopholes resulted in ever-tightening settings that increased exclusion and override behaviour. In both cases, the system’s behaviour diverged from its original intent, without any explicit decision to change that intent.

Another pattern was copying configuration between contexts. An age control configured for a high-risk environment was reused in a lower-risk one because it was already available and "known to work". The same thresholds, retry limits and escalation rules were applied, even though the consequences of error were very different.

Operationally, this created friction where none had previously existed. Users were subjected to controls that felt excessive. Staff struggled to explain why simple interactions required complex checks. Over time, workarounds emerged, undermining the control's purpose.

Yet from a systems perspective, nothing appeared wrong. The configuration was "standard". The method was "approved". The problem lay in the mismatch between configuration and context.

Configuration drift was another common feature. Systems rarely remained static. Usage patterns changed. Threat models evolved. User populations shifted. Each change prompted small configuration adjustments. Rarely were these reviewed holistically. More often, they accumulated as a series of reactive fixes.

What the system did in practice gradually diverged from what anyone believed it did.

In some cases organisations discovered this only after an incident or external scrutiny. Logs showed decisions being made in ways that surprised those responsible. Thresholds had been altered years earlier. Fallbacks were being triggered far more often than expected. Escalation paths had become default paths.

At that point, reconstructing *why* the system behaved as it did was difficult. Configuration history was incomplete. Rationale was undocumented. Decisions that had significant policy implications had been made incrementally, by different teams, under different pressures.

From an operational standpoint, configuration choices often felt reversible and low-risk. A threshold could be adjusted. A retry added. A fallback widened. In reality, each change reshaped user behaviour, staff behaviour and system outcomes in ways that were hard to predict.

Configuration also interacted with acceptability in powerful ways. Settings that increased friction encouraged disengagement. Settings that allowed repeated retries encouraged gaming. Settings that relied on fallback pathways shifted decision-making to less visible parts of the system. Each adjustment altered incentives and behaviours, often in ways that were only apparent months later.

Two organisations using the same underlying approach could therefore experience radically different outcomes. One might report smooth operation and low complaint volumes, while quietly accepting higher risk. Another might report strict enforcement and high exclusion, accompanied by frequent overrides and workarounds.

The difference was not the method. It was how the system was configured and how those configurations evolved over time.

It became clear that configuration was not a neutral technical layer sitting beneath policy. It was where policy was enacted, modified and, sometimes, undermined. Treating configuration as invisible meant treating real-world outcomes as accidental rather than as the result of choices.

Once age-based decisions moved into large-scale systems, those choices needed to be made visible, deliberate and reviewable. Without that, systems could not be said to implement policy at all, they merely approximated it, unpredictably.

This recognition did not arise from theory. It arose from lived experience: from systems that behaved "correctly" in design documents but very differently in operation; from teams struggling to explain outcomes they did not intend; and from organisations discovering that the same control could produce radically different results depending on how it was set up.

1.8 What we mean by "age assurance"

At its simplest, age assurance is about answering one question:

Is this person old enough for this?

Age assurance refers to the ways organisations gain confidence about a person's age or age range, in order to support an age-based eligibility decision. The outcome is usually limited: above or below a threshold or within a defined range. It is rarely about establishing a specific age.

What distinguishes age assurance is that it focuses on eligibility, not identity.

Age assurance is contextual. The level of confidence required depends on what is at stake. Different decisions justify different levels of friction, intrusion and certainty.

It does not promise perfect accuracy. It accepts uncertainty and manages it deliberately. Its purpose is to reduce foreseeable harm while avoiding unnecessary secondary harms created by poorly aligned systems. Age-based decisions involve unavoidable tensions.

Effectiveness competes with privacy. Assurance competes with accessibility. Consistency competes with context. Automation competes with judgement. No system can optimise all of these simultaneously and pretending otherwise produces brittle, untrustworthy outcomes.

This is why age assurance is best understood not as a single mechanism or solution, but as a response to systemic misalignment: between policy intent and operational reality, between stated values and lived experience and between what systems are assumed to do and what they actually do in practice.

Chapter 2 – Age Assurance Is a System, Not a Check

2.1 The temptation of the "age check"

When people first encounter age assurance, they often imagine a single moment of truth. A screen appears, a question is asked, a result is returned and the problem is solved.

This instinct is understandable. Many familiar safeguards work this way. We show identification at a door. We tick a box online. We enter a date of birth and move on. These interactions are brief, transactional and easy to explain. It feels natural to assume that age assurance should follow the same pattern: one action, one answer, one decision.

For a long time, many systems were designed on exactly this assumption.

What experience revealed, however, is that this mental model does not survive contact with real-world use at scale. Not because the checks themselves were poorly designed, but because age assurance does not operate as a single action. It operates within a wider environment of people, incentives, expectations, technologies and rules. When age assurance is treated as a momentary check, most of the forces that shape its effectiveness remain invisible.

Age assurance is not a moment.

It is a system.

2.2 Beyond the single check

Real age assurance systems operate across time, across interactions and across changing conditions. Users return. Contexts shift. Risk profiles evolve. Decisions are revisited, implicitly or explicitly.

Confidence can degrade or strengthen depending on what happens next. A model that treats age assurance as a one-off decision struggles to accommodate this reality.

One of the first signs of the mismatch is repetition. In many services, age-related decisions are not made once, but repeatedly. Access may be requested again after time has passed. Different features may carry different thresholds. Users may move between devices, locations or accounts. Each repetition introduces questions about whether earlier decisions still apply and what should happen when they do not.

In a "single check" model, repetition is awkward. Either the check is repeated mechanically creating friction and frustration or it is assumed to remain valid indefinitely, increasing exposure to risk. Neither approach is inherently wrong, but both are system design choices, not properties of the check itself.

A second limitation is pass/fail thinking. Checks are often described as if they produce a binary answer: old enough or not, allowed or denied. In practice, age assurance rarely operates with such clarity. Even where the outcome must ultimately be binary, the confidence behind it is not. Systems that acknowledge uncertainty can respond proportionately, using alternative routes or safeguards when confidence is low. Systems that insist on definitiveness tend to push uncertainty out of sight, where it reappears later as complaints, workarounds or unexpected harm.

Failure handling exposes this most clearly. In a simple "single check" model, failure is treated as an endpoint: access is denied and the interaction ends. In real systems, failure is rarely that simple. Users may try again, seek help, switch channels or persist until they find a path that works. Staff may intervene. Exceptions may be made. Each of these responses becomes part of how the system actually behaves and, overall, how effective it is.

What matters, then, is not only whether a check passes or fails, but what the system does next. How failure is handled, explained, appealed or mitigated often has as much influence on outcomes as the initial decision. A model that focuses narrowly on the decision point struggles to account for this.

Importantly, the shortcomings of the "single check" model are not a sign that age assurance cannot work. They are a sign that the model is incomplete. Many early implementations disappointed not because the underlying tools were incapable, but because they were placed into systems that expected them to behave as isolated gatekeepers rather than as contributors to an ongoing decision process.

Once this is recognised, the question changes. It is no longer "how do we design a better check?", but "how do we design a system in which age-related decisions remain appropriate, proportionate and effective over time?" That shift opens a more constructive design space.

Age assurance can be made to work but only once it is understood as something more than a single moment of decision.

2.3 Age assurance as decision support, not truth discovery

A key step in understanding age assurance is recognising what it is actually trying to do.

Age assurance is not about discovering an objective or absolute truth about a person's age. In most contexts, it does not need to establish an exact date of birth or a permanent fact about someone's identity. What it is doing instead is supporting a decision: whether to allow, restrict or modify access in a particular situation.

Every age-based decision involves judgement. Decisions differ in what is at stake, in how much risk is acceptable and in how errors are handled. The level of confidence required to access low-risk content is not the same as that required to enter a regulated venue or purchase a restricted product. Nor are the consequences of a wrong decision the same in every case.

2.4 What we mean by a "system" in age assurance

If age assurance is more than a single check, the obvious next question is: what is it instead?

When people hear the word "system", they often think first of technology: software, services, interfaces or devices. In age assurance, this is a tempting shortcut. A particular tool is deployed, a service is integrated and it is described as "the age assurance system".

This way of speaking is convenient, but it is incomplete.

In age assurance, a system is the whole arrangement through which age-related decisions are produced and acted upon. That arrangement includes technology, but it also includes people, processes, rules, incentives and oversight. None of these elements is optional and none operates independently.

A helpful way to think about a system is to ask not "what does it consist of?", but "what does it do?". In this case, it enables age-based eligibility decisions to be made repeatedly, at scale, in a way that aligns with intent and manages risk over time. If an element influences that outcome in practice, it is part of the system, whether or not it was formally designed as such.

This perspective helps explain why age assurance often felt more difficult than expected in early deployments. Attention was focused on individual tools or checkpoints, while much of the surrounding system that shaped their behaviour remained implicit. Decisions were treated as if they were being discovered by a mechanism, rather than produced by an arrangement.

That distinction matters. Age assurance systems produce a decision by combining inputs, assumptions, thresholds and responses within a defined context. The confidence attached to that decision is not an intrinsic property of a tool; it is an outcome of how the system is designed and operated.

It is therefore useful to distinguish between components, services and systems. A component is a discrete part that performs a function. A service is a packaged offering that may include one or more components, often delivered by an age assurance service provider. A system is the wider arrangement in which components and services are selected, configured, combined, overseen and responded to in practice.

Confusion between these levels has been a recurring source of misunderstanding. When a component performs well in isolation, it is easy to assume that deploying it will produce good outcomes. When a service is evaluated, it is tempting to treat that evaluation as a proxy for system effectiveness. In reality, neither assumption holds reliably without considering how the surrounding system behaves.

Outcomes belong to systems, not tools.

This becomes clearer when system boundaries are drawn too narrowly. If the boundary is drawn tightly around a technical capability, many influences are pushed outside the frame: user behaviour, staff intervention, exception handling, communication and feedback loops. The system appears simpler, but only because much of its behaviour has been excluded from view. In practice, those excluded elements continue to shape outcomes. They are not disturbances; they are part of how the system functions.

Drawing the system boundary more honestly does not make age assurance harder. It makes it more understandable. It becomes easier to see why the same tool can produce very different outcomes in different contexts, why improvements often come from changes in process or configuration rather than replacement and why responsibility and risk cannot be localised to a single step.

Crucially, this framing makes it clear that age assurance is achievable. The challenge has never been the absence of capable tools. It has been the tendency to treat tools as if they could carry system-level responsibility on their own. Once that burden is lifted, age assurance becomes something that can be designed, operated and improved deliberately.

2.5 Components, interactions and emergent behaviour

Once age assurance is understood as a system rather than a single check, attention naturally turns to its parts. Systems are made up of components and it is tempting to assume that if each component performs well, the system as a whole will behave as intended.

In practice, this assumption rarely holds.

The reason is not that components are unimportant. It is that system behaviour is shaped less by what components do individually than by how they interact with one another and by how those interactions evolve over time.

Components are usually designed, tested and evaluated in isolation. When a component meets its criteria, it is reasonable to describe it as "working". What that description does not capture is how the component behaves once it is placed into a live system, connected to other components, operated by people and exposed to the real world.

Age assurance systems are not static assemblies. They are networks of interaction. Information flows between parts. Decisions in one place shape behaviour elsewhere. Small mismatches accumulate. Over time, the system begins to behave in ways that no single component was designed to produce.

This is often described as emergent behaviour. The term can sound abstract, but the idea is simple: emergent behaviour is what happens when a system does something meaningful that cannot be attributed to any one part alone.

In age assurance, this can take many forms. A component may be accurate in controlled conditions, but when integrated into a broader service its outputs are used in ways the designers did not anticipate. A retry mechanism intended to help legitimate users may also enable repeated attempts until a desired outcome is reached. A fallback designed for rare failures may quietly become the default path for many users. None of these outcomes requires a faulty component. They arise from interaction.

Interfaces are especially important here. Interfaces are where components meet: where data is passed, decisions are handed off or responsibility shifts. In many systems, these interfaces matter more than the internal workings of the components themselves. Information that is meaningful in one context may be misunderstood in another. Confidence may be flattened into a binary signal. Nuance may be lost as decisions propagate. Over time, these small distortions shape behaviour.

This helps explain why systems that appear to work well in testing or early deployment may behave differently once scaled. Testing environments are necessarily bounded. They fix assumptions, limit interaction and constrain behaviour. Live systems do not. As systems are used repeatedly, users learn how they respond and adapt. Staff learn where the system struggles and compensate. Operators tune settings to manage load or complaints. Each adjustment is rational in isolation. Together, they change how the system behaves.

Importantly, this change is not random. Systems tend to stabilise around patterns that balance effort, risk and reward. If a pathway is easier, it will be used more. If a failure mode is costly, it will be avoided or softened. Behaviour evolves through interaction, not through a single decision to change the system.

Seen through this lens, emergent behaviour is not a flaw to be eliminated. It is a property to be understood and managed. Systems that acknowledge emergence can monitor behaviour over time, adjust interactions deliberately and create feedback loops that support learning. Systems that ignore it tend to chase symptoms: a component is tightened or replaced and new behaviour emerges elsewhere.

For age assurance, this is an encouraging conclusion. It suggests that effectiveness does not depend on finding a perfect component or a flawless design. It depends on understanding how components interact, how behaviour emerges and how the system responds over time.

2.6 Actors, roles and invisible labour

Age assurance systems do not operate on their own. They are sustained, interpreted and corrected by people.

Some roles are obvious. Users interact with systems directly. Staff handle questions, complaints or exceptions. Providers design and operate services that perform age-related functions. Relying parties use system outputs to make decisions. Regulators and oversight bodies respond when expectations change.

Other roles are less visible, but no less important.

A defining feature of age assurance systems in practice is the amount of unplanned human effort required to keep them functioning acceptably. This work is rarely captured in system diagrams or design documents, yet it plays a decisive role in shaping outcomes. It includes the informal, reactive and adaptive effort that keeps a system usable and defensible at scale.

Invisible labour appears wherever a system's assumptions meet reality. Frontline staff encounter users who do not fit expected patterns, struggle with interfaces or are unfairly excluded by default paths. In responding, staff make judgement calls: when to escalate, when to allow a retry, when to apply discretion and when to intervene manually. These actions are rarely framed as age assurance decisions, but they directly affect who gains access and under what conditions.

Users also perform their own version of invisible labour. They learn how systems behave, which paths are smoother and what actions lead to success. Some of this learning supports legitimate access, helping users navigate unfamiliar processes. Some of it exploits gaps or inconsistencies. In both cases, user behaviour feeds back into system operation.

Operators and administrators perform another kind of invisible labour. They monitor metrics, respond to incidents, adjust settings and manage trade-offs between risk, performance and user experience. A threshold is tweaked to reduce false rejections. A fallback is expanded to manage volume. A warning is softened to reduce complaints. Each change makes sense locally. Collectively, they reshape the system.

Much of this effort sits outside formal responsibility structures. Design documents describe intended behaviour. Policies describe desired outcomes. Contracts describe roles at a high level. The day-to-day work that reconciles these elements is often unacknowledged.

This matters because responsibility tends to follow effort. When outcomes are contested, attention often turns to those closest to the point of failure. Frontline staff are asked why they allowed access. Operators are asked why settings were changed. Users are blamed for misuse. These responses can obscure a simpler truth: the system was already relying on these actors to compensate for its limitations.

Recognising invisible labour does not mean criticising it. It is often the reason systems succeed at all. Human flexibility allows systems to cope with ambiguity, diversity and change. The problem arises when systems quietly depend on that flexibility while formally denying its existence. When discretion is exercised but not recognised, it cannot be supported, reviewed or improved. When responsibility is implicit, accountability becomes confused. When people are expected to absorb risk without authority, trust erodes.

Making roles visible is therefore not about adding bureaucracy. It is about aligning responsibility with reality. It also helps explain why similar tools can produce different outcomes across organisations: the surrounding practices, such as training, escalation norms, tolerance for risk and organisational culture, shape behaviour as much as the components do.

2.7 Practices, not just design

Age assurance systems are often described in terms of design: the rules they apply, the steps users are expected to follow and the safeguards meant to operate under defined conditions. These descriptions are necessary, but they are never sufficient.

What ultimately determines how an age assurance system behaves is not just what is written down, but what people actually do.

This difference between documented process and lived practice exists in all complex systems, but it is especially pronounced in age assurance. This is not a sign that the original design was flawed. It is a sign that design alone cannot anticipate every context, user or interaction. Practice fills the gaps.

The difficulty arises when systems depend on practice while pretending they do not. When formal descriptions assume ideal behaviour, but real outcomes rely on informal adaptation, a disconnect emerges. Decisions are made, but the basis for those decisions is obscured. Responsibility is exercised but not clearly allocated. Risk is managed, but not transparently.

In age assurance, this disconnect often surfaces around uncertainty. Formal processes may describe clear decision points, but lived practice deals with ambiguity: borderline cases, partial failures, conflicting signals or users who do not fit expected profiles. Practice determines whether such cases are resolved through escalation, discretion, repetition or exclusion.

Because these responses are rarely captured formally, they can undermine assurance in subtle ways. A system may appear strict on paper but permissive in practice. It may appear consistent while relying on discretionary judgement applied unevenly. Conversely, a system may appear exclusionary, while informal practices quietly soften its impact. None of these outcomes is inherently wrong. The problem is not that practice exists, but that it is often invisible to those who assume the system behaves as designed.

This invisibility makes learning difficult. If practice is not acknowledged, it cannot be reviewed, improved or aligned with intent. Adjustments happen locally and reactively. Over time, the system evolves without a shared understanding of how or why.

There is also a fragility to informal practice. It depends on experience, local culture and tacit knowledge. Staff turnover organisational change or external scrutiny can disrupt it suddenly, exposing assumptions that were never made explicit.

From a system perspective, this is a missed opportunity. Practices are not just workarounds. They are sources of insight. They reveal where design assumptions are strained, where configuration choices are misaligned and where user needs are not fully met. They show how people interpret rules, manage risk and balance competing demands in real time.

Systems that recognise this can treat practice as something to be surfaced and shaped, rather than tolerated quietly. They can decide deliberately where discretion should live, rather than letting it drift. This does not require rigid formalisation. It requires acknowledgement, reflection and alignment.

In effective age assurance systems, there is an explicit relationship between design, configuration and practice. Design sets the intended structure. Configuration expresses policy choices in operational form. Practice reflects how those choices play out in reality. When these layers are aligned, systems are more resilient, more transparent and easier to govern. When they are misaligned, assurance becomes performative rather than real.

2.8 Why system thinking changes everything that follows

By this point, the limits of thinking in terms of single checks should be clear. Not because checks are useless, but because they are only ever one part of a much larger picture.

Age assurance outcomes emerge from systems. They are shaped by interactions, by configuration, by practice and by the way responsibility and judgement are distributed across people and processes. Once this is recognised, many of the frustrations that have surrounded age assurance begin to make sense.

What once appeared to be failures of tools are more accurately understood as mismatches between mental models and operational reality. What seemed like inconsistency often turns out to be unmanaged discretion. What felt like overreach or underperformance frequently reflects unexamined configuration choices or informal practices doing essential work.

Seen through a system lens, these are not reasons to abandon age assurance. They are reasons to approach it more deliberately.

This shift in perspective changes the kinds of questions that matter. Instead of asking whether a particular method is "good enough" in isolation, attention turns to how approaches behave in context, how they interact with users and operators and how they perform over time. Instead of searching for a definitive solution, the focus moves to managing trade-offs transparently and proportionately.

This is where age assurance becomes governable.

System thinking makes it possible to talk sensibly about outcomes. Outcomes are not simply the result of individual decisions; they are patterns that emerge across repeated interactions. They reflect how risk is managed in practice, how access is enabled or constrained and how confidence is maintained as conditions change.

Age assurance is not a single check to be passed or failed. It is an ongoing capability that can be designed, operated and improved over time. Understanding it as a system is what makes that possible.

Chapter 3 – What Is Age Assurance For?

3.1 Outcomes first: what are we really trying to decide?

Age assurance debates often begin with the wrong question. They start by asking how old someone is or how accurately that age can be determined. This framing feels natural, but it obscures the real problem.

Age assurance systems are not built to discover truth for its own sake. They are built to support decisions under uncertainty, decisions about access, protection, participation and risk. When those decisions are poorly understood, no amount of technical sophistication can compensate.

This chapter reframes age assurance around outcomes. It explains why age is a proxy rather than a target, why certainty is rarely achievable or necessary and why many failures in age assurance can be traced back to decisions that were never properly defined.

The most instinctive way to think about age assurance is also the most misleading. It frames the problem as one of discovery: *How old is this person?* If that question can be answered accurately enough, the rest appears straightforward.

This framing feels natural because it mirrors how age works in everyday life. Age is treated as an immutable attribute, anchored to a date of birth and increasing predictably over time. When age matters socially or legally, it often appears as a simple fact to be checked and confirmed. From this perspective, age assurance looks like a simple problem of measurement.

In practice, this intuition leads systems in the wrong direction.

Organisations do not need to know how old someone is in the abstract. They need to decide what to do next. Age matters only because it is used to support decisions about access, protection, participation or exposure. Once this is recognised, the apparent centrality of "knowing age" begins to dissolve.

Age, in age assurance, is not the target. It is a proxy.

3.2 Age as a proxy for risk and capacity

Age is used because it correlates, imperfectly but usefully, with other factors: vulnerability, legal responsibility, cognitive capacity, social expectations and exposure to harm. These are the things decision-makers actually care about. Age is a shorthand that allows those concerns to be operationalised at scale.

This proxy role is crucial. It explains why age thresholds exist at all, why they vary across jurisdictions and why they are periodically revised. Thresholds are not discoveries about human biology; they are judgements about risk tolerance and social policy.

Once age is understood as a proxy, it becomes clear why exact age is often unnecessary. Many age-based decisions do not become better simply because the system knows whether someone is fourteen years and three months old rather than fourteen years and nine months old. The decision rarely turns on that distinction. What matters is whether the person is likely to fall on one side or the other of a boundary that has been set for a particular purpose.

In these cases, demanding precision is not neutral. It reshapes systems toward greater data collection, stronger identity binding and higher friction – often without improving the quality of the decision being made.

A useful way to clarify this distinction is to separate *facts* from *decisions*.

Facts are claims about the world: a recorded date of birth, a historical event, a verified document. Decisions are actions taken under conditions of uncertainty, guided by rules, values and risk assessments.

Age assurance operates squarely in the second domain. Even when it draws on factual inputs, it does so in order to support a choice: allow or deny access, permit or restrict participation, escalate or proceed.

Confusing these domains leads to persistent problems. Systems are judged by how well they appear to establish facts – their classification accuracy, rather than by how well they support decisions responsibly. Failures are framed as inaccuracies rather than misalignments between outcome and purpose. Technical debates substitute for unresolved policy questions.

Reframing age assurance as decision support cuts through this confusion. It forces attention onto what the system is actually expected to do and under what conditions it can be said to have succeeded.

Many of the most common age-based decisions require surprisingly little information.

A service deciding whether to apply child protections does not need a full identity profile. A venue deciding whether to allow entry does not need a precise age. A platform moderating content exposure does not need a permanent record of who a user is.

What these decisions require is *sufficient confidence* that a person falls into a relevant category for the duration of the interaction. That confidence may come from different sources, vary in strength and degrade over time, but it is always tied to the decision being made, not to an abstract notion of truth.

Over-precision in this context can be actively harmful. It increases the amount of personal data processed. It raises expectations of certainty that cannot be sustained. It hardens boundaries that are, in reality, socially constructed and context dependent.

Paradoxically, systems that aim to "know age" too precisely often perform worse at the task that actually matters making proportionate, defensible decisions in the real world.

3.3 The cost of over-precision

The harms of over-precision are not theoretical. They appear repeatedly in practice.

When systems are designed to extract exact age, they tend to accumulate data beyond what is necessary for the decision at hand. This increases privacy risk, even when the additional data is rarely used. It also increases the consequences of error, because precise claims invite stronger reliance.

Over-precision also reduces resilience. Systems optimised for narrow, deterministic outcomes struggle when inputs are ambiguous, environments change or users behave unexpectedly. Edge cases become failures rather than normal conditions to be managed.

Finally, over-precision distorts accountability. When a system claims certainty, any failure appears exceptional and blameworthy. When uncertainty is acknowledged, responsibility can be distributed more realistically across design, governance and use.

Recognising that precision has costs as well as benefits is a necessary step toward more mature age assurance systems.

The central question of age assurance is therefore not *"How old is this person?"* but *"What decision do we need to make and how confident do we need to be to make it responsibly?"*

This reframing has far-reaching implications. It shifts attention from tools to outcomes, from accuracy to proportionality and from certainty to judgement. It also makes visible the fact that different decisions legitimately require different answers to that question.

Some decisions justify higher confidence and greater friction. Others do not. Some errors are tolerable; others are not. These distinctions cannot be resolved by technical means alone. They are inherent to the decision itself.

By starting with the decision rather than the fact, age assurance becomes easier to reason about, even if it becomes harder to oversimplify.

3.4 Classes of age-based decisions

Once age assurance is understood as decision support rather than fact-finding, an immediate complication emerges not all age-based decisions are the same.

In practice, age is used to support a wide variety of decisions, each with different purposes, risks and consequences. Treating them as interchangeable leads to poorly aligned systems and misplaced expectations. Yet this is exactly what often happens. A control designed for one kind of decision is reused for another and when it fails, the failure is blamed on technology rather than on outcome design.

To reason clearly about age assurance, it is therefore necessary to distinguish between different *classes* of age-based decisions. These classes are not rigid categories, but they capture recurring patterns that matter for how outcomes should be framed.

Protection decisions

Protection decisions are concerned primarily with preventing harm. Their purpose is to reduce the likelihood that children or vulnerable individuals are exposed to content, interactions or environments that could reasonably be expected to cause damage.

Examples include decisions about access to explicit material, exposure to high-risk online interactions or participation in environments known to create particular vulnerabilities for younger users.

In protection decisions, the dominant concern is *risk avoidance*. The cost of allowing access to someone who should have been protected is often seen as high, while the cost of restricting access to someone who could safely proceed is sometimes treated as secondary. As a result, protection decisions often tolerate higher rates of exclusion in order to minimise exposure.

This asymmetry matters. Systems designed around protection outcomes frequently err on the side of caution and they often justify friction, false negatives or repeated challenges as acceptable safeguards. Whether that judgement is appropriate depends on context, but the underlying logic is distinct.

Problems arise when protection-oriented outcomes are silently reused elsewhere. Controls optimised to avoid harm can become unnecessarily restrictive when applied to decisions where participation, autonomy or inclusion are more central concerns.

Eligibility decisions

Eligibility decisions determine whether an individual is legally or contractually permitted to access goods, services or a space. These decisions are often closely tied to regulation, liability and enforcement.

Examples include purchasing restricted products, entering age-regulated venues or engaging in activities where legal thresholds are explicit and consequences for non-compliance are significant.

In eligibility decisions, accuracy and defensibility are often prioritised. Organisations are concerned not only with making the right call, but with being able to demonstrate that the call was made responsibly. This tends to raise the bar for confidence and encourages more formalised outcomes.

However, eligibility decisions are still decisions under uncertainty. They do not magically become factual simply because a legal threshold is involved. The appearance of certainty can mask the same trade-offs present elsewhere: exclusion versus access, burden versus risk, enforcement versus proportionality. Importantly, most of the laws globally dictating these eligibility requirements also provide that systems are "reasonable" and "operated with diligence" – not that they are foolproof or 100% accurate.

When eligibility outcomes are treated as universally applicable, they can crowd out other decision types. Systems begin to assume that every age-based interaction requires the same level of assurance, even when the underlying risks differ substantially.

Participation decisions

Participation decisions shape how and whether individuals can engage in social, educational or digital spaces. Unlike protection or eligibility decisions, participation is not always about prohibition. It is often about *modulation* or the delivery of age-appropriate experience.

Examples include decisions about account features, modes of interaction, levels of autonomy or the availability of safeguards as users move through different stages of development.

Participation decisions recognise that age is not a binary switch but a continuum. They often involve graduated outcomes rather than simple allow-or-deny logic. The aim is not merely to prevent harm or enforce rules, but to support appropriate engagement over time.

These decisions are particularly sensitive to acceptability. Excessive restriction can undermine trust, discourage participation or push users toward less visible or more harmful spaces. Under-restriction can expose users to risks they are not prepared to manage.

When participation outcomes are forced into rigid, eligibility-style frames, systems become brittle. They struggle to accommodate growth, variation and context and they often provoke workarounds that defeat their original purpose.

Exposure decisions

Exposure decisions focus on what someone encounters, rather than whether they are allowed to participate at all. They are common in content-rich environments, where the question is not access versus denial, but *degree* and *type* of exposure.

Examples include content ranking, filtering, recommendation systems or the presentation of warnings and prompts. These decisions often operate continuously and adaptively, rather than at a single checkpoint.

Exposure decisions tolerate ambiguity by design. They rarely require strong claims about age. Instead, they adjust experience based on signals, patterns and inferred categories. Their effectiveness depends less on precision and more on responsiveness.

However, exposure decisions can create cumulative effects. Small adjustments, applied repeatedly, can shape behaviour, expectations and opportunities over time. When exposure outcomes are poorly framed, they can lead to subtle forms of exclusion or over-surveillance.

Treating exposure decisions as if they required the same certainty as eligibility decisions often leads to over-collection of data and disproportionate controls, undermining the very flexibility that makes them effective.

3.5 Why different classes imply different tolerances

Each class of decision carries different implications for:

- acceptable uncertainty,
- tolerable error,
- reversibility of outcomes,
- and distribution of harm.

Protection decisions may tolerate higher false negatives. Participation decisions may not. Eligibility decisions often prioritise auditability. Exposure decisions prioritise adaptability.

These differences are not technical. They are normative. They reflect judgements about risk, responsibility and social values. When they are ignored, systems default to the most restrictive assumptions, because restriction feels safer than discretion.

This is one reason age assurance systems often become more intrusive over time. Outcomes drift toward the strictest interpretation, not because it is always justified, but because distinctions between decision types were never made explicit.

A recurring failure mode in age assurance is the reuse of outcomes across decision classes.

A threshold designed to protect children from harm is reused to determine participation rights. An eligibility control is applied to exposure management. A system built to satisfy regulatory scrutiny becomes the template for all age-based interactions.

Initially, this appears efficient. Over time, it creates friction, exclusion and loss of trust.

Users experience controls as arbitrary or excessive. Staff struggle with edge cases. Organisations face pressure to soften enforcement informally. The system still appears to "work" on paper, but its real-world behaviour drifts.

These failures are often misdiagnosed as problems of accuracy or implementation. In reality, they stem from outcome mismatch: the system is answering the wrong question for the decision at hand.

3.6 Why regulation matters and where its limits lie

Regulation plays a critical role in age-based eligibility requirements. It does not merely constrain behaviour, it communicates social norms, expectations and boundaries. Prohibitions on selling alcohol or tobacco to children, for example, remain appropriate even though they are not perfectly enforced. Their value lies not in eliminating all violations, but in making clear what society considers acceptable and unacceptable and thus significantly reducing exposure to harm if not wholly eliminating it.

Age assurance operates within this normative framework. Regulation establishes the *why* of age restrictions, what is being protected, restricted or enabled and on whose behalf. Without regulation, age assurance would lack legitimacy and coherence.

At the same time, law must generalise. It expresses intent at a high level, using thresholds and categories that can be applied consistently across diverse contexts. This generalisation is a strength, not a flaw. It allows expectations to be shared and responsibilities to be assigned.

Difficulties arise not because regulation exists, but because it is sometimes treated as if it were a complete specification for system behaviour.

When distinctions between different classes of age-based decisions are not recovered at the design and operational level, compliance can become a proxy for good outcomes. Organisations focus on meeting formal requirements rather than on supporting the underlying decisions in context. Systems may then satisfy regulatory tests while behaving in ways that feel misaligned with the intent those regulations were meant to express.

When such misalignments surface, the instinctive response is often to tighten controls or increase enforcement. While sometimes necessary, this can also reinforce a cycle in which regulation is asked to do work better suited to system design, governance and practice.

Recognising different classes of age-based decisions does not weaken regulation. It strengthens its application. It allows regulatory intent to be translated into outcomes that are proportionate, comprehensible and aligned with real-world behaviour, rather than relying on uniform controls to solve fundamentally different decision problems.

3.7 Thresholds, categories and grey areas

Age-based eligibility decisions are almost always structured around boundaries. A person is old enough or they are not; permitted or restricted; treated as a child or as an adult. These thresholds create the appearance of clarity and in policy terms they often serve an important purpose. They translate complex social judgements into rules that can be applied consistently.

In practice, however, thresholds do not eliminate ambiguity. They concentrate it.

Every age threshold produces a zone of uncertainty around itself. People near the boundary are not rare exceptions; they are a predictable and recurring feature of age assurance systems. Most operational complexity, user friction and dispute arises not far from the threshold, but right on top of it.

Understanding this is essential. Grey areas are not a failure mode to be engineered away. They are an inherent consequence of using age as a decision criterion.

Binary thresholds are attractive because they are simple. They reduce decisions to a pass or fail outcome and appear easy to explain, audit and enforce. From a distance, they look clean and objective.

At scale, their limitations become apparent.

A binary threshold collapses a continuous attribute into a single dividing line. On one side, access is granted; on the other, it is denied. The difference between a person just above the threshold and one just below it may be negligible in terms of risk or capacity, yet the outcome changes abruptly.

This creates pressure at the boundary. Users test it. Systems see repeated attempts clustered around it. Small variations in inputs lead to large changes in outcomes. What appears to be a simple rule becomes a source of instability.

Binary thresholds therefore do not remove judgement from age-based decisions. They merely relocate it – into system design, configuration and exception handling.

To manage this instability, many systems implicitly or explicitly introduce categories.

Instead of a single boundary, there may be ranges: younger children, adolescents, young adults. Instead of a single outcome, there may be graduated responses: additional safeguards, reduced functionality, warnings or prompts.

These tiered outcomes acknowledge a basic reality: age-related capacity and risk do not change abruptly at a single moment. They shift gradually, unevenly and contextually.

Categorisation does not eliminate ambiguity, but it distributes it. It allows systems to respond proportionately rather than absolutely. It also makes visible what binary thresholds often conceal: that age-based decisions are always approximations.

However, categories introduce their own challenges. They require clearer outcome definitions, more nuanced communication and more deliberate configuration. When they are bolted onto systems designed for pass/fail logic, they can appear inconsistent or arbitrary.

The presence of categories is therefore not a sign of indecision. It is a sign that the system is grappling with reality.

A common mistake in age assurance design is to treat borderline cases as exceptional.

In practice, they are not.

Designing systems as if the majority of interactions will be clear-cut leads to brittle behaviour. Systems perform well in idealised cases but struggle precisely where they are most needed.

Recognising borderline ages as the operational norm rather than the exception changes design priorities. It shifts attention from optimising average performance to managing uncertainty responsibly.

3.8 Binding: why correct attachment is a functional requirement, not a detail

One of the most common sources of failure in age assurance systems is not the choice of method, the accuracy of a model or the strength of a security control. It is a quieter and more fundamental problem: whether the result of an age assurance process is correctly attached to the right person, session, device or interaction it is meant to govern.

This property is referred to as binding.

Binding describes how an age assurance outcome – for example, “over 18”, “under 16” or “age verified” – remains meaningfully connected to the correct subject at the point where a decision is actually made. It is the difference between an answer that is technically correct and one that is *operationally valid.*

Crucially, binding is not the same thing as identity. A system can be strongly bound without knowing who a person is and it can be weakly bound even when extensive identity data is collected. Binding is about attachment and continuity, not about naming.

In practice, binding answers questions such as:

- Who or what, is this result attached to?
- For how long does that attachment remain valid?
- Can it be reused, shared, replayed or transferred?
- What happens when the context changes – device, location, session, assistance?
- What assumptions are being made about user behaviour?

These questions are rarely asked explicitly, yet they determine whether an age assurance system functions as intended once it leaves the diagram and enters the real world.

Poor binding explains many familiar real-world problems. Results that can be reused too easily are shared. Results that are weakly tied to a session are replayed. Results that rely on assumptions about single-user devices break down in shared or assisted environments. Results that are bound only to a moment, but treated as persistent, drift out of context. In response, staff intervene, users retry, workarounds emerge and the system quietly stops behaving as designed.

None of this requires malicious intent. It is the predictable outcome of systems that answer the age question but fail to manage how that answer travels.

This is why binding is a functional characteristic, not a security afterthought. A system that produces an accurate age result but cannot ensure that the right result reaches the right decision point is not functionally effective. Equally, a system that compensates for weak binding by collecting more identity data has not solved the problem – it has merely displaced it.

Binding choices are often encoded in configuration rather than architecture: session lifetimes, retry limits, device assumptions, fallback paths, staff override rules. Because these choices feel technical or operational, they are rarely treated as policy decisions. Yet they shape who is excluded, who is waved through and how risk is distributed in practice.

Importantly, there is no single correct binding model. What constitutes "sufficient" binding depends on context of use, risk tolerance, user population and the consequences of error. A one-time check for low-risk content will require a very different binding posture from repeated access to a regulated service. The mistake is not choosing one model over another; it is failing to recognise that a choice has been made at all.

Once binding is made visible, many downstream design questions become clearer. Privacy trade-offs can be assessed more honestly. Acceptability issues can be anticipated rather than discovered. Security controls can be targeted where they actually matter. Governance discussions move from abstract assurance to concrete behaviour.

3.9 Why pass/fail oversimplifies reality

Pass/fail logic suggests that a single decision point can resolve age-related risk. In reality, many risks are cumulative, contextual or reversible.

A single failed check may not justify exclusion. A single passed check may not justify unrestricted access. Yet pass/fail framing encourages systems to behave as if one outcome settles the matter conclusively.

This oversimplification creates downstream problems. Systems become rigid. Users experience outcomes as unfair or disproportionate. Staff are forced to compensate through discretion, undermining consistency.

More importantly, pass/fail outcomes obscure the fact that age assurance is often part of a broader risk management strategy. It rarely operates in isolation. Treating it as a definitive gate exaggerates its role and raises expectations it cannot meet.

Where pass/fail logic dominates, retries and second chances inevitably emerge.

Users who are denied access try again. Systems allow reattempts to reduce false exclusion. Staff introduce escalation paths to manage complaints. These behaviours are not anomalies; they are compensatory mechanisms.

Retries are a signal that uncertainty has not been resolved, not that it has disappeared. Each retry trades one kind of risk for another. Excessive retries undermine safeguards. Excessive denial undermines trust.

The presence of retries and escalation is therefore diagnostic. It reveals where outcome framing is misaligned with reality. Systems that acknowledge this explicitly can manage it. Systems that pretend it does not exist cannot.

3.10 Why ambiguity is unavoidable

Ambiguity persists in age assurance because age itself is an imperfect proxy. It correlates with risk and capacity, but it does not determine them. No amount of refinement can eliminate this gap entirely.

Technical improvements may reduce uncertainty at the margins, but they do not change the underlying structure of the problem.

As long as age-based decisions rely on thresholds applied to human variation, grey areas will exist.

Treating ambiguity as a design flaw leads to escalation: more data, stricter controls, tighter binding. Treating it as a normal condition leads to different choices: proportionality, transparency and resilience.

The latter approach does not deny the need for boundaries. It recognises their limits.

3.11 Having confidence in age assurance results

Confidence is often spoken about as though it were something a system simply possesses. Age assurance systems are described as offering higher or lower confidence, as if confidence were a measurable quality that could be attached to a tool and carried with it wherever it is deployed.

This way of thinking is appealing, but it obscures how confidence actually operates in practice.

Age assurance systems do not generate confidence in isolation. They are used to support decisions and it is those decisions, made in specific circumstances and with particular consequences, that may or may not be taken with confidence. The same system can inspire confidence in one context and undermine it in another, without any change in its underlying behaviour.

Seen in this way, confidence belongs not to methods, but to the act of deciding.

Every age-based decision carries its own stakes. Some decisions are low risk and easily reversible. Others are consequential, difficult to undo or carry legal or social implications. The amount of confidence required to act responsibly varies accordingly.

A level of uncertainty that is acceptable when moderating content exposure may be entirely unacceptable when determining access to a regulated service. Conversely, a decision that demands high confidence in one context may require far less in another, simply because the consequences differ.

When confidence is treated as an intrinsic property of a method, these distinctions are flattened. Systems are labelled as sufficiently confident or insufficiently confident without reference to what they are being asked to support. This leads to mismatches that are often discovered only after deployment, when outcomes begin to feel disproportionate or misaligned.

Reframing confidence as decision-dependent brings those distinctions back into view.

Age assurance methods do have properties that matter. They may behave consistently under similar conditions, degrade in predictable ways or handle uncertainty more gracefully than alternatives. These characteristics influence how much weight a decision-maker might place on the information they provide.

But these properties are inputs to a decision, not substitutes for judgement.

A method that performs reliably does not automatically justify confident action. Its outputs still need to be interpreted in light of what is being decided, who is affected and what happens if the decision is wrong. Treating method performance as equivalent to decision confidence skips over this interpretive step.

This distinction helps explain why disputes about "accuracy" so often fail to resolve disagreements in age assurance. Measures of performance can be correct and yet still irrelevant to the decision at hand.

3.12 Why accuracy alone is an unreliable guide

Claims about classification accuracy – the likelihood that an age assurance system delivers a correct age assurance result – are frequently used as shorthand for confidence. A system that is described as highly accurate is assumed to support confident decisions, while one that is less accurate is treated with suspicion.

In practice, accuracy is a narrow lens.

Accuracy is always defined relative to particular assumptions: about populations, environments, thresholds and evaluation criteria. Even where these assumptions are reasonable, the resulting figures do not capture how errors are distributed, how they cluster near boundaries or how they interact with user behaviour and operational constraints.

More importantly, accuracy says nothing about the consequences of error. A system may be accurate on average while still producing outcomes that are unacceptable in context, because the remaining errors fall on those who bear the greatest cost.

When accuracy becomes a proxy for confidence, systems are judged by how well they perform in abstraction rather than by how well they support real decisions. This creates a persistent gap between technical claims and lived experience.

Confidence is also shaped by how systems behave over time, not just by how they perform in principle.

Operational confidence emerges from patterns of use. It is influenced by whether outcomes are consistent, whether edge cases are handled predictably and whether users and staff can understand and navigate the process without constant friction.

A system may be technically sound and yet inspire little confidence if it produces frequent disputes, requires repeated retries or forces staff to improvise solutions. Conversely, a system that openly acknowledges uncertainty and provides clear paths for escalation may be trusted even if its limitations are well understood.

This operational dimension explains why confidence can erode even when systems are unchanged. Behaviour adapts, expectations shift and what once felt acceptable may no longer be so.

Beyond operation lies another layer: confidence in how decisions are governed.

Governance confidence depends on whether age-based decisions can be explained, reviewed and, where necessary, challenged. It is shaped by transparency, accountability and the perceived fairness of outcomes.

Systems that claim certainty often struggle here. When outcomes are presented as definitive, there is little room to acknowledge uncertainty or error. When things go wrong, explanations feel evasive or defensive, undermining trust.

By contrast, systems that frame confidence as provisional are often easier to justify. Admitting uncertainty does not weaken governance; it allows responsibility to be exercised more honestly.

This distinction matters because age assurance operates in contested spaces. Public trust depends less on claims of technical perfection than on the sense that decisions are being made thoughtfully and proportionately.

Confidence is not fixed at the moment a system is introduced. It changes as conditions change.

User populations evolve. Incentives shift. Contexts of use expand. What once supported confident decision-making may become less reliable as assumptions drift out of alignment with reality.

Systems that treat confidence as a one-time achievement struggle to respond to this drift. Those that treat it as something to be maintained through observation and adjustment are better able to remain aligned with their purpose.

Recognising confidence as dynamic rather than static helps explain why ongoing practice, configuration and review matter – themes that recur later in this book.

Once confidence is understood as a property of decisions, an unavoidable implication follows: confident decisions still sometimes turn out to be wrong.

3.13 Error is inherent, not exceptional

In many discussions of age assurance, error is treated as a flaw to be eliminated. Systems are evaluated in terms of how close they come to perfection and improvement is framed as a steady march toward zero mistakes.

This framing is unrealistic.

Age assurance operates under uncertainty by design. It relies on proxies, thresholds and incomplete information. As a result, error is not an anomaly that appears only when something goes wrong; it is a normal and persistent feature of decision-making.

Treating error as exceptional encourages systems to conceal it. Treating error as inevitable encourages systems to manage it.

This difference in attitude has significant consequences for how systems are designed, explained and governed.

Errors in age-based decisions come in different forms and they do not carry the same consequences.

Denying access to someone who should have been permitted has different implications from allowing access to someone who should have been restricted. The former may inconvenience, exclude or frustrate; the latter may expose individuals or organisations to harm, liability or public concern.

Which error is considered more serious depends on context. In some settings, exclusion is the greater harm. In others, exposure is. There is no universal answer.

What matters is that these trade-offs are recognised explicitly. When they are left implicit, systems drift toward whichever error appears safer from an institutional perspective, often at the expense of users who have little voice in the outcome.

Every error imposes a cost, but that cost is not borne equally. Some errors fall on individuals, who may be excluded, delayed or forced to disclose more information than expected. Others fall on organisations, through enforcement action, reputational damage or operational burden. Still others fall on society more broadly, through loss of trust or the normalisation of intrusive controls.

Deciding which errors are acceptable therefore involves deciding who is expected to absorb their impact.

These decisions are rarely neutral. When costs are pushed onto users, systems may appear effective while quietly eroding trust. When costs are pushed onto providers, controls may be softened informally. When costs are deferred until harm becomes visible, responses tend to be reactive and punitive.

Making these distributions explicit is uncomfortable, but necessary. It brings policy choices into the open, where they can be examined rather than encoded invisibly into system behaviour.

Because error involves trade-offs, deciding what is acceptable cannot be delegated to technology alone.

A system cannot determine whether an error rate is tolerable without reference to values, priorities and consequences. These judgements belong to governance: to those responsible for setting policy, overseeing implementation and answering for outcomes.

This does not mean that technical analysis is irrelevant. Evidence about system behaviour is essential. But evidence does not resolve value judgements. It informs them.

When acceptable error is framed as a purely technical question, debates become circular. Stakeholders argue about metrics while talking past one another about underlying priorities. Clarity emerges only when the policy layer is acknowledged.

The way systems handle error has a direct impact on privacy. When errors are treated as intolerable, systems often respond by collecting more data, increasing scrutiny and tightening controls. Each step may reduce one kind of error while increasing others, including privacy harm and exclusion.

Conversely, when uncertainty and error are acknowledged, systems can make different choices. They can limit data collection to what is proportionate, accept residual risk and rely on safeguards beyond age assurance alone.

Trust is shaped by these choices. Users are more likely to accept systems that occasionally get things wrong but do so transparently, than systems that claim perfection while quietly imposing disproportionate costs.

Chapter 4 – Understanding ISO/IEC 27566 as a Framework, Not a Rulebook

4.1 Why age assurance resists simple rules

Age assurance has an unusual relationship with rules. From the outside, it looks like the kind of problem that ought to yield to prescriptive laws and standards. There is an age threshold, a legal requirement, a harm to be prevented. It seems reasonable to expect that a clear rule could be written, a compliant process defined and the problem closed.

What experience revealed instead was something far messier.

The first difficulty lies in the sheer diversity of situations in which age-related decisions are made. Age assurance is not a single use case replicated at scale. It appears in online services, physical venues, retail transactions, automated systems and mediated interactions. Some contexts involve fleeting, low-risk encounters; others involve irreversible or high-consequence decisions. Some operate under close supervision; others are fully automated. The meaning of "getting it wrong" shifts dramatically between these settings.

Rules that appear sensible in one context often fail in another. A process designed to minimise risk in a high-stakes environment may be intolerably burdensome when applied to everyday interactions. Conversely, a lightweight approach that works well at scale may be wholly inadequate where the consequences of error are severe. Attempts to collapse this diversity into a single set of instructions tend to produce systems that are either overbearing or under-protective and sometimes both at once.

The second difficulty is time. Age assurance systems do not exist in a static environment. Technologies evolve, but so do the behaviours of those subject to them. As soon as a rule is deployed, it becomes part of the environment to which users adapt. Patterns emerge. Weak points are discovered. Informal knowledge circulates about how systems behave and how they might be circumvented or endured.

Static rules struggle in the face of this adaptation. Measures that initially appear robust gradually lose their effectiveness, not because the technology fails, but because behaviour shifts around it. Prescriptions that once looked proportionate become brittle. Updating them is slow, often requiring formal processes that lag behind real-world change. What was meant to provide certainty instead becomes a source of fragility.

There is also a deeper conceptual mismatch between rules and the nature of age assurance itself. Rules are most effective when the thing being regulated is discrete and observable. Age assurance is neither. It does not operate on a simple fact, but on signals, proxies and judgements made under uncertainty. The decision it supports is rarely binary in practice, even when it is framed that way in law.

This is why the focus on "doing the right check" proved so persistent and so misleading. It suggested that compliance could be achieved through the correct sequence of actions, rather than through an ongoing alignment between purpose, behaviour and outcome. Systems built around this assumption often appeared rigorous while quietly drifting away from the decisions they were meant to support.

Behavioural adaptation amplifies this problem. When systems are designed around fixed rules, users learn to interact with the rule rather than the underlying intent. They optimise for passing the check, not for complying with the spirit of the decision. Organisations respond by tightening controls, increasing friction or collecting more data, which in turn provokes further adaptation. A feedback loop emerges in which rules beget complexity and complexity begets evasion.

None of this implies that rules are useless. Age assurance operates within legal and regulatory boundaries that are necessarily rule-based. The problem is assuming that those rules can be translated directly into technical prescriptions without loss. Experience shows that this translation is where failure often occurs.

ISO/IEC 27566 reflects the recognition that age assurance cannot be stabilised through instruction alone. It accepts that systems will operate in diverse contexts, evolve over time and provoke behavioural response. Rather than attempting to freeze that complexity into static requirements, it takes a different approach: providing a structure within which change, disagreement and uncertainty can be reasoned about without collapsing into chaos.

This is not a retreat from rigour. It is an acknowledgement of where rigour must live. In age assurance, discipline is not achieved by writing ever more detailed rules, but by creating frameworks that make the consequences of decisions visible and the need for judgement unavoidable.

4.2 From prescription to characteristics

Once it became clear that simple rules could not carry the weight placed upon them, a deeper question emerged. If age assurance could not be stabilised through instructions, how could it be reasoned about at all without descending into ad-hoc judgement or purely political debate?

The answer was not to abandon structure, but to change what that structure described.

Prescription focuses on actions. They tell systems what to do: perform a check, collect a signal, apply a threshold. Characteristics focus on qualities. They describe how a system behaves, what kinds of outcomes it produces and how it affects the people subject to it. This shift may seem subtle, but its implications are profound.

Actions can be followed mechanically. Qualities cannot. They are relational, emerging from the interaction between a system, its users, its operators and its context. A system is not private or intrusive in the abstract; it is so in relation to the data it collects, how long it retains it, how it is reused and how visible those practices are to users. A system is not effective in general; it is effective at supporting a particular decision, under particular conditions, with particular tolerances for error.

By focusing on characteristics, the framework moves the discussion away from isolated steps and toward the lived behaviour of systems. It asks not whether the right box was ticked, but what kind of system results from the choices that were made.

This orientation also recognises that characteristics describe tensions rather than targets. They are not destinations that can be reached once and declared complete. They are dimensions along which systems are continually negotiated. Improving a system along one dimension almost always reshapes it along another. These shifts are not failures of execution; they are consequences of operating in a constrained space.

Crucially, characteristics survive technological change. Methods come and go. Signals that once seemed authoritative lose their force. New techniques emerge with different strengths and weaknesses. Yet the underlying questions remain. How confident should a decision be? How much intrusion is justified? Who bears the burden when uncertainty cannot be resolved? Because characteristics describe these enduring concerns, they remain meaningful even as implementations change.

This durability is not accidental. It reflects an understanding that disagreement is unavoidable. Reasonable actors will differ on what matters most in a given context and those differences cannot be eliminated through better specification. What can be done is to provide a structure within which disagreement can occur without becoming incoherent.

Characteristics allow that. They enable people to disagree about trade-offs without needing to agree on methods. They make it possible to say that two systems are different in principled ways, rather than treating one as compliant and the other as defective. They support conversation across disciplines precisely because they do not presuppose technical consensus.

There is also a governance dimension to this shift. Prescription tends to concentrate authority at the point of rulemaking. Once written, they invite deference. Characteristics distribute responsibility more widely. They require designers, operators and decision-makers to justify how their systems behave, not simply to demonstrate that a procedure was followed.

This is more demanding, not less. It removes the comfort of mechanical compliance and replaces it with the obligation to explain and defend choices through transparent practice statements. In doing so, it aligns more closely with the reality of age assurance, where the most important decisions are rarely captured by a single rule or check.

The move from prescription to characteristics therefore represents a change in what counts as rigour. Rigour is no longer located in detailed instruction, but in clarity of reasoning. It lies in being explicit about what is being optimised, what is being sacrificed and why those choices are considered acceptable in a given context.

ISO/IEC 27566 embodies this shift. It does not tell the reader what to build. It tells them what to pay attention to. And in a domain as contested and consequential as age assurance, that change of focus is not a compromise. It is the only way the problem can be approached without pretending that it is simpler than it really is.

4.3 The mischiefs the framework is trying to contain

The purpose of ISO/IEC 27566 becomes much clearer when it is read not as an abstract framework, but as a response to patterns of failure that repeatedly emerged in real deployments. These failures were rarely the result of negligence or bad faith. More often, they arose from reasonable decisions taken in isolation, without a structure that made their wider consequences visible.

One recurring mischief stems from the pursuit of certainty. When age-related decisions are treated as if they require definitive proof, systems tend to accumulate signals. Each additional data point promises to reduce doubt: another document, another biometric check, another record retained "just in case". Over time, this accumulation becomes normalised. Data collected for one purpose is retained for another. Temporary measures become permanent. What began as an effort to support a specific decision quietly transforms into a system that knows far more about individuals than the original context justified.

This is not usually driven by malice. It is driven by anxiety about edge cases, about auditability and about being unable to explain a past decision. Yet the effect is the same. Privacy costs rise incrementally, often without a clear moment at which anyone consciously chose to pay them. The framework exists in part to surface this dynamic, to make visible the way that the language of assurance can be used to justify disproportionate data practices long after their original rationale has faded.

A different mischief appears when systems succeed technically but fail socially. Some age assurance mechanisms perform exactly as specified: they return consistent results, resist attack and enforce thresholds reliably. And yet they generate friction that excludes legitimate users, disproportionately affects particular groups or creates barriers that feel arbitrary or degrading. In these cases, effectiveness on paper masks a deeper problem. The system may be correct, but it is not acceptable.

When acceptability fails, users adapt. They abandon processes, seek workarounds or route around controls entirely. Informal practices emerge to "help people through". What looks like compliance at the system boundary dissolves into inconsistency in operation. The framework treats this not as a soft concern, but as a central risk. A system that cannot be lived with cannot reliably support the decisions it claims to enforce.

There are also mischiefs that arise from composition rather than design. Age assurance systems are rarely monolithic. They are assembled from components that may each function well in isolation. One component may be accurate, another privacy-preserving, another robust against attack. Yet when combined, they can interact in ways that undermine the system as a whole. Signals may be reused beyond their original context. Results may be cached and replayed inappropriately. Escalation paths may exist on paper but be impractical in use.

These failures are particularly hard to diagnose because no single part is obviously at fault. Each component behaves as expected. The problem emerges only at the level of the system, where interactions produce outcomes that no one explicitly intended. The framework responds by insisting that effectiveness is a property of systems, not components and that analysis must account for how parts combine, not just how they perform individually.

Perhaps the most insidious mischief of all lies in configuration. Thresholds, defaults, retry limits and fallback behaviours are often treated as neutral technical settings. In practice, they encode value judgements. They determine how strict a system is, how forgiving it can be and who bears the cost of uncertainty. A default setting can decide whether a user is blocked, escalated or trusted without any human intervention at the point of decision.

When these choices remain implicit, they escape scrutiny. Decisions appear to be made by "the system" rather than by the people who configured it. Responsibility becomes diffuse. When harm occurs, it is difficult to locate the moment at which a different choice could have been made. The framework seeks to counter this by drawing attention to configuration as a locus of control, where policy is enacted in practice even when no policy document exists.

Taken together, these mischiefs explain why a framework was necessary. They show that the risks of age assurance do not arise solely from technical weakness, but from the way systems evolve over time, respond to pressure and embed decisions invisibly. ISO/IEC 27566 does not claim to eliminate these problems. Its purpose is more modest and more demanding: to make them harder to ignore.

4.4 Why trade-offs are central, not accidental

Once age assurance is understood in terms of characteristics rather than prescription, trade-offs stop looking like unfortunate side effects and start to look like the core of the problem. They are not evidence that something has gone wrong. They are evidence that the system is operating in the real world.

Age assurance systems are pulled in different directions simultaneously. Increasing confidence in a decision often increases friction for users. Reducing friction frequently requires tolerating greater uncertainty. Measures that strengthen resistance to abuse can introduce barriers that exclude legitimate users. Efforts to minimise data collection can make auditing or investigation more difficult. These tensions are not anomalies to be engineered away; they are structural features of the space.

The language of optimisation obscures this reality. It suggests that systems can be tuned until all desirable qualities are maximised at once, as though the problem were one of calibration rather than judgement. In practice, improvements are local and contingent. Gains in one area tend to create costs elsewhere and those costs are often borne by different actors. A change that benefits operators may disadvantage users. A measure that reassures regulators may impose burdens on service providers. No amount of technical sophistication removes the need to decide where those burdens should fall.

Trade-offs also shift over time. What appears proportionate at deployment may become excessive as contexts change. Early conservatism may give way to evidence that allows relaxation. Conversely, new forms of misuse may require tightening controls that were once sufficient. Systems that treat trade-offs as solved problems tend to become brittle. They lock in assumptions that no longer hold and resist adjustment because change itself is seen as a failure.

Hiding trade-offs creates a different kind of risk. When systems present themselves as neutral or fully optimised, they invite misplaced confidence. Decisions appear automatic rather than contingent. When harm occurs, it is difficult to explain because the choices that shaped the outcome were never acknowledged as choices. Responsibility dissolves into complexity.

Frameworks like ISO/IEC 27566 respond to this by surfacing trade-offs rather than resolving them. They provide a structure within which competing qualities can be examined together, rather than optimised in isolation. They encourage designers and decision-makers to be explicit about what is being prioritised and why and to accept that reasonable people may disagree about those priorities.

This approach is explanatory rather than justificatory. It does not seek to defend particular outcomes or to normalise discomfort. It seeks to make clear why discomfort arises at all. In doing so, it reframes success. A well-designed age assurance system is not one that avoids trade-offs, but one that recognises them, manages them openly and revisits them as conditions change.

Seen this way, characteristics are not constraints imposed by the framework. They are lenses that bring trade-offs into focus. They allow tensions to be discussed without pretending that they can be eliminated. And they remind everyone involved that judgement is not a flaw in the system, but the work the system exists to support.

4.5 Context as the unifying thread

If characteristics explain what matters and trade-offs explain why tensions arise, context explains why none of this can be decided once and for all. Context is the thread that holds age assurance together, not as an abstract concept, but as a lived practice.

Age assurance systems do not exist in the abstract. They are deployed somewhere, for someone, for a particular purpose, under particular constraints. Remove that setting and the system becomes impossible to judge in any meaningful way. Claims about effectiveness, proportionality or acceptability lose their reference point. What remains is architecture divorced from consequence.

This is why the same system can appear responsible in one setting and inappropriate in another. A design that is proportionate when applied to a high-risk, tightly regulated interaction may be excessive when used for everyday access. A level of friction that is tolerable in a supervised environment may be exclusionary in an unsupervised one. A degree of uncertainty that is acceptable for a reversible decision may be unacceptable when the outcome cannot easily be undone.

Context shapes not only what outcome is sought, but how characteristics should be interpreted. Effectiveness is not a universal measure; it depends on what decision is being supported and what failure would mean in practice. Privacy is not an abstract property;

it depends on what data is collected, how it is used and what expectations users bring with them. Acceptability is not static; it is mediated by culture, accessibility, trust and experience.

This dependence on context is often uncomfortable for those seeking uniform solutions. It complicates procurement, oversight and regulation. It resists centralisation. Yet it reflects the reality that age assurance operates at the boundary between technical systems and social judgement. Attempting to strip away context in the name of simplicity tends to produce systems that are either overly rigid or quietly misaligned with their purpose.

Context also explains why solutions do not travel well. An approach that works in one jurisdiction may fail elsewhere, not because it is flawed, but because the surrounding assumptions differ. Legal thresholds, social norms, expectations of authority and tolerance for error all shape how systems are perceived and how they function. Treating portability as the default risks exporting misalignment along with technology.

The framework does not attempt to collapse context into a single variable. Instead, it treats context as the environment within which characteristics acquire meaning. It asks readers to consider how and where a system is used before asking whether it performs well. In doing so, it resists the temptation to judge systems solely by their design intent or headline claims.

This orientation also limits the extent to which judgement can be centralised. While high-level principles can be shared, their application cannot be fully predetermined. Decisions about what is proportionate, acceptable or sufficient must be made close to use, where consequences are visible. The framework supports this by providing a structure for reasoning that can be applied locally without abandoning coherence.

Seen this way, context is not an additional factor to be considered after the fact. It is the condition that gives all other considerations their force. Characteristics without context are empty. Trade-offs without context are arbitrary. Systems without context are diagrams.

By making context the unifying thread, ISO/IEC 27566 reinforces a simple but demanding idea: age assurance cannot be judged from a distance. It must be understood where it operates, in the conditions it creates and in the lives it affects.

4.6 Why configuration and practice matter more than architecture

When age assurance systems are discussed at a distance, attention tends to settle on architecture. Diagrams are drawn, components are named and boundaries are defined. This way of thinking is reassuring. Architecture appears stable, intentional and legible. It suggests that control lies in design.

In practice, however, architecture is rarely where the most consequential decisions are made.

The behaviour of an age assurance system is shaped far more by how it is configured and how it is used than by the abstract structure of its components. Two systems built from the same architectural pattern can behave very differently in the real world, not because they were designed differently, but because they were configured differently and operated under different assumptions.

Configuration is where policy quietly enters the system. Thresholds determine how confident the system must be before allowing an interaction to proceed. Retry limits determine how much effort a user is expected to expend. Timeouts, caching rules and result lifetimes determine whether decisions are treated as momentary judgements or enduring facts. Escalation paths determine whether uncertainty leads to human review, additional checks or outright refusal.

None of these choices are neutral. Each encodes a judgement about risk, burden and trust. Yet they are often treated as technical details, set once during deployment and revisited only when something goes wrong. Over time, these settings harden into defaults. They become invisible, not because they are unimportant, but because they are familiar.

This invisibility is dangerous. It allows systems to drift away from their original intent without any explicit decision being made. A threshold set conservatively to manage early uncertainty may remain long after evidence suggests it could be relaxed. A fallback introduced to handle rare failures may become the dominant path for a subset of users. What looks like stability can mask quiet transformation.

Practice amplifies this effect. Age assurance systems are not self-contained machines that run untouched once deployed. They are embedded in organisations and operated by people. Staff intervene when users struggle. Informal guidance circulates about how to handle edge cases. Exceptions are made, then repeated, then normalised. Over time, these practices shape how the system actually functions, regardless of how it was designed to function.

This is not a failure of discipline. It is a natural response to systems that encounter real users and real pressure. Practice fills the gaps that design cannot anticipate. It smooths rough edges, resolves ambiguity and keeps services running. But it can also undermine the characteristics the system was meant to preserve. A privacy-preserving design can be weakened by operational logging. A carefully balanced process can become skewed by informal shortcuts. A system intended to escalate uncertainty can quietly convert it into routine acceptance.

The framework's emphasis on configuration and practice reflects an uncomfortable truth: control does not reside solely with designers. It is exercised continuously, through everyday choices that are rarely labelled as policy decisions even though that is exactly what they are.

This is why focusing exclusively on architecture creates a false sense of security. A well-designed system can behave poorly if configured incautiously or operated under pressure without reflection. Conversely, a modest architectural approach can perform well if its configuration is carefully managed and its operation aligned with its purpose.

Frameworks attend to configuration and practice because they are where characteristics are realised or eroded. They are where trade-offs are enacted, often repeatedly, often quietly. By drawing attention to these loci of control, ISO/IEC 27566 shifts the conversation away from idealised designs and toward lived systems.

This shift also reframes responsibility. When outcomes are attributed solely to architecture, accountability tends to stop at deployment. When configuration and practice are acknowledged as central, responsibility becomes ongoing. Decisions are not finished when the system goes live; they continue to be made every time a setting is adjusted, an exception is granted or a workaround becomes routine.

Seen in this light, the framework's concern with how systems are used is not an add-on. It is a recognition that age assurance systems are dynamic, adaptive and socially embedded. What matters is not only what was built, but what is being done with it now.

4.7 What a framework can (and cannot) do

By this point in the chapter, it should be clear that ISO/IEC 27566 was never intended to behave like a conventional rulebook. That makes it important to be explicit about what a framework of this kind is capable of doing and, just as importantly, what it cannot do without being misused.

A framework provides a way of thinking. It offers shared reference points that allow different actors to reason about the same system without having to agree in advance on methods, technologies or outcomes. It creates a common vocabulary for describing behaviour, surfacing assumptions and making trade-offs visible. In doing so, it supports comparison, explanation and scrutiny without forcing convergence.

This is a subtle form of power. It does not compel agreement, but it makes disagreement intelligible. It allows one system to be distinguished from another on principled grounds, rather than on branding or assertion. It gives regulators, designers and operators a way to ask whether a system behaves as claimed and whether those claims remain credible as context changes.

What a framework does not do is remove responsibility. It does not decide what is acceptable, sufficient or fair. It cannot determine where lines should be drawn, because those lines are shaped by law, culture, risk appetite and social values that lie outside the reach of technical abstraction. Attempting to use a framework to settle those questions once and for all misunderstands its role.

Nor does a framework absolve organisations of judgement. On the contrary, it exposes where judgement is being exercised, even when that judgement is hidden behind configuration settings or operational routines. It resists the comfort of mechanical compliance by refusing to translate complex questions into simple checkmarks. This can feel unsettling, particularly in regulatory environments accustomed to clear-cut obligations. Yet it reflects the reality that responsibility in age assurance cannot be delegated entirely to standards or systems.

Misuse of frameworks often takes a familiar form. They are treated as checklists, mined for phrases that can be cited as evidence of alignment or invoked as authority to justify predetermined choices. When this happens, the framework's most valuable function is lost. Instead of supporting reasoning, it becomes a shield against it. Instead of illuminating trade-offs, it conceals them.

ISO/IEC 27566 is deliberately designed to resist this kind of misuse. Its non-prescriptive nature is not a gap to be filled by supplementary rules, but a boundary that signals where accountability must remain human and contextual. The framework does not claim to guarantee good outcomes. It claims only to make the reasoning behind outcomes more legible.

This distinction matters. In domains where harm is possible and values conflict, the absence of guaranteed answers is not a failure of governance. It is an honest acknowledgement of complexity. Frameworks operate in that space. They do not promise certainty; they promise structure.

Understanding this helps set appropriate expectations. The value of ISO/IEC 27566 lies not in its ability to tell organisations what to do, but in its ability to make clear what they are doing and why. When used in this way, it strengthens accountability rather than weakening it. When treated as a substitute for judgement, it does the opposite.

Seen clearly, the framework does not compete with policy, regulation or organisational responsibility. It supports them by providing a disciplined way to think about systems whose behaviour cannot be reduced to simple rules. That is both its power and its limit.

4.8 Reading the framework as a guide to judgement

Having walked through why age assurance resists simple rules, why characteristics replace prescription and why trade-offs, context, configuration and practice sit at the centre of the problem, one conclusion should now feel unavoidable. Age assurance cannot be reduced to a technical exercise. It is, at its core, a matter of judgement.

ISO/IEC 27566 should therefore be read not as an authority that delivers answers, but as a guide that shapes how questions are asked. Its value lies in how it disciplines thinking rather than how it directs action. It encourages readers to slow down, to surface assumptions and to recognise where decisions are being made implicitly rather than explicitly.

This way of reading the framework changes what it means to disagree. Disagreement is no longer a sign that the framework has failed to provide clarity. It is evidence that the framework is doing its work. Reasonable people will reach different conclusions about what is proportionate, acceptable or sufficient in a given context. What matters is not that those conclusions align, but that the reasoning behind them can be articulated, examined and compared.

Judgement, in this sense, is not arbitrary. It is structured. The framework provides a set of lenses through which systems can be examined consistently, even when outcomes differ. It allows decisions to be revisited as conditions change, without treating revision as a loss of credibility. On the contrary, the willingness to adjust in light of new evidence becomes a mark of responsible governance rather than a sign of instability.

Reading the framework this way also guards against a common temptation. When faced with complexity, there is a strong pull toward seeking definitive answers – a preferred method, a minimum threshold, a single correct configuration. ISO/IEC 27566 resists that pull. It insists that certainty has limits and that pretending otherwise creates new risks. By doing so, it invites a more mature engagement with uncertainty, one that acknowledges its presence without allowing it to paralyse decision-making.

Chapter 5 – Methods in the Real World: Verification, Estimation and Inference

5.1 Why methods are not solutions

When age assurance enters public or regulatory debate, discussion tends to crystallise around methods. Verification is framed as "stronger" than estimation. Estimation is presented as more "privacy preserving" than inference. Inference is defended as "proportionate" where other approaches are seen as excessive. These framings suggest that the central challenge of age assurance is choosing the correct technical approach.

This assumption is deeply appealing and fundamentally flawed.

Methods are not solutions. They are tools that shape how age-related decisions are made, contested and experienced. Choosing a method does not resolve the underlying tensions in age assurance; it merely relocates them. Questions about uncertainty, proportionality, privacy, exclusion and accountability do not disappear when a method is selected. They re-emerge elsewhere in the system, often in less visible ways.

The persistence of method-centric thinking is not accidental. It offers psychological and political comfort. For policymakers, it suggests that difficult social problems can be addressed through specification rather than ongoing judgement. For organisations, it creates the impression that compliance is a matter of implementation rather than governance. For technologists, it aligns with a familiar pattern in which better tools are expected to yield better outcomes.

Method prescription often hides ulterior motives. Requiring use of identity to prove age can be a method for governments to achieve ubiquitous deployment of digital identity services at substantial cost to the user both in terms of inherent costs of identity systems (even if taxpayer funded) but also risks to their autonomy, privacy, security and exposure of their digital footprint.

In practice, method-centric logic rarely survives contact with deployment.

Age assurance problems are not static. They are shaped by context, incentives, behaviour and evolving expectations. No method can neutralise these forces. A system that relies on verification inherits dependencies on records, identity infrastructures and user willingness to engage. A system built around estimation inherits uncertainty, edge cases and sensitivity to environment. A system grounded in inference inherits reliance on contextual signals and governance choices about what counts as reasonable evidence.

Operational reality is less forgiving. Systems built around methods inherit their limitations as structural features. When those systems encounter friction, exclusion or privacy harm organisations often respond by intensifying the method-tightening thresholds, adding retries, escalating checks. This rarely resolves the underlying issue. It simply amplifies the side-effects.

5.2 What age assurance methods are actually doing

At a practical level, age assurance methods do not establish facts in the abstract. They generate *grounds for action*. They provide reasons (sometimes strong, sometimes tentative) for a relying party to allow or restrict access, escalate a check or apply additional safeguards. Each method does this in a different way and each frames uncertainty differently.

Understanding this distinction helps explain why debates about "accuracy" or "strength" often miss the point. Methods do not compete to discover the same truth. They answer different kinds of questions under different assumptions and they distribute responsibility for error and judgement differently across the system.

Age verification operates by relying on an external assertion. It takes a claim about a person's date of birth that has been established elsewhere and treats that claim as sufficiently authoritative for the purpose at hand. The method itself does not create certainty; it borrows it. The confidence associated with verification flows from the perceived reliability of the source being relied upon, the integrity of the binding to the individual and the context in which the assertion is reused.

This reliance on external assertions gives verification a particular character. It feels definitive because it anchors decisions to something that exists beyond the immediate interaction. For many regulated contexts, this is precisely its appeal. It supports auditability, accountability and retrospective justification. Decisions can be explained by pointing to records rather than to judgement.

At the same time, verification shifts the centre of gravity away from the moment of decision. Questions about access become questions about documentation, identity infrastructure and eligibility to participate in record-based systems. The method supports a clear answer, but only for those who can reach it. In doing so, it makes participation conditional on factors that may have little to do with the risk being managed and potentially generate high friction.

Age estimation functions very differently. Instead of borrowing certainty from the past, it generates evidence in the present. It observes something about the user, often including their biometrics and produces an assessment expressed in terms of likelihood. Even when its outputs are simplified into binary signals, the underlying logic remains probabilistic. However, the instant and present nature of estimation make binding the result to the individual more straightforward.

This means that estimation does not offer a single, stable answer. It offers a degree of confidence that must be interpreted. Thresholds, buffers and fallback paths are not peripheral details; they are the mechanism by which estimation becomes operational. Without them, an estimate is simply information. With them, it becomes a decision.

The significance of this is often underappreciated. Estimation does not fail because it is "less accurate" than verification. It fails when systems pretend that uncertainty has been eliminated rather than managed. When estimates are treated as facts, small uncertainties produce disproportionate harm. When uncertainty is acknowledged and designed for, estimation can support decisions that are proportionate, reversible and responsive to context.

Age inference occupies a third functional space. It does not rely on formal records or observable physical characteristics. Instead, it reasons from context. It draws on facts, behaviours or signals that correlate with age-related attributes and uses those correlations to support an eligibility decision.

Inference is often invisible to users, which gives it both power and risk. It can operate with minimal friction, using information that is already present in the interaction. In low-risk contexts, this can be an advantage, allowing systems to adapt without demanding additional effort from users.

However, inference does not create certainty. It creates plausibility. Its strength lies in proportionality rather than precision. The reasonableness of an inference depends not only on the signals used, but on how narrowly and transparently the reasoning is bounded. Without clear limits, inference can drift from contextual reasoning into persistent profiling, shifting its function from decision support to categorisation.

Across all three methods, a common pattern emerges. None of them answers the question "How old is this person?" in any absolute sense. They answer questions like "Is it reasonable to allow access now?", "Is further checking warranted?" or "Is this interaction consistent with expected age-related behaviour?". These are operational questions, not metaphysical ones.

This is why confidence does not reside inside methods. Confidence emerges from how their outputs are interpreted and acted upon. A verification result can be undermined by poor binding, compromised identity attributes or inappropriate reuse. An estimation result can be trusted when used conservatively and questioned when used rigidly. An inference can be acceptable when scoped narrowly and harmful when allowed to persist.

Seen this way, methods are not rivals in a race toward certainty. They are different ways of managing uncertainty. Each offers a distinct balance between friction, confidence and responsibility. Each requires judgement to translate output into action.

The tendency to rank methods obscures this reality. It encourages systems to be designed around method capabilities rather than decision needs. It frames uncertainty as a technical defect rather than a design parameter. Most importantly, it shifts attention away from how people experience age assurance in practice.

5.3 Behaviour changes everything

No aspect of age assurance is more decisive and more consistently underestimated than user behaviour.

Methods are often evaluated as if users were passive inputs to a system, responding predictably to prompts and controls. In practice, user behaviour dominates outcomes. How people react to age assurance mechanisms, how they adapt over time and how they interpret friction or failure shapes system performance far more than technical properties alone.

Age assurance does not take place in a vacuum. It occurs in environments where users have motivations, incentives and constraints of their own. Some users want access quickly. Some want to avoid sharing information. Some are uncertain about what is being asked of them. Others, particularly children and young people, are experimenting, testing boundaries or responding to peer behaviour. These motivations are situational rather than fixed and they change over time.

One of the most persistent mistakes in age assurance design is to assume that misrepresentation is primarily malicious. In reality, most age-related misrepresentation is opportunistic and context dependent. Users respond to perceived friction and consequence. When the cost of honesty feels higher than the cost of misrepresentation, honesty declines. When the system feels reasonable and proportionate, compliance increases.

This dynamic explains why the same method can produce radically different outcomes in different contexts. A verification step that feels acceptable for one-off access to a regulated service may feel excessive when encountered repeatedly. An estimation process that feels low-friction in isolation may become frustrating when users are asked to repeat it frequently. An inference mechanism that works quietly in the background may provoke resistance when users become aware of how conclusions are being drawn.

Friction is not merely an inconvenience; it is a behavioural signal. It communicates how much the system values certainty relative to user effort. Systems that demand high effort for low perceived benefit invite circumvention. Systems that balance effort and outcome more carefully tend to elicit cooperation.

Circumvention rarely takes a single form. It reflects whatever adaptations are easiest or most socially acceptable in a given context. Sometimes this means technical workarounds, such as altering apparent location or network characteristics to avoid triggering controls. In other cases, it involves social strategies, using shared accounts, relying on older siblings or parents to complete checks or informally reusing credentials that were never intended to be transferable. In still other cases, circumvention takes the form of record or persona fabrication, where users supply information that fits the system's expectations rather than their own circumstances.

What matters is not the specific tactic, but the underlying pattern. Users do not experience these actions as "attacks" on a system. They experience them as problem-solving responses to friction or trying to prevent the system from working as intended. The more effort a system demands, the more inventive and normalised these responses become especially when they are reinforced by peer behaviour or tacit adult cooperation. Once circumvention becomes socially embedded, tightening controls does not eliminate it, it simply changes its form.

Repetition intensifies these effects. Age assurance is rarely a single encounter. Over time, users learn how systems behave. They discover which paths lead to success, which lead to dead ends and which are easiest to bypass. Even well-intentioned users begin to optimise their behaviour. This learning process is inevitable and it steadily erodes assumptions made during design.

Laboratory evaluations rarely capture this. Controlled testing environments assume static behaviour, fixed incentives and isolated interactions. Real-world systems encounter feedback loops. Behaviour adapts. What worked on day one may behave very differently after months of use, especially when users share experiences and expectations.

Adversarial behaviour, where it exists, is often a response to system design rather than an inherent trait of users. Framing all misrepresentation as attack encourages defensive design that increases friction for everyone. This, in turn, creates new incentives for avoidance and exclusion. The system becomes locked in a cycle where tightening controls produces diminishing returns.

Behaviour also interacts with trust. Users make rapid judgements about whether a system is fair, predictable and respectful. When outcomes feel arbitrary or opaque, trust declines. When users do not understand why a decision was made or how to recover from failure, frustration replaces cooperation. Over time, trust erosion manifests as dropout, avoidance or reliance on unofficial workarounds.

These behavioural patterns matter because age assurance systems rely on participation to function. A method that performs well under idealised conditions can fail operationally if users disengage or adapt in unexpected ways. Conversely, a method that is less precise in theory can support better outcomes if it aligns with how people actually behave.

The dominance of behaviour also explains why technical improvements do not always translate into better results. Increasing confidence thresholds, adding retries or escalating checks may improve theoretical assurance while degrading real-world effectiveness. As friction increases, honest users are disproportionately affected, while motivated users find new paths around controls.

Understanding behaviour requires abandoning the idea that users are obstacles to be managed. They are participants whose responses shape system dynamics. Designing age assurance without accounting for this is equivalent to designing traffic systems without considering how drivers behave.

This insight is particularly important for acceptability, which is often framed as a secondary concern or a matter of user experience design. In reality, acceptability is the behavioural foundation of age assurance. Without it, methods do not fail loudly. They fail quietly, through disengagement and drift.

Recognising that behaviour changes everything forces a re-evaluation of how success is measured. High technical performance does not guarantee sustained participation. Low error rates do not ensure fairness if exclusion accumulates invisibly. Systems that appear robust in isolation may become brittle when behaviour shifts.

This does not mean that age assurance systems must capitulate to every user preference. It means they must be designed with a realistic understanding of how people respond to effort, uncertainty and consequence. Behaviour is not noise to be filtered out. It is the medium through which age assurance operates.

Repetition intensifies these effects. Age assurance is rarely a single encounter. Over time, users learn how systems behave. They discover which paths lead to success, which lead to dead ends and which are easiest to bypass. Even well-intentioned users begin to optimise their behaviour. This learning process is inevitable and it steadily erodes assumptions made during design.

Laboratory evaluations rarely capture this. Controlled testing environments assume static behaviour, fixed incentives and isolated interactions. Real-world systems encounter feedback loops. Behaviour adapts. What worked on day one may behave very differently after months of use, especially when users share experiences and expectations.

Adversarial behaviour, where it exists, is often a response to system design rather than an inherent trait of users. Framing all misrepresentation as attack encourages defensive design that increases friction for everyone. This, in turn, creates new incentives for avoidance and exclusion. The system becomes locked in a cycle where tightening controls produces diminishing returns.

Behaviour also interacts with trust. Users make rapid judgements about whether a system is fair, predictable and respectful. When outcomes feel arbitrary or opaque, trust declines. When users do not understand why a decision was made or how to recover from failure, frustration replaces cooperation. Over time, trust erosion manifests as dropout, avoidance or reliance on unofficial workarounds.

These behavioural patterns matter because age assurance systems rely on participation to function. A method that performs well under idealised conditions can fail operationally if users disengage or adapt in unexpected ways. Conversely, a method that is less precise in theory can support better outcomes if it aligns with how people actually behave.

The dominance of behaviour also explains why technical improvements do not always translate into better results. Increasing confidence thresholds, adding retries or escalating checks may improve theoretical assurance while degrading real-world effectiveness. As friction increases, honest users are disproportionately affected, while motivated users find new paths around controls.

Understanding behaviour requires abandoning the idea that users are obstacles to be managed. They are participants whose responses shape system dynamics. Designing age assurance without accounting for this is equivalent to designing traffic systems without considering how drivers behave.

This insight is particularly important for acceptability, which is often framed as a secondary concern or a matter of user experience design. In reality, acceptability is the behavioural foundation of age assurance. Without it, methods do not fail loudly. They fail quietly, through disengagement and drift.

Recognising that behaviour changes everything forces a re-evaluation of how success is measured. High technical performance does not guarantee sustained participation. Low error rates do not ensure fairness if exclusion accumulates invisibly. Systems that appear robust in isolation may become brittle when behaviour shifts.

This does not mean that age assurance systems must capitulate to every user preference. It means they must be designed with a realistic understanding of how people respond to effort, uncertainty and consequence. Behaviour is not noise to be filtered out. It is the medium through which age assurance operates.

Parental involvement is sometimes described, pejoratively, as "parental collusion". This framing is misleading. Parents are not external adversaries attempting to defeat age assurance systems; they are participants acting within family relationships, values and practical constraints. In many contexts, parents actively support children in navigating systems they perceive as confusing, disproportionate or misaligned with their child's maturity.

This behaviour does not invalidate age assurance. It reveals a basic truth: age assurance does not operate outside families, but through them. Systems that treat parental involvement as a failure mode to be eliminated tend to undermine trust and legitimacy, while systems that recognise it as a contextual reality are better able to manage risk proportionately.

5.4 Privacy harms as method side-effects

Privacy harms in age assurance are often discussed as if they were policy failures: a system collected too much data, stored it insecurely or shared it improperly. While such failures do occur, they are not the most common or the most consequential sources of harm.

In practice, many privacy risks arise not because systems are badly designed, but because they are doing exactly what they were optimised to do.

Age assurance methods are routinely deployed in environments where decision-makers seek certainty, defensibility and auditability. These goals are understandable. They also exert a powerful gravitational pull on system design. Over time, they encourage the accumulation of data, the extension of retention periods and the reuse of information beyond its original purpose. Privacy harm emerges not from a single misstep, but from a series of seemingly reasonable choices.

This is why privacy issues in age assurance are best understood as side-effects rather than flaws. They are emergent properties of how methods interact with institutional incentives and operational pressures.

One of the strongest drivers of privacy harm is the pursuit of certainty. When organisations are uncomfortable with uncertainty, they respond by collecting more information, retaining it longer and linking it more extensively. Verification systems encourage this by making historical records central to decision-making. Estimation systems can encourage repeated capture to improve confidence or resolve edge cases. Inference systems invite accumulation of contextual signals to strengthen plausibility over time.

None of these practices is inherently abusive. Each can be justified in isolation. Together, they produce systems that steadily expand their data footprint.

The most significant privacy risks often do not occur at the moment of collection. They arise later, through persistence and reuse. Data gathered to answer a narrow question is retained "just in case". Signals intended to be ephemeral become durable attributes. What began as decision support slowly becomes categorisation and tracking.

This process is rarely explicit. It unfolds through configuration changes, incident responses and incremental extensions of scope. A retention period is lengthened to support investigation. A dataset is reused to improve consistency. An inference signal is stored to reduce friction next time. Each step feels operationally sensible. The cumulative effect is identity creep.

Identity creep is particularly insidious because it is rarely framed as a privacy failure. Sometimes it is even mandated by laws or even developed by design. Systems may comply with formal data protection requirements while still producing harm through aggregation and linkage. A method may minimise data in a single interaction yet contribute to a broader ecosystem in which user activity becomes increasingly traceable and persistent.

Claims of "privacy-preserving" design often obscure this dynamic. They tend to focus on how little data is collected at one moment, rather than on how data behaves over time. A system can be privacy-preserving in isolation and privacy-degrading in context. What matters is not only what is collected, but what is remembered, reused and recombined.

Another source of harm arises when methods migrate across contexts. Techniques designed for high-stakes, regulated environments are often repurposed elsewhere because they appear robust or compliant. When transplanted into lower-risk or higher-frequency settings, the same methods can become intrusive. The problem is not the method itself, but the mismatch between its assumptions and the new context of use.

This mismatch is particularly visible where age assurance becomes persistent. What is acceptable as a one-time check may be harmful when encountered repeatedly. What is proportionate for access to restricted services may be excessive for routine interaction. Methods do not automatically adapt to these shifts. Systems must be designed to recognise them.

Privacy harm also arises when systems treat data as the primary means of resolving uncertainty. Instead of designing for graceful failure, fallback paths or proportional escalation organisations often default to collecting more information. This reinforces the belief that confidence can be purchased through data accumulation, rather than earned through careful system design.

The irony is that such accumulation often undermines trust. Users become more guarded. They disengage or seek workarounds. Systems respond by tightening controls further, deepening the cycle. They worry that governments are "watching" them, which in less progressive cultures can be a real worry and have real world consequences.

Importantly, none of this requires malicious intent. Privacy harms emerge even in systems built by conscientious teams operating under regulatory pressure. The harm lies in how methods interact with organisational incentives, not in the presence or absence of bad actors.

Understanding privacy in this way shifts the focus of responsibility. It moves attention away from individual technical safeguards and toward systemic behaviour. It raises questions about why data is retained, how long it persists and how easily it can migrate across purposes.

This reframing is uncomfortable because it challenges the idea that privacy can be "solved" through method choice. Selecting a method labelled as privacy-preserving does not guarantee privacy-preserving outcomes. Those outcomes depend on governance, configuration and restraint.

Recognising privacy harms as side-effects also helps explain why they are so often discovered late. By the time concerns surface, systems have already adapted, expanded and entrenched certain practices. Reversing those practices is far harder than preventing them.

The implication for age assurance is clear. Privacy protection cannot be bolted onto methods after the fact. It must be understood as a property of how systems evolve over time. Methods shape that evolution, but they do not control it.

5.5 Acceptability is what keeps methods alive

Acceptability is often treated as a secondary concern in age assurance. It is discussed in terms of user experience, interface design or public perception and it is frequently subordinated to goals of accuracy, security or compliance. In practice, this hierarchy is inverted. Acceptability is what allows age assurance methods to function at all.

Methods do not fail dramatically when they become unacceptable. They fail quietly. Users disengage. Completion rates decline. Legitimate attempts are abandoned. Staff intervene to bypass controls. Over time, the system continues to operate, but the quality and meaning of its outputs deteriorate.

These failures are easy to miss because they rarely present as technical errors. Logs may show that checks are being performed. Dashboards may indicate high confidence among completed transactions. What is not visible is the population that never reaches the point of completion.

This invisibility makes acceptability failures particularly dangerous. When systems exclude users before a decision is recorded, exclusion leaves no trace. The system appears to function well precisely because those most affected by its demands are no longer participating.

In operational environments, acceptability problems surface indirectly. Organisations notice rising support requests. Front-line staff develop informal overrides. Exception handling becomes routine. These adaptations are often framed as necessary pragmatism, but they are signals that the formal system is no longer aligned with real-world conditions.

Acceptability failures are frequently misdiagnosed. When dropout increases, it is often attributed to user error or non-compliance. When workarounds proliferate, they are treated as discipline problems rather than design issues. The response is to tighten controls, add instructions or increase enforcement. Each of these measures increases friction further, accelerating disengagement.

The result is a downward spiral. As participation declines, confidence in the system's representativeness erodes. Decisions are made on the basis of an increasingly narrow subset of users. Bias and exclusion intensify, even if the method itself remains unchanged.

This dynamic helps explain why "technically strong" methods so often fail socially. Strength is typically defined in terms of resistance to error or attack. Social viability depends on whether users can and will complete the process without undue burden. A method that excludes large numbers of legitimate users does not produce stronger outcomes. It produces distorted ones.

Acceptability is also deeply context dependent. A method that is acceptable in one setting may be unacceptable in another, even if the risk being managed appears similar. Frequency of use matters. Visibility matters. Cultural expectations matter. Systems that ignore these factors often appear robust on paper and fragile in practice.

One of the most common sources of acceptability failure is the mismatch between method assumptions and user reality. Verification assumes access to documentation, authoritative sources and familiarity with formal processes. Estimation assumes comfort with biometric observation and occasional error. Inference assumes trust in contextual judgement. When these assumptions do not hold, the burden shifts to users to adapt. Those who cannot adapt are excluded.

Exclusion is rarely experienced as a single event. It accumulates through repeated friction, failure and uncertainty. Users who are repeatedly challenged, delayed or rejected begin to disengage pre-emptively. Over time, they stop attempting access altogether. The system does not record this as a failure, but it is.

Acceptability also shapes how errors are tolerated. In systems that users perceive as fair and proportionate, occasional failures are often accepted. In systems perceived as arbitrary or burdensome, even small errors provoke resistance. Trust amplifies tolerance; frustration amplifies conflict.

Importantly, acceptability is not about making age assurance pleasant or invisible. It is about ensuring that the burdens imposed by a system are aligned with the value of the decision it supports. When users perceive this alignment, cooperation increases. When they do not, resistance becomes rational.

Acceptability therefore cannot be treated as a cosmetic concern. It is an operational requirement. Systems that ignore it may satisfy formal criteria while failing to support real-world decision-making.

Recognising acceptability as a sustaining force rather than an optional feature changes how success is understood. A system that produces highly confident decisions for a narrow subset of users is not necessarily more effective than one that produces less certain decisions across a broader population. The question is not which method is strongest, but which system remains viable over time.

5.6 Why methods are combined in practice

In real-world deployments, age assurance systems rarely rely on a single method from start to finish. Even where a system is described as "verification-based" or "estimation-led", closer inspection usually reveals layers, sequences and fallbacks that involve more than one approach.

These combinations are not typically the result of a single design decision. They emerge over time, as systems encounter edge cases, operational pressures and conflicting expectations. Each addition is usually justified as a pragmatic response to a specific problem. Taken together, they transform how the system behaves.

One of the most common drivers of combination is uncertainty. No method produces uniform confidence across all users and contexts. Designers respond by introducing secondary checks to handle cases where confidence falls below an acceptable threshold. Estimation may be used to filter routine cases, with verification reserved for those near a boundary. Inference may operate quietly until behaviour triggers escalation.

Another driver is friction management. Systems often attempt to minimise burden for most users while retaining the ability to intervene when risk appears higher. Combining methods allows friction to be distributed unevenly. Some users encounter little resistance, while others face more demanding processes.

Fallbacks play a particularly important role. When a primary method fails-due to technical issues, user inability or environmental conditions, systems must decide whether to deny access, retry or escalate. Introducing an alternative method can seem like a humane and inclusive choice. It also introduces new complexity.

Each combination creates transitions: moments where the system decides to change how it is interacting with the user. These transitions are where confusion, frustration and error are most likely to occur. Users often experience them as arbitrary, especially when escalation is poorly explained or inconsistently applied.

Combination also complicates accountability. When a decision is based on multiple methods, it becomes harder to explain which element was decisive. Responsibility can diffuse across components, teams and organisations. This diffusion makes governance more challenging, particularly when outcomes are contested.

Importantly, combining methods does not automatically improve outcomes. It changes the trade-offs. Layering can reduce uncertainty in some cases while increasing friction and exclusion in others. Sequential use can smooth initial interactions while making failure more punishing. Fallbacks can improve accessibility while weakening the clarity of decision criteria.

These effects are rarely anticipated at design time. Combinations evolve in response to operational feedback, regulatory scrutiny or public concern. Over time, systems can accumulate methods that were never intended to interact. The resulting behaviour is shaped less by any individual method than by how they have been stitched together.

This is why it is misleading to treat combinations as inherently superior. They are responses to complexity, not solutions to it. Each additional layer increases the number of configuration choices that must be managed and the number of assumptions that must hold for the system to behave as intended.

5.7 Configuration determines method behaviour

If methods are tools and combinations are responses to complexity, configuration is where age assurance systems actually take shape.

Configuration choices determine how methods behave in practice. They decide when a method is invoked, how its outputs are interpreted, what happens when confidence, binding and security is low and how users move through the system. While methods are often discussed in abstract terms, configuration translates them into lived experience.

These choices are rarely treated as policy decisions, yet they function as such. Thresholds define who is challenged and who passes without friction. Retry limits decide how much effort is expected of users before access is denied. Timeouts determine whether failure feels temporary or final. Escalation paths shape who bears the burden of uncertainty. Binding determines if the age assurance result relates to the right individual.

Defaults are particularly powerful. They are often inherited from vendor settings, early prototypes or regulatory assumptions and then left unchanged. Over time, defaults harden into norms. They become the behaviour of the system, even when no one can clearly explain why they were chosen.

This is why the same method can behave very differently across deployments. Two systems may both rely on estimation, yet one may challenge users frequently while another rarely does. The difference lies not in the algorithm, but in how its outputs are analysed and acted upon. Configuration determines whether uncertainty is tolerated, concealed or punished.

Configuration also mediates how systems respond to failure. When a method does not produce a usable result, the system must decide what to do next. Does it retry automatically? Does it ask the user to try again? Does it escalate to a different method? Does it deny access outright? Each option communicates something about trust, responsibility and proportionality.

These decisions are not merely technical. They encode values about fairness, inclusion and risk tolerance. Yet they are often made under operational pressure, without explicit reflection. Incident response, regulatory scrutiny or public controversy can drive rapid configuration changes that persist long after the triggering event has passed.

Over time, configuration drift becomes a significant source of divergence between intended and actual system behaviour. Adjustments accumulate. Exceptions become standard paths. Security can be degraded. What began as a carefully balanced design gradually shifts in response to short-term pressures.

Governance mechanisms rarely keep pace with this drift. Configuration is often managed by technical teams, while accountability sits elsewhere in the organisation. Documentation lags behind reality. Assumptions made during design are no longer tested. The system continues to function, but it no longer behaves as originally understood.

This gap is one of the reasons why age assurance outcomes can surprise their designers. When systems are evaluated or challenged, attention often focuses on the method, even though the decisive factors lie in configuration choices that have evolved quietly over time.

Configuration also interacts with behaviour in powerful ways. Small changes in thresholds or retries can alter user experience dramatically. What feels like a minor adjustment to improve assurance can trigger significant increases in dropout or exclusion. Conversely, small relaxations can change how users perceive fairness and effort.

Because these effects are nonlinear, configuration choices are difficult to optimise. There is no setting that is universally appropriate. What works in one context may fail in another. What is proportionate at one point in time may become excessive as use patterns change.

Despite this, configuration is often treated as a one-time task rather than an ongoing responsibility. Systems are deployed with settings that are assumed to be stable, even as context, behaviour and expectations evolve. When problems arise, they are addressed reactively rather than through systematic review.

Recognising configuration as the real control surface of age assurance has important implications. It shifts responsibility away from abstract debates about method superiority and toward concrete decisions about how systems operate. It makes visible the fact that many of the most consequential choices in age assurance are not made by algorithms, but by people adjusting parameters.

5.8 Why method debates distract from the real work

Despite decades of experience and repeated evidence from deployment, debates about age assurance continue to centre on methods. Verification is promoted as definitive. Estimation is criticised as unreliable. Inference is alternately praised as proportionate or condemned as opaque. These debates recur across policy consultations, procurement processes and public discourse.

Their persistence is revealing.

Method debates endure not because they are particularly informative, but because they are comforting. They offer a way to talk about age assurance that feels concrete and bounded. Choosing a method suggests decisiveness. Comparing methods suggests progress. Mandating a method suggests control.

Most importantly, method debates allow responsibility to be relocated. If outcomes are unsatisfactory, the method can be blamed. If harms occur, the technology can be questioned. Attention is directed away from the harder work of system design, configuration and governance.

This displacement is understandable. The real work of age assurance is uncomfortable. It requires acknowledging uncertainty, making trade-offs explicit and accepting that no configuration will satisfy all objectives simultaneously. It demands ongoing judgement rather than one-time decisions.

Method debates simplify this reality. They imply that better tools will resolve social and organisational tensions. They encourage the belief that confidence can be specified rather than cultivated.

Reframing is therefore necessary. The question is not which method is strongest, but how systems distribute effort, risk and responsibility. The question is not how much certainty a method claims to deliver, but how uncertainty is managed and communicated. The question is not whether a method is privacy preserving in theory, but how data behaves over time in practice.

When debates are reframed in this way, methods do not disappear from view. They become contextualised. They are understood as components whose effects depend on how they are embedded and governed.

This reframing also clarifies why age assurance resists simple answers. Systems must balance competing objectives that cannot be fully reconciled. They must operate across diverse contexts with differing expectations. They must adapt as behaviour and norms evolve.

Chapter 6 – From Methods to Systems: Components, Flows and Dependencies

6.1 Why systems matter more than components

Age assurance becomes genuinely difficult only after the technology starts working.

Before deployment, the problem appears tractable. Methods can be compared, accuracy figures can be cited, security properties can be asserted and components can be evaluated in isolation. From that vantage point, it is tempting to believe that building a good system is primarily a matter of choosing good parts and assembling them correctly. If each component does what it claims to do, the system should behave well.

This belief does not survive contact with the real world.

In operational environments, age assurance systems fail even when every identifiable component appears to function as intended. No algorithm crashes. No service goes offline. No obvious defect presents itself. Yet users are wrongly excluded, inappropriate access is granted, disputes multiply and trust erodes. Investigations struggle to identify a single point of failure because there is none.

The reason is simple and uncomfortable: system behaviour is not the sum of component behaviour.

Components operate locally. Systems operate across time, context, interpretation and responsibility. Between the moment evidence is generated and the moment a decision is experienced, that evidence is transformed (sometimes repeatedly) by orchestration logic, thresholds, interfaces, policies and human intervention. Each transformation is small, reasonable and defensible in isolation. Collectively, they produce outcomes that no individual component "intended". This is not a flaw in implementation. It is a normal property of socio-technical systems.

One of the most persistent misconceptions in age assurance is not that certification is unhelpful, but that certification of methods or components is assumed to say more than it can. Certification at the component level plays an important role. It can establish that a method meets defined characteristics under stated conditions and that it behaves consistently within a known scope. What it cannot do is predict how that method will behave once it is embedded in a live service, combined with other components, shaped by configuration choices and exposed to real users over time.

Those questions are not about whether a component works, but about how a system behaves. Addressing them requires system-level certification that looks across components, interfaces and configuration in operation and that considers behaviour over time rather than at a single point. The complementary roles of component-level and system-level certification and how they should be understood together, are explored in more detail in Chapter 12.

Not understanding the difference between methods, components and systems is why systems can fail without fault. A verification component may bind a date of birth correctly. An estimation component may produce statistically sound classifications. An inference component may draw reasonable conclusions from contextual signals. Each can be "correct" on its own terms. Yet the system that combines them may behave erratically, unfairly or disproportionately.

A confidence score generated by a method is not the same thing as confidence in the resulting decision. Confidence is accumulated, attenuated or amplified as outputs pass through thresholds, fallbacks, escalation paths and human interpretation. At each step, uncertainty is handled, sometimes explicitly, often implicitly. By the time a final outcome is reached, the system may present certainty that no single component would have claimed on its own.

This is one reason why age assurance systems often appear more decisive at their edges than they are at their core. The further a decision is from the evidence that generated it, the more final it tends to appear. This is not because the evidence has become stronger, but because the system has exhausted its mechanisms for expressing uncertainty.

6.2 Drawing the system boundary (and why it's hard)

Every claim about how an age assurance system behaves rests on a prior decision that is rarely made explicit: where the system is assumed to begin and end.

This boundary setting is so fundamental and so often implicit, that it shapes almost every subsequent misunderstanding about responsibility, failure and accountability. When age assurance systems disappoint or worse, cause harm, the problem is frequently traced to a method, a vendor or a design choice. Far less often is attention paid to the quieter question of whether the system under discussion was ever correctly bounded in the first place.

In practice, age assurance systems do not have natural edges. They fade into surrounding technical infrastructure, organisational processes, human judgement and downstream consequences. The boundary is therefore not something that can be discovered; it is something that is chosen. And that choice is rarely neutral.

From a technical perspective, it is convenient to draw the system boundary tightly. The system becomes the service that generates an age signal or decision and everything else is treated as context. Inputs arrive from outside; outputs are handed off. Once the output has been delivered, the system's responsibility is considered complete.

From a user's perspective, this framing makes little sense. Users experience age assurance as a single journey: from the moment they are asked to prove or demonstrate eligibility, through the interaction itself and into whatever consequences follow. Whether an access denial is generated by a model, a policy rule or a downstream interpretation is irrelevant. For the user, it is all "the system".

Regulatory and governance perspectives introduce further tension. Oversight bodies are often concerned not just with the moment of decision, but with how evidence is stored, how outcomes are audited, how disputes are handled and how results are reused over time. These activities are routinely placed outside the "technical system" boundary, even though they materially affect fairness, proportionality and harm.

The result is a persistent mismatch: systems are designed and assessed as if they are smaller than the systems users and regulators actually encounter.

Boundary choices are not simply analytical conveniences. They are shaped by incentives, certification requirements, liability concerns, organisational structure and procurement models. Drawing a narrow boundary limits formal responsibility. It simplifies contracts, reduces apparent scope and makes assurance claims easier to defend. It also pushes complexity and risk outward.

In many deployments, the boundary is drawn precisely at the point where accountability becomes uncomfortable. The system "ends" before human review begins. It "ends" before appeals are processed. It "ends" before logs are examined or patterns are analysed. These activities are treated as operational or organisational matters, rather than as part of the age assurance system itself.

This boundary setting has consequences.

When systems fail, the failure often occurs in spaces that were declared out of scope. Decisions are overturned by humans who lack context. Appeals rely on incomplete records. Users are asked to resubmit evidence without understanding why their previous attempt failed. From the narrow system perspective, nothing has gone wrong. From the lived system perspective, trust is breaking down.

Boundaries are also political in a more subtle sense. They determine whose values are embedded in system behaviour. A boundary drawn tightly around technical components privileges engineering considerations over user experience. A boundary drawn around contractual responsibilities has the effect of privileging organisational convenience over accountability. A boundary drawn without reference to downstream impact privileges short-term decision-making over long-term consequences.

Age assurance systems are particularly sensitive to these dynamics because they operate at points of exclusion. Decisions are binary or at thresholds. Errors are often experienced as personal, not abstract. The system boundary determines whether those experiences are treated as anomalies, expected friction or systemic failure.

There is also a temporal dimension to boundary-setting that is frequently overlooked. Systems are often bounded as if decisions are instantaneous and disposable. In reality, age assurance outcomes persist. They influence future access, create records and shape user behaviour. A decision made today can affect a user's experience tomorrow, even if the technical system no longer "remembers" making it.

When boundaries ignore this persistence, accountability gaps open up. No single actor feels responsible for accumulated effects. Patterns emerge that no one is tasked with noticing.

Another complicating factor is that different actors operate with different implicit boundaries simultaneously. A provider may treat the system as ending at the delivery of an age assurance result. A relying party may treat it as ending at an access decision. A user may treat it as ending only when they get to what they want. These perspectives coexist, but they are rarely reconciled.

The consequence is not just confusion, but systemic fragility. When something goes wrong, each actor can truthfully claim that the failure occurred outside their boundary. Responsibility becomes fragmented without being denied outright. Everyone is partially responsible; no one is fully accountable.

This is why governance mechanisms that focus narrowly on technical performance struggle to address real-world harms. They assess the system that was declared, not the system that actually exists. They reinforce boundary choices rather than interrogating them.

Drawing system boundaries explicitly does not solve these problems on its own, but failing to do so guarantees they will persist. Once boundaries are acknowledged as choices rather than facts, it becomes possible to ask harder questions. Why is this activity outside the system? Who benefits from that choice? Who bears the cost? What assumptions are being made about behaviour beyond the boundary?

6.3 Components, interfaces and the spaces between

In practice, interfaces are where most age assurance systems acquire their risk. An interface is not just a technical connection. It is a moment of translation. Something understood in one context must be re-expressed in another. Evidence becomes output. Output becomes input. A nuanced internal assessment becomes a simplified external signal. Each translation discards information, whether intentionally or not.

At these points, uncertainty is not resolved; it is reshaped. A component may generate a confidence score, a probability distribution or a bounded estimate. The next component may accept only a binary input. A threshold is applied. The result crosses an interface as "pass" or "fail," with no trace of how close the decision was, what assumptions were made or how stable the result might be under slightly different conditions.

Nothing has gone wrong technically. The interface has done exactly what it was designed to do. Yet something important has been lost.

Timing mismatches compound this effect. Components operate at different speeds, under different assumptions about freshness and relevance. One part of the system may rely on real-time evidence; another may reuse cached results. Decisions are sometimes made using information that was valid minutes, hours or days earlier, without that delay being visible to the user or the operator.

These mismatches are rarely documented as risks because each component is behaving reasonably in isolation. Only when viewed as a system does the fragility become apparent.

Format mismatches are equally consequential. Information that is meaningful to one component may be ambiguous or misleading to another. A result intended as advisory may be treated as authoritative. A signal intended to reduce risk may be interpreted as proof. Interfaces rarely communicate intent; they communicate data points.

When automated components disagree, fail or produce unexpected results, the system often hands control to a person. This handoff is an interface like any other, but one that is far less visible in design documentation. The person receiving the handoff is expected to resolve ambiguity using limited information, under time pressure and often without clear authority.

Frontline staff, moderators or support agents become the de facto integrators of the system. They reconcile outputs that were never designed to be reconciled. They explain decisions they did not design. They manage user frustration caused by interactions they cannot see. These human interfaces are where responsibility weakens most sharply. The system's logic becomes opaque, even to those operating it. Decisions are justified post hoc. Escalation becomes a coping mechanism rather than a designed pathway.

The more components a system contains, the more interfaces it has. Risk does not increase linearly with complexity; it concentrates at these junctions. Each interface introduces a small loss of fidelity, a small shift in interpretation, a small assumption about context. Over time, these losses accumulate.

This is why age assurance systems often exhibit patterns that no single component predicts. Users encounter inconsistent outcomes. Edge cases cluster around thresholds. Similar interactions produce different results depending on timing or pathway. Appeals reveal gaps in explanation rather than errors in calculation.

These are not signs of malfunction. They are signs that the system is operating across interfaces that were never designed to carry the full weight placed upon them.

A common response is to try to strengthen interfaces through standardisation. Clearer schemas, richer metadata, more explicit signals are introduced. While this can help, it does not eliminate the underlying problem. Interfaces cannot fully preserve the meaning, context or uncertainty of what passes through them. They can only manage loss, not prevent it.

The mistake is to assume that better interfaces will make systems behave like components. They will not. They merely shift where interpretation occurs.

Understanding age assurance at system level therefore requires accepting that interfaces are not neutral conduits. They are active sites where evidence is simplified, confidence is reshaped and responsibility is quietly transferred.

6.4 Data flows are not decision flows

Data flows describe how information moves. Decision flows describe how authority is exercised. In many age assurance systems, data moves smoothly while decision authority becomes increasingly unclear. Evidence is collected, transformed, transmitted, stored and audited, yet no single point in the system can convincingly answer the question: *who decided and on what basis?*

This distinction matters because age assurance is not merely an informational activity. It is an exercise of power. It determines access, exclusion, escalation and sometimes suspicion. The legitimacy of those outcomes depends not just on the availability of data, but on the clarity of decision-making authority.

In practice, age assurance systems are often designed with meticulous attention to data provenance. Inputs are logged. Outputs are timestamped. Records are retained. From a technical perspective, the system appears transparent and traceable. Yet when outcomes are contested, this apparent transparency dissolves.

Audit trails show *what* happened without explaining *why* it happened in a way that is intelligible to users, operators or oversight bodies. The system can replay a sequence of data transformations without identifying where discretion was exercised, where assumptions were applied or where uncertainty was resolved into a final outcome.

This is because decisions are rarely made at a single point. They emerge gradually as evidence passes through thresholds, policies and interpretations. A probabilistic output becomes a categorical signal. A contextual qualifier is dropped. A fallback is triggered.

Each step feels operational rather than decisional, yet together they produce a decision with real consequences.

The further a decision is from the original evidence, the harder it is to locate responsibility for it.

This problem becomes especially visible during appeals or disputes. Users ask why they were denied access, escalated or required to provide additional evidence. The system can respond with data scores, flags and timestamps but struggles to articulate a reasoned judgement. The explanation becomes procedural rather than substantive.

From the user's perspective, this feels evasive. From the system's perspective, it is accurate: no single component "decided" in the way the question implies.

Decision authority is often assumed to lie downstream, where the outcome is experienced. A relying party may believe that the age assurance provider made the decision. The provider may believe it merely supplied a signal. The system designer may believe the decision lies in policy configuration. Each belief is plausible and together they leave a vacuum.

Another complicating factor is the transformation of evidence over time. Age assurance systems often reuse data or decisions beyond their original context. A result generated for one interaction may influence later ones. A signal intended to be advisory may become determinative when cached or reused. Evidence ages, but systems rarely surface that ageing.

As a result, decisions are sometimes made on stale or partially transformed evidence without this being apparent to anyone involved. The data flow is intact; the decision context is not.

This is why strong data governance does not automatically produce strong decision governance. Knowing where data came from does not tell you who was authorised to rely on it, under what conditions or for how long. Provenance is not legitimacy.

The distinction between data flows and decision flows also exposes a deeper tension in system design. Data flows are relatively easy to automate, optimise and audit. Decision flows are harder to formalise without confronting uncomfortable questions about discretion, authority and accountability.

Many systems avoid this confrontation by letting decisions "emerge" from configuration and thresholds. No one explicitly decides; the system simply behaves. This can be efficient, but it obscures the fact that decisions are still being made-just without a clear locus of responsibility.

In age assurance, where decisions directly affect access and participation, this obscurity is particularly damaging. It undermines trust, complicates redress and weakens the basis for assurance. A system that cannot clearly explain how decisions are made cannot convincingly claim that those decisions are fair, proportionate or accountable.

Understanding that data flows are not decision flows is therefore a turning point. It forces a recognition that evidence alone does not justify outcomes. Decisions require authority, context and explanation. Systems that fail to make these visible will continue to struggle under scrutiny.

6.5 Dependencies, assumptions and fragility

In design and procurement, dependencies are frequently categorised informally as "critical" or "non-critical". Critical dependencies are the ones whose failure is assumed to stop the system outright: the core service, the network connection, the database. Non-critical dependencies are expected to degrade gracefully or not to matter very much if they fail.

Real-world deployments repeatedly show that this distinction is unreliable. Dependencies that are considered non-critical often become critical precisely because systems are not designed around their failure. When an upstream data source becomes less reliable or an external service degrades rather than fails cleanly, the system continues to operate, but on distorted inputs. Decisions are still made. Outcomes still occur. The failure is silent.

Age assurance systems are particularly vulnerable to this kind of silent degradation because they rely on signals whose validity depends on context. Device quality, environmental conditions, data freshness and user behaviour all influence outcomes. When these factors change, systems rarely stop. They simply become less accurate, less fair or less proportionate.

Latency is a common example. Small increases in response time rarely trigger alarms, yet they change user behaviour. Users retry, abandon or escalate. Systems interpret this behaviour as risk or non-compliance, triggering stricter pathways. A dependency that merely slowed down has reshaped system outcomes.

Availability is another. Partial outages, rate limits or degraded performance in external services often lead systems to rely on cached results, fallbacks or alternative signals. These substitutes are rarely equivalent to the primary pathway, but they are treated as such because the system must continue to operate.

Upstream data quality is an even more subtle dependency. Age assurance systems often rely on records, attributes or signals that are assumed to be accurate enough. When those assumptions are violated through outdated information, inconsistencies or biased coverage, the system has no way to detect the problem. It continues to function, producing decisions that appear legitimate but rest on unstable foundations.

These dependencies interact with each other in ways that amplify fragility. A small degradation in data quality combined with a slight increase in latency and an aggressive threshold can produce outcomes that are wildly different from those observed in testing or pilots. No single factor is sufficient to explain the change. Together, they form a failure cascade.

Resilience is rarely distributed evenly across the system. Core components may be monitored, tested and hardened. Peripheral dependencies-especially those outside organisational or contractual control-are often left unexamined. When stress arrives, it concentrates in these weaker areas.

Because many dependencies sit outside formal system boundaries, their impact is easy to deny. When failures occur, they are described as environmental issues, user behaviour or exceptional circumstances. The system itself is declared healthy because its internal components are operating as designed.

From the perspective of the user or the relying party, this distinction is meaningless. They experience a system that behaves unpredictably, inconsistently or unfairly. From the perspective of governance, it is dangerous. It creates the illusion of robustness while fragility accumulates unseen.

The deeper problem is that dependencies carry assumptions that are rarely articulated. Assumptions about how users will behave, how often conditions will deviate, how external services will evolve and how quickly issues will be noticed. When these assumptions fail, systems lack the conceptual tools to recognise the failure as systemic.

This adaptive behaviour can be mistaken for resilience. In reality, it is often a sign that fragility is being managed by shifting burden onto users and frontline actors.

6.6 Where confidence is gained, lost and misplaced

Confidence is the quiet currency of age assurance systems. Every age-related decision implies a judgement about how sure the system is, even when that judgement is never stated explicitly. Confidence determines whether access is granted immediately, whether additional steps are required, whether a result is accepted as final or whether a human is asked to intervene. Yet despite its centrality, confidence is rarely treated as something that moves through a system. It is treated as something that exists at a point.

In practice, confidence does not sit still. It flows.

At the point where evidence is first generated confidence is often relatively well understood. Methods produce outputs that are probabilistic, conditional or bounded. Uncertainty is visible, at least internally. Designers and engineers know where the limits lie.

As that output moves through the system, however, confidence is transformed.

Thresholds convert ranges into categories. Policies convert likelihoods into permissions. Interfaces convert nuanced assessments into simplified messages. At each step, the system resolves uncertainty not by reducing it, but by hiding it. What emerges downstream is often a decision that appears more certain than the evidence that originally supported it.

This is not usually the result of overconfidence at the point of measurement. It is the result of abstraction.

Systems are good at abstracting complexity away from users and operators. That is one of their purposes. The problem arises when uncertainty is treated as a form of complexity to be abstracted, rather than as a property that must be preserved or managed. Once abstracted away, it cannot be recovered.

Confidence therefore degrades as it moves through a system, even as its outward expression becomes firmer. The system behaves as if it knows more, when in fact it has merely stopped expressing what it does not know.

This effect is amplified at system edges.

Decisions presented to users or relying parties are often binary or final. "Access granted." "Access denied." "Further verification required." These outcomes carry an implicit claim of certainty, regardless of how provisional or conditional the underlying evidence may have been.

Ironically, this means that the parts of the system that are furthest from the evidence often project the highest confidence. Scrutiny is lowest where certainty appears greatest.

Downstream components tend to trust upstream outputs because questioning them would require access to information they do not have. The interface does not communicate uncertainty, so the receiving component treats the signal as authoritative. This effect is amplified when confidence is carried in shared artefacts such as signals, tokens, credentials or passkeys. Once uncertainty has been collapsed into a portable assertion, it becomes easy to reuse, relay or cache without re-examining the conditions under which it was generated. Over time, this trust becomes structural. The system behaves as if confidence has been validated at each step, when in reality it has merely been inherited and propagated.

Assurance boundaries reinforce this effect. When assurance activities focus on individual components or stages, they validate confidence locally. The system as a whole may never be assessed for how confidence accumulates, degrades or is misapplied across boundaries. Each part is "assured," yet the overall confidence story remains incoherent.

Edge cases cluster around thresholds because that is where confidence is thinnest. Small changes in input produce large changes in outcome because the system has no way to express partial confidence. Users experience these shifts as arbitrariness, even when the underlying method behaves consistently.

Appeals and disputes further expose misplaced confidence. When users challenge outcomes, systems often struggle to explain not just what happened, but how sure they were meant to be. Explanations fall back on procedure rather than judgement. The system can describe its steps, but not its confidence.

Another subtle effect is that confidence often migrates away from evidence and toward process. If the system followed its rules, the outcome is treated as legitimate, regardless of whether the evidence was strong. Process compliance becomes a proxy for confidence.

This is particularly problematic in age assurance because process compliance is easier to demonstrate than evidential adequacy. A system can show that it applied thresholds consistently, logged decisions correctly and escalated according to policy, while still making decisions on weak or inappropriate evidence.

Over time, this dynamic encourages systems to optimise for procedural certainty rather than evidential robustness. The system becomes confident that it is operating correctly, even as its decisions drift away from their original purpose.

Confidence also accumulates unevenly. Some users are consistently subject to higher scrutiny because the system lacks confidence in their signals, devices or contexts. Others pass through with minimal friction. These patterns are rarely visible at component level, but they shape lived experience and perceptions of fairness. Chapter 8 explores some of these trade-offs in more detail including those associated with demographic consistency.

Because confidence is not tracked explicitly as it flows, systems have little ability to correct these imbalances. They can adjust thresholds or add fallbacks, but they cannot easily see where confidence is being lost or assumed.

Understanding confidence as something that moves and is distorted as it passes through systems is essential for meaningful assurance. Without this understanding, confidence claims remain superficial. Systems appear confident where they should be cautious and cautious where they should be confident.

6.7 Configuration as system behaviour, not tuning

In age assurance systems, configuration *is* behaviour. It is where abstract intent becomes operational reality and where policy choices are translated into lived experience. Long after methods and components have stabilised, configuration continues to determine who is admitted, who is challenged and who is excluded.

Thresholds are the most obvious example. They appear technical, even mathematical, but they encode judgements about acceptable error, risk tolerance and harm distribution. A threshold defines how much uncertainty the system is willing to tolerate before acting. Raising or lowering it changes not just accuracy metrics, but who bears the cost of caution.

Retries and timeouts carry similar weight. Allowing multiple attempts may improve inclusion but increase exposure to misuse. Limiting retries may reduce abuse but disproportionately affect users who struggle with the interface, environment or device. These are not implementation details; they are policy decisions expressed in code.

Fallback paths are where configuration choices become particularly visible. When a primary method fails or produces low confidence, the system must decide what happens next. Does it escalate to a more intrusive method? Does it deny access? Does it defer the decision? Each option reflects a different view of proportionality and responsibility.

Defaults are even more powerful, precisely because they are rarely questioned. Default thresholds, default retry limits, default escalation rules persist because they "work well enough." As contexts change-user populations, threat models, regulatory expectations-those defaults remain. Configuration drift becomes normal.

This drift is rarely visible. Systems do not announce that their behaviour has changed relative to their original intent. They simply adapt to operational realities. Engineers tweak settings to reduce load. Operators adjust rules to handle complaints. Each change is locally rational. Collectively, they transform the system.

From the outside, the system still appears to be doing the same thing. From the inside, its behaviour may have shifted substantially.

Configuration also determines how confidence, discussed in the previous section, is expressed and resolved. Thresholds decide where uncertainty becomes certainty. Escalation rules decide when doubt triggers friction. Timeouts decide when silence is interpreted as failure. These choices govern how confidence flows through the system more directly than any method characteristic.

Because configuration is often treated as operational rather than conceptual, it is rarely subject to the same scrutiny as method choice. It is adjusted by different actors, under different incentives and often without clear ownership. Documentation lags behind reality. Assurance focuses on what was designed, not what is currently configured.

This separation creates a dangerous illusion: that the system being assured is the system being operated.

In age assurance, where outcomes are sensitive and often contested, this illusion matters. Users experience configuration, not architecture. They encounter thresholds, retries and fallbacks, not abstract methods. When outcomes feel arbitrary or unfair, it is often configuration-not technology-that is responsible.

This perspective also reveals why configuration choices are so rarely reviewed holistically. They sit at the intersection of technical, operational and policy domains. No single role owns them fully. As a result, they accumulate quietly until their effects become visible through failure or controversy.

6.8 Why system thinking changes what "good" looks like

Once age assurance is understood as a system phenomenon, it becomes difficult to hold on to familiar ideas of what it means for a solution to be "good".

Many of the measures that dominate early discussions around accuracy, speed, conversion rates, false positives and false negatives, remain relevant, but they are no longer sufficient. They describe how parts behave under certain conditions, not how systems perform over time, under pressure and in the presence of disagreement.

A system that "works as designed" can still fail in every way that matters.

Design intent is necessarily partial. It reflects assumptions about users, contexts, dependencies and behaviour that rarely survive intact. Systems that cling too tightly to their original design parameters often become brittle. They perform well in the narrow conditions they anticipated and poorly everywhere else.

System thinking therefore shifts attention away from optimisation and toward robustness. A highly effective age assurance system needs to not only work as intended but be robust. The question is no longer how precisely a method performs, but how the system behaves when inputs are messy, signals are ambiguous, dependencies degrade or users act in unexpected ways.

In age assurance, these conditions are not edge cases. They are normal.

Resilience matters more than precision because the cost of failure is unevenly distributed. Small errors in controlled settings may look acceptable on a dashboard, but they can accumulate into systematic exclusion or disproportionate burden in practice. A system that tolerates uncertainty and degrades gracefully will often produce fairer outcomes than one that insists on maximal confidence at all times.

System thinking also reframes performance. Speed and efficiency are valuable, but they are not neutral. Faster systems tend to surface decisions more quickly than they surface understanding. Efficiency gains often come from suppressing ambiguity rather than resolving it. In sensitive contexts, that trade-off deserves scrutiny.

What looks like good performance from an operational perspective may feel like arbitrary rigidity from a user's perspective. System thinking insists that both views matter.

This reframing has consequences for procurement and governance. Selecting a solution based on component-level claims or benchmark results says little about how it will behave once integrated into a larger environment. Evaluating systems requires attention to interfaces, configuration practices, escalation paths and responsibility structures, factors that are rarely visible in marketing materials or technical specifications.

It also changes how assurance should be understood. Assurance is not a badge that can be attached to a component or a system at a point in time. It is an ongoing practice of observing behaviour, questioning assumptions and responding to drift. Systems that cannot be adjusted without undermining trust are not well assured, no matter how strong their initial credentials.

Perhaps most importantly, system thinking changes how success is judged over time.

A "good" age assurance system is not one that never fails. It is one that fails in predictable ways, recognises those failures and provides mechanisms for recovery and learning. It is one where uncertainty is managed rather than denied, where responsibility is visible rather than displaced and where confidence is earned rather than assumed.

This does not mean abandoning ambition or rigour. It means directing them toward the properties that actually matter in practice: adaptability, transparency and proportionality.

Chapter 7 – Context of Use: The Variable that Changes Everything

7.1 Why context is the first question, not the last

When organisations first encounter the need for age assurance, the question they ask is almost never about context. It is about solutions. What technology exists? What method is recommended? What system has been used elsewhere? The search begins with tools rather than conditions.

This ordering feels natural because solutions are tangible. They can be demonstrated, compared and procured. They promise progress in an area that otherwise feels ambiguous, contested and politically sensitive. Context, by contrast, feels vague and difficult to pin down. It resists neat specification. It does not fit easily into procurement documents or architectural diagrams. So it is deferred.

That deferral is where problems begin.

Age assurance is not, at its core, a technology problem. It is a decision problem. It exists to support judgements about eligibility, access or protection in situations where age matters and certainty is imperfect. Those judgements only make sense in relation to the circumstances in which they are made. Remove those circumstances and the idea of an "effective" solution quickly becomes meaningless.

Effectiveness cannot be assessed in isolation because there is no such thing as context-free effectiveness. A system that appears accurate, efficient or acceptable in one situation may be harmful, exclusionary or fragile in another. The same error can be trivial in one setting and serious in another. The same friction can be reassuring in one environment and intolerable in the next. Context determines which outcomes matter and which failures are acceptable.

Despite this organisations routinely treat context as something to be "applied" after a solution has been selected. They choose a method or system first, then ask how it can be deployed across multiple uses. This sequencing locks in assumptions early, often without recognising them as such. Decisions about thresholds, interfaces, escalation paths and configuration are made under an implicit picture of how the system will be used. When reality diverges from that picture, the system is blamed rather than the assumptions that shaped it.

Context-free solutions are especially appealing because they promise transferability. If a system works somewhere, it is tempting to believe it will work elsewhere. This belief is reinforced by demonstrations, pilots and case studies that highlight success while quietly embedding the conditions that made that success possible. Those conditions are rarely portable.

Early deployments often occur in unusually favourable contexts. Attention is high. Use is limited. Participants are motivated or supervised. Support is readily available. Under these conditions, many systems appear robust. The danger lies in mistaking this early success for general suitability.

Once a system is scaled or reused, context reasserts itself. Users encounter it more often. Incentives change. Edge cases multiply. What was once rare becomes routine. Behaviour adapts. The system has not changed, but its meaning has. Friction accumulates. Errors cluster. Complaints rise. At this point organisations often describe the system as failing in practice despite having "worked" before.

What has actually failed is the sequencing. By treating context as the last question rather than the first organisations postpone the hardest judgements until they are embedded in deployed systems.

By then, choices are constrained. Technical integrations are complete. Contracts are signed. Changing course is costly, politically and operationally.

Asking about context first does not eliminate difficulty. It brings it forward. It forces organisations to confront uncomfortable questions early: who bears the cost of being wrong, how often decisions will occur, what happens when users do not behave as expected and how assumptions will be revisited over time. These questions resist definitive answers, but avoiding them does not make them go away.

Once age assurance is understood as a system – rather than a method or a check – the centrality of context becomes unavoidable. Systems do not operate in abstraction. They operate in lived environments, shaped by human behaviour organisational practices and evolving conditions. Context is not an external variable acting on a finished system. It is part of the system itself.

For this reason, context cannot be treated as a refinement step or a deployment detail. It is the foundation on which all subsequent decisions rest. Without a clear understanding of the context in which age-related decisions are made, questions about methods, configurations or performance have no stable meaning.

Context is therefore not the last thing to consider once a solution has been chosen. It is the first question that gives every other question its shape.

7.2 What we mean by "context of use"

When the phrase "context of use" appears in discussions of age assurance, it is often treated as a label rather than an idea. It becomes shorthand for a sector, a channel or a deployment setting – online versus physical, supervised versus unsupervised, public versus private. These labels are convenient, but they obscure more than they reveal.

Context of use is not a category into which a system can be placed. It is the set of conditions under which age-related decisions are actually made, experienced and relied upon. Those conditions are not static and they are rarely singular. They form a living environment in which technical systems interact with people organisations and time.

At its simplest, context is about the situation in which a decision occurs. But even that simple framing quickly expands. A decision is not just a moment of classification or verification. It is part of a sequence of actions. Someone approaches a system with a purpose. They bring expectations shaped by past experience. They encounter instructions, interfaces and constraints. An outcome is produced and something happens next. That "next step" may be access, refusal, delay, escalation or substitution. Each of these possibilities feeds back into how the system is understood and used in the future.

It is the concept that you can't jump into the same river twice. The first time a user encounters an age assurance system, much of this is unknown. They do not yet know how intrusive it will feel, how long it will take, how likely it is to fail or what happens if it does. They proceed cautiously, often patiently. By the second or third encounter, those uncertainties have diminished. Users know where the friction lies, how deep the process goes, how cold it feels and how to get out if they need to. The system has not changed, but the experience of it has and with that, the context in which decisions are made.

Context therefore includes not only the decision itself, but what surrounds it before and after. It includes how often decisions occur, whether they are rare interruptions or routine interactions. It includes whether users experience them alone or in the presence of others, whether help is available and whether outcomes can be questioned or reversed. It includes what is at stake if the system is wrong and who feels the consequences of that error.

These conditions shape behaviour in ways that are difficult to predict from design documents alone. A system that is encountered once, in a low-pressure situation, invites patience and cooperation. The same system encountered repeatedly, under time pressure or emotional stress, invites avoidance, optimisation and circumvention. Nothing about the technology has changed, but the context has transformed its practical meaning.

Context also extends beyond users to organisations. How staff are trained, how exceptions are handled, how complaints are managed and how performance is monitored all contribute to the environment in which the system operates. An age assurance outcome does not end at the technical result; it becomes part of an organisational process that interprets, records and acts on that result. Those processes vary widely, even when systems appear similar.

Time is an inseparable part of context. At launch, a system exists in a moment of heightened attention. Assumptions are fresh. Edge cases are rare. Over time, familiarity sets in. Users learn how the system behaves. Organisations adjust configurations. Surrounding technologies evolve. Policies shift. What began as a carefully bounded use gradually stretches, often without anyone explicitly deciding to expand it.

This temporal dimension means that context cannot be fully specified in advance. Some conditions can be anticipated, but others only emerge through use. Early descriptions of context tend to reflect intentions rather than reality. They describe how a system is meant to be used, not how it will actually be used once it becomes part of everyday activity.

For this reason, context is always plural. Even within a single deployment, there are multiple contexts operating at once. There is the intended context imagined by designers and policymakers. There is the typical context experienced by most users. There are edge contexts where assumptions break down. There are emergent contexts created by repetition, scale or adaptation. These contexts overlap and interact, sometimes reinforcing each other, sometimes pulling in different directions.

Attempts to reduce this complexity to a single "context of use" description are understandable. They simplify communication and decision-making. But they also create a false sense of stability. They suggest that once context has been defined, it can be treated as fixed. In practice, the most important contextual shifts are those that go unnoticed because they do not announce themselves as changes.

Understanding context, then, is not about producing a definitive description. It is about recognising that age assurance systems are always situated, always contingent and always operating under conditions that influence how their outputs are generated and interpreted. Context is not something applied to a finished system; it is part of what the system is.

This perspective also explains why context cannot be treated as a purely technical matter. Social norms, organisational incentives and user expectations are not externalities. They shape behaviour just as surely as thresholds or configurations do. A system that ignores these factors may still function technically, but it will not function as intended.

By the time age assurance outcomes are relied upon – to allow or deny access, to trigger safeguards or to allocate responsibility – context has already done much of the work. It has shaped who engages, how they engage and what the outcome means in practice.

To understand age assurance without understanding context is therefore to misunderstand the problem itself. Context of use is not an optional framing device or a preliminary note. It is the environment in which age assurance acquires meaning and without which discussions of effectiveness, fairness or proportionality cannot be grounded in reality.

7.3 How the same system behaves differently in different contexts

One of the most persistent sources of confusion in age assurance is the belief that systems have a single, stable behaviour that can be observed, measured and relied upon regardless of where they are deployed. This belief is reinforced by technical documentation, demonstrations and evaluations that present systems as bounded artefacts: inputs go in, outputs come out and performance can be summarised.

In real use, this picture rarely survives contact with context.

When the same age assurance system is placed in different environments, its behaviour changes – not because the technology malfunctions, but because the conditions under which it operates alter the meaning and impact of its outputs. What looks like the same system on paper becomes a different system in practice.

Consider how behaviour shifts across settings that differ only slightly. In one environment, users may encounter the system occasionally, perhaps unexpectedly. The interaction feels like an interruption rather than a routine. Users take time to read instructions, follow prompts carefully and accept the result, even if it is inconvenient. A small amount of friction feels appropriate, even reassuring, because the interaction is framed as protective or exceptional.

In another environment, the same system is encountered repeatedly. It becomes part of a habitual flow. Users approach it with expectations shaped by prior encounters. They know roughly how long it will take, where it is likely to fail and what happens if it does. Under these conditions, patience erodes. The same friction that once felt tolerable now feels unnecessary. Errors that were once rare now feel frequent, simply because they are experienced more often.

Nothing about the method or configuration has changed. What has changed is repetition. Frequency alone can transform the user experience of an age assurance system, turning a manageable inconvenience into a persistent burden.

Supervision introduces another axis of variation. When interactions occur under observation (whether by staff, peers or authority figures) behaviour tends to align with expectations. Users comply, even when outcomes are unfavourable. They may ask for help, but they are less likely to abandon the process or attempt to circumvent it.

Remove that supervision and behaviour shifts. Users are left alone with the system. They explore its boundaries. They try different approaches. They abandon attempts that feel unfair or opaque. The same system, operating without oversight, produces different patterns of completion, failure and complaint.

Channels matter in similar ways. An interaction mediated through one channel may feel formal, constrained or consequential. The same interaction through another channel may feel casual or disposable. These differences influence how seriously users take the outcome, how willing they are to retry and how they respond to rejection or delay.

These contextual effects are not limited to users. Organisations experience them as well. In some environments, age assurance outcomes are treated as advisory signals, one input among many. In others, they are treated as definitive. The same technical result may be subject to review in one setting and accepted without question in another. These downstream interpretations shape how much weight the system effectively carries.

Because these differences emerge from use rather than design, they are often invisible to those evaluating systems in isolation. A system may appear to perform consistently in tests, yet produce very different real-world outcomes once embedded in different operational flows.

Acceptability is especially sensitive to these shifts. A level of friction that feels proportionate when stakes are high may feel arbitrary when stakes are low. A system that is tolerated as a safeguard in one context may be rejected as intrusive in another. These judgements are not errors of perception; they are rational responses to differing circumstances.

Importantly, these changes do not require dramatic contextual differences. Small shifts in how often a system is encountered, how quickly a decision is needed or how easily outcomes can be challenged can produce disproportionately large effects. What begins as an edge case can become a dominant pattern once conditions change.

This is why organisations are often surprised by how systems behave outside their original deployment setting. They observe outcomes that feel inconsistent or unstable and attribute them to flaws in the technology. In reality, the system is behaving consistently with its context. What has changed is not the system, but the environment in which its outputs are produced and interpreted.

Understanding this helps explain why attempts to standardise behaviour across contexts often fail. Configuration changes intended to "fix" problems in one setting can create new problems in another. Thresholds tuned for speed may increase exclusion elsewhere. Escalation paths that work under supervision may break down when users are alone.

From a distance, these effects can look like poor design or lack of robustness. From a contextual perspective, they are simply the predictable consequences of deploying the same system under different conditions.

Recognising this does not mean that systems cannot be compared or evaluated. It means that evaluation must always be situated. Observations about behaviour must be tied to the circumstances under which they were made. Claims about effectiveness must be understood as contingent, not universal.

7.4 Context, risk and proportionality

Discussions of age assurance are often framed in the language of risk. Certain uses are described as "high risk," others as "low risk," and systems are evaluated in terms of how well they manage those risks. This framing feels objective and reassuring. Risk appears to be something that can be identified, classified and mitigated through appropriate technical measures.

Risk is not an abstract property of an age assurance system or of an age-related decision. It is experienced by people in particular situations and it takes its meaning from what happens when things go wrong. The same technical error can be inconsequential in one context and deeply harmful in another. Without understanding context, risk assessments quickly become detached from lived reality.

Proportionality is meant to bridge this gap. It is the idea that the intrusiveness, friction and certainty of an age assurance system should be aligned with what is at stake. Where the consequences of error are severe, higher levels of assurance may be justified. Where the consequences are minor, lighter-touch approaches may be appropriate.

But proportionality is not a formula. It cannot be derived from risk labels alone. It depends on how risk manifests in a particular context and on whose interests are prioritised when trade-offs are made.

Consider how differently risk is experienced across contexts that appear similar on the surface. In one setting, a false rejection may mean a brief delay or inconvenience. In another, it may result in exclusion from something essential or time-sensitive. In one environment, a false acceptance may have little immediate impact. In another, it may expose someone to significant harm or legal consequence.

These differences do not arise because the system behaves differently in a technical sense. They arise because the context changes what follows from the decision. Risk is realised downstream, not at the point where an age assurance result is produced.

This is why attempts to classify contexts as inherently "high risk" or "low risk" often fail to travel well. Such labels flatten complex situations into single descriptors and obscure the distribution of harm. They hide questions about who bears the cost of being wrong and how often that cost is paid.

Proportionality decisions are therefore inseparable from value judgements. They involve choices about acceptable exclusion, acceptable intrusion and acceptable uncertainty. These choices are rarely neutral and they cannot be resolved by technical optimisation alone.

Context also determines how proportionality is perceived by users. A level of friction that feels reasonable when stakes are clear may feel arbitrary when stakes are opaque. A system that is tolerated as protective in one environment may be rejected as excessive in another. These reactions are not failures of communication; they are reflections of differing contextual expectations.

Importantly, proportionality is not a one-time decision. It evolves as context changes. Early deployments often operate under assumptions that do not hold at scale. As systems are used more frequently, by more diverse populations and under different conditions, the balance between caution and accessibility may need to be revisited.

What once felt proportionate can come to feel burdensome or exclusionary. Conversely, what once seemed sufficient may no longer provide adequate protection as behaviour adapts or as reliance on the system increases.

This temporal aspect of proportionality is often overlooked. Organisations may treat proportionality as something that can be "designed in" at the outset, rather than as an ongoing judgement that must be revisited. When context shifts quietly, proportionality can drift out of alignment without anyone explicitly deciding to change course.

Context also shapes how risk is distributed across actors. In some environments, users bear most of the risk of error. In others, organisations or third parties absorb it. These distributions influence behaviour. Where users bear the cost, they may resist or avoid the system. Where organisations bear the cost, they may seek higher assurance or tighter controls.

Understanding proportionality therefore requires looking beyond the technical characteristics of a system to the wider decision environment in which it operates. It requires asking not just whether a system reduces risk in some abstract sense, but how it reallocates risk across people and over time.

This perspective explains why debates about proportionality are often contentious. Different stakeholders experience risk differently and reasonable people can disagree about what level of intrusion or certainty is justified. Context does not eliminate these disagreements; it makes them visible.

Recognising the contextual nature of risk and proportionality does not undermine the case for age assurance. It grounds it. It shifts the focus from seeking universally "appropriate" solutions to making context-sensitive judgements that can be explained, revisited and, when necessary, revised.

7.5 When context assumptions break down over time

Every age assurance system is built on assumptions about how it will be used. These assumptions are rarely careless or naïve. They are typically grounded in research, consultation and early deployment experience. They reflect how designers, policymakers and implementers believe the system will fit into the world.

The problem is not that assumptions exist. It is that they are treated as stable.

At design time, assumptions often feel well founded because they are made under conditions of relative control. Early deployments involve limited user groups, heightened attention and a shared understanding that the system is new. Users are cautious. Operators are attentive. Support is readily available. Edge cases are rare. Under these conditions, systems tend to perform well. Error rates appear manageable. Feedback is broadly positive. It is easy to conclude that the system is fundamentally sound.

What this early success often conceals is how sensitive the system is to changes in use. As deployment widens and becomes routine, the context in which the system operates shifts. User populations broaden. Motivation varies. Some users encounter the system for the first time; others have interacted with it repeatedly. What once felt novel becomes familiar. What once felt acceptable becomes frustrating. Assumptions that held during early stages begin to erode.

Designers may have assumed occasional use, only to find the system embedded in repeated workflows. They may have assumed a certain level of digital literacy or access to devices, only to discover far greater diversity in practice. They may have assumed broadly cooperative behaviour, only to see incentives emerge that favour avoidance, optimisation or circumvention.

When these assumptions no longer hold, systems rarely fail dramatically. Instead, they begin to exhibit patterns that feel puzzling or disproportionate. Certain users are rejected more often than expected. Complaints cluster around particular interactions. Escalation mechanisms are used in ways that were not anticipated. Support teams encounter the same issues repeatedly, without a single technical fault to point to.

These signals are often treated as operational noise rather than as evidence of deeper misalignment. The response is incremental: adjust thresholds, tweak interfaces, add guidance, expand support. While such changes may alleviate symptoms, they do not address the underlying issue that the system is now operating in a context different from the one it was designed for.

Time compounds this effect. Users learn how the system behaves and adapt their actions accordingly. Workarounds spread. Predictability replaces uncertainty and predictability invites optimisation. At the same time, organisations change. Staff turnover erodes institutional memory. Configuration decisions made under specific pressures persist long after their rationale is forgotten. What began as a temporary adjustment becomes the default.

External conditions shift as well. Devices update. Platforms change policies. New integrations are added. Legal and organisational environments evolve. None of these changes is dramatic in isolation, but together they quietly alter the context in which the system operates.

Because this change is gradual, it often goes unnoticed. The system continues to function. Decisions continue to be made. Logs continue to be generated. From an operational perspective, nothing appears broken. Yet the relationship between the system's outputs and the decisions they are meant to support grows weaker.

Over time, this can produce a form of assurance decay. The system still produces results, but those results carry less substantive meaning. They signal process or compliance rather than providing confidence that decisions are being supported in the way originally intended.

7.6 Why context breaks comparisons and benchmarks

The desire to compare age assurance systems is understandable. Comparison promises clarity. It offers a way to choose between options, justify decisions and demonstrate diligence. Numbers, rankings and benchmarks appear to provide an objective basis for action in a space that otherwise feels complex and contested.

This desire is not misplaced. Measurement and evaluation are essential tools. The problem arises when comparison is treated as context-free.

Every comparison is made under particular conditions. Measurements are generated from specific populations, behaviours, environments and configurations. They capture how a system behaves *in that setting*, at that moment in time. When those results are lifted out of their original context, much of their meaning is lost.

Performance metrics are especially vulnerable to this problem. A measure that is informative in one environment may be misleading in another. An error rate that appears low when interactions are rare may feel intolerable when interactions are frequent. A latency that seems acceptable in a low-pressure setting may be disastrous where time is critical. Without context, the same number can signal very different things.

Benchmarks compound this issue by encouraging generalisation. They invite the belief that systems can be ranked independently of use and that higher performance in one context implies higher performance everywhere. This belief is comforting, but it rarely holds.

Context shapes not only system behaviour, but what is being measured. Differences in user populations, incentives, supervision and repetition all influence observed outcomes. Two systems compared under different conditions may appear meaningfully different when, in practice, they would behave similarly if placed in the same context. Conversely, systems that perform similarly in evaluation may diverge sharply once deployed elsewhere.

This is why cross-context comparisons often produce false confidence. They obscure the fact that what is being compared are not just systems, but the environments in which those systems were observed. When context is flattened, differences are attributed to technology rather than to use.

The appeal of benchmarks also lies in their apparent neutrality. Numbers feel authoritative. They seem to remove judgement from decision-making. In reality, benchmarks encode a host of contextual assumptions about what matters, what is measured and what is ignored. These assumptions are rarely visible to those relying on the results.

This does not mean that comparison is futile. It means that comparison without interpretation is dangerous. Metrics and benchmarks are starting points for understanding, not substitutes for it. They require contextual framing to be meaningful.

Interpreting comparison results responsibly involves asking how closely the evaluation conditions resemble the intended use. It involves understanding which aspects of context were present and which were absent. It involves recognising that results are provisional, contingent on conditions that may not persist.

In practice, this kind of interpretation is often neglected. Comparisons are simplified for communication, procurement or assurance purposes. Nuance is lost. Contextual caveats are omitted. What remains is a set of numbers that appear definitive but are, in fact, highly situational.

Understanding why context breaks comparisons does not require rejecting measurement or evaluation. It requires recognising their limits. It requires treating comparisons as evidence of behaviour under specific conditions, not as universal indicators of quality.

7.7 Context as a governance responsibility

As discussed earlier in this Chapter, context is often treated as something that should be surfaced in the early stages of system design. It is discussed when requirements are gathered, when scope is defined and when initial decisions are made about methods or architecture. Once those decisions are taken, context quietly recedes into the background, replaced by operational concerns: uptime, performance, integration and compliance.

However, context is not just a design input. It is an ongoing condition that shapes how a system behaves, how it is relied upon and where responsibility ultimately sits. For that reason, context is not merely a technical concern or an implementation detail. It is a matter of governance.

To govern an age assurance system responsibly is, in part, to govern the context in which it operates. This involves deciding what the system is intended to support, under what conditions and with what limitations. It also involves noticing when those conditions change and determining whether the system should continue to be relied upon in the same way.

These decisions are rarely framed explicitly as governance choices. More often, they are made implicitly through inaction. A system is deployed for one use and gradually adopted for others. Its outputs are treated as increasingly authoritative. Assumptions about who uses it, how often and with what consequences drift without formal acknowledgement.

When this happens, responsibility shifts silently. Decisions that were once bounded and contextualised become generalised. Outputs that were once advisory become definitive. A system designed to support judgement begins to replace it, not because anyone decided this should happen, but because no one decided it should not.

This is where governance matters most.

Someone, somewhere, defines the context in which an age assurance system is considered appropriate. That definition may be explicit or implicit, narrow or broad. But it carries weight. It shapes procurement, integration and reliance. It signals what kinds of use are expected and which are out of scope.

Equally important is who monitors whether actual use continues to align with that definition. Context does not drift loudly. It drifts quietly, through incremental changes in behaviour, scale and reliance. Without active attention, systems can be used in ways that no one would have endorsed if asked directly.

Governance failures around context rarely look like failures at first. Systems continue to operate. Decisions continue to be made. Metrics remain within acceptable ranges. The appearance of normality masks the fact that the system is now operating under assumptions that no longer hold.

When context is treated as fixed, governance mechanisms tend to freeze around an initial picture of use. Reviews focus on whether the system continues to meet technical criteria, rather than on whether those criteria remain appropriate. Questions about scope, proportionality and reliance are assumed to have been settled once and for all.

This freezing effect is particularly pronounced when systems become embedded in organisational routines. Over time, the system's presence is taken for granted. It becomes part of "how things are done." Challenging its context of use can feel disruptive, unnecessary or even disloyal to earlier decisions.

Yet this is precisely when governance is most needed.

Context-aware governance does not require constant redesign or perpetual upheaval. It requires the capacity to ask uncomfortable questions at appropriate moments. Are we still using this system in the way we originally intended? Have patterns of use changed? Are new groups affected? Have the consequences of error shifted?

These questions do not have purely technical answers. They require judgement and they often require balancing competing interests. But avoiding them does not make those trade-offs disappear. It simply allows them to be resolved implicitly, without scrutiny.

Another governance challenge arises from the distribution of responsibility across systems. Age assurance rarely exists as a single, self-contained service. It sits within ecosystems of relying parties, intermediaries, platforms and users. Each actor may have a partial view of context, but no single actor sees the whole picture.

When context shifts, its effects may be felt in one part of the ecosystem but originate in another. Without coordination, each actor may assume that someone else is responsible for noticing and responding. Context drift then becomes a collective blind spot.

Effective governance must therefore grapple with questions of ownership. Who is responsible for defining context? Who is responsible for monitoring it? Who has the authority to revise assumptions when reality diverges from design?

These are not abstract questions. They shape how age assurance systems are trusted, challenged and evolved over time. When they are left unanswered, context governs by default rather than by design.

Understanding context as a governance responsibility also clarifies why disputes and failures often feel uncomfortable or politicised. When context has not been explicitly governed, disagreements about appropriate use surface only after harm or controversy has occurred. At that point, positions harden and accountability becomes contested.

By contrast, when context is treated as something that must be actively managed, there is space for disagreement without crisis. Changes in use can be recognised as such. Assumptions can be revisited without implying that past decisions were reckless or wrong.

This perspective reframes governance not as enforcement, but as stewardship. It is about maintaining alignment between what a system is designed to do and how it is actually used, in a world where both behaviour and conditions change.

Seen this way, context is not a peripheral concern to be handled at the margins of age assurance. It is central to how responsibility is exercised over time. Ignoring it does not simplify governance; it undermines it.

7.8 Why context forces judgement

By this point in the chapter, one conclusion should be difficult to avoid: context resists closure. It cannot be fully specified, stabilised or encoded. However carefully an age assurance system is designed, there will always be conditions it does not anticipate, behaviours it does not predict and consequences it does not fully control.

This is not a failure of design or engineering. It is a reflection of what age assurance exists to do.

Age assurance systems do not make decisions in isolation. They support decisions that matter to people, organisations and societies, under conditions of uncertainty. Those conditions are shaped by context and context is irreducibly complex. It includes human behaviour, social norms organisational practices and time. No model, configuration or rule set can capture all of this in advance.

For this reason, attempts to automate judgement away are ultimately self-defeating. Systems can produce signals, scores or classifications. They can apply thresholds consistently and at scale. But they cannot determine, on their own, how those outputs should be interpreted when circumstances change or when values come into conflict.

Context forces judgement because it forces choices between competing goods. Inclusion versus protection. Efficiency versus care. Certainty versus accessibility. These choices are not technical optimisation problems. They are normative decisions that depend on how harms are understood and whose interests are prioritised.

Different people, acting in good faith, will weigh these considerations differently. What feels proportionate to one stakeholder may feel excessive to another. What seems cautious in one context may feel negligent in another. These disagreements are not anomalies to be eliminated. They are a natural consequence of operating in diverse and changing environments.

Recognising the inevitability of judgement does not weaken age assurance. It strengthens it by placing systems in their proper role. Systems provide structure, consistency and evidence. They do not absolve organisations of responsibility for deciding how that evidence is used.

This perspective also explains why debates about age assurance are often frustrating when framed purely in technical terms. Disputes that appear to be about accuracy, performance or thresholds are frequently about context and values. When those underlying issues are not acknowledged, discussions become circular. Each side talks past the other, armed with different assumptions about what the system is for and how it should be used.

Context also explains why disagreement persists even when evidence is abundant. Data can illuminate how systems behave under certain conditions. It cannot tell us, on its own, what should be done when those conditions change or when trade-offs become sharper. That gap can only be bridged by judgement.

Importantly, judgement does not mean arbitrariness. It does not mean abandoning structure or accountability. On the contrary, recognising where judgement is required allows it to be exercised deliberately, transparently and revisited over time. It makes space for explanation, challenge and revision.

When organisations pretend that judgement has been eliminated – that systems decide for themselves – responsibility does not disappear. It simply becomes harder to locate. Decisions still happen, but no one feels accountable for them. Context then governs by default, rather than by choice.

Chapter 8 – The Trade-offs You Cannot Eliminate

8.1 What do we mean by trade-offs?

Age assurance systems are often introduced with an implicit promise: that with sufficient care, expertise and rigour, it should be possible to design a system that is accurate, fast, secure, privacy-preserving and acceptable to users all at once.

This chapter exists to dismantle the idea that age assurance can be optimised into harmony. Not because designers are careless or technologies immature, but because the goals age assurance systems are expected to satisfy are in structural tension with one another. Functionality, performance, security, privacy and acceptability are not independent attributes that can be tuned in isolation. They are competing pressures. Every real system resolves them somehow.

Sometimes that resolution is explicit and carefully reasoned. More often, it is implicit, embedded in configuration choices, defaults, operational shortcuts and assumptions about user behaviour. When those trade-offs are not surfaced and owned, they tend to reappear later as failures, disputes or loss of trust.

8.2 Why trade-offs are structural, not accidental

Age assurance systems are rarely introduced with the explicit intention of making trade-offs. On the contrary, most are conceived with a genuine aspiration to "get it right": to be accurate without being intrusive, robust without being exclusionary, efficient without being careless and protective without being punitive. Early design conversations often assume that these qualities can be layered together, each addressed in turn, until a balanced system emerges.

This assumption is understandable. In many technical domains, improvements along one dimension can be achieved without visibly degrading others. Faster hardware does not necessarily reduce correctness. Better cryptography does not automatically make systems harder to use. It is therefore tempting to believe that with sufficient care, age assurance systems can be engineered into alignment.

Age assurance brings trade-offs to the surface earlier and more forcefully than many other systems because it sits directly at the point where technical outputs become social consequences. Its purpose is not merely to process information, but to enable or deny access. Its decisions are experienced personally, often repeatedly and often under conditions where the cost of being wrong is unevenly distributed. As a result, tensions that might remain abstract elsewhere become tangible very quickly.

What is crucial to understand is that these tensions do not arise only when systems fail. They arise when systems work exactly as intended.

A system can be functionally correct – producing age-related outputs within expected parameters – and still create outcomes that feel unreasonable, exclusionary or brittle in use. It can meet performance targets while quietly narrowing the space for discretion or appeal. It can apply strong security controls while steadily increasing friction for legitimate users. It can minimise data collection in one respect while enabling extensive reuse through configuration elsewhere. None of these effects require malfunction. They are expressions of how competing pressures have been resolved.

This is why trade-offs in age assurance are structural rather than accidental. They are not introduced by poor implementation or lack of diligence. They are the result of trying to satisfy multiple legitimate objectives within environments that cannot be fully stabilised.

At a high level, age assurance systems are expected to do several things at once: to produce reliable age-related signals, to do so quickly and at scale, to resist misuse and circumvention, to limit unnecessary data exposure and to be tolerated by the people required to use them. Each of these expectations pulls on the system in a different direction. Strengthening one changes the conditions under which the others operate.

What often obscures this reality is that many trade-offs are resolved implicitly. They are not framed as choices between competing values, but as technical necessities or operational conveniences. A shorter timeout is justified as efficiency. A retained log is justified as auditability. A simplified flow is justified as usability. Each decision is defensible in isolation. Taken together, they encode a particular balance of risks and burdens.

Because these balances are rarely articulated, they are also rarely revisited. Systems accumulate assumptions about "normal" users, "typical" environments and "acceptable" error that harden over time. When contexts change through scale, repetition, regulatory attention or behavioural adaptation, those assumptions begin to misalign with reality.

At that point, it can appear as though the system has failed. In truth, it is behaving consistently with choices that were made earlier, often without recognising them as trade-offs at all.

Understanding trade-offs as structural changes how systems are evaluated. It shifts attention away from the question of whether a system meets its specifications and toward the question of how it distributes uncertainty, friction and harm in practice. It also reframes later difficulties creating complaints, exclusion, avoidance, erosion of trust, not as aberrations, but as signals that the existing balance no longer fits the context in which the system is now operating.

This perspective does not imply that better design is futile. It implies that better design requires honesty about tension. Age assurance systems cannot be tuned into harmony because the world they operate in is not harmonious. Users differ. Stakes vary. Incentives conflict. Adversarial behaviour evolves. Any system that claims to have eliminated trade-offs is almost certainly hiding them.

8.3 Functionality: when "working" is not the same as working well

Functionality is usually the first characteristic to be defined and the easiest to mistake for success. An age assurance system is said to "work" when it produces an age-related output in the form expected: a pass or fail, a threshold decision, a range or a confidence-weighted result. If that output is generated consistently and in line with specification, functional requirements are often considered satisfied.

In practice, this definition is too thin to carry the weight placed upon it.

Age assurance does not exist to generate age signals for their own sake. It exists to support age-related decisions in real contexts, with real consequences. A system can therefore be functionally correct while still failing to produce outcomes that are meaningful, proportionate or trustworthy in use. The gap between "the system works" and "the system works well here" is where many difficulties originate.

This gap emerges because functional goals are rarely defined with full reference to how outputs will be interpreted, reused and relied upon over time. A function such as "determine whether a user is over a specified age" appears straightforward. Yet it silently embeds assumptions: about how often the determination will be made, what happens when the result is uncertain, whether the output will be cached or shared and how disputes will be handled.

When those assumptions hold, functionality appears robust. When they do not, the same functional behaviour produces outcomes that feel unreasonable.

Edge cases are often the first signal. Users who do not conform to typical patterns because of appearance, disability, environment, device limitations or behaviour, they expose the boundaries of functional assumptions. What was framed as a rare exception becomes a recurring experience for some users. Over time, edge cases stop being exceptional. They reveal what the system was never designed to consider.

This is why asking "does it work?" is rarely the right functional question. The more relevant question is "what kind of work is this function actually doing in this context?" Producing an age signal is one kind of work. Producing a decision that can be relied upon, contested and explained is another.

Functional definitions also shape downstream trade-offs in less obvious ways. A narrowly defined function encourages narrow optimisation. If success is defined purely in terms of output generation, then anything that slows or complicates that output appears as inefficiency. Fallback paths, retries, graduated responses and human review become costs rather than integral parts of functionality. Over time, these elements are minimised or removed in the name of "making it work".

The result is often a system that functions cleanly under ideal conditions but poorly under variation. It produces decisive outputs quickly, but offers little support when those outputs are disputed or inappropriate. Users experience this not as technical failure, but as inflexibility or unfairness.

Another source of functional mischief lies in the reuse of outputs beyond their original scope. An age signal generated for one decision context is often attractive for reuse elsewhere. Caching, sharing or persisting that signal improves efficiency and consistency. Yet the moment an output is reused, it begins to carry weight beyond what its original functional definition contemplated.

A signal intended as provisional may become definitive. A result generated under one set of assumptions may be relied upon under another. Functionality that appeared sufficient at the moment of generation becomes fragile when detached from its context.

None of this requires malfunction. The system continues to do exactly what it was designed to do. What changes is how much is asked of the function and how little of that demand was anticipated.

Functional success is therefore deeply entangled with performance, security, privacy and acceptability. A function that insists on certainty may demand more data. A function that must respond instantly may discard nuance. A function that resists abuse aggressively may exclude legitimate users. A function that is simple to explain may fail under adversarial pressure.

Treating functionality as a neutral baseline obscures these interactions. It encourages the belief that once the "right" function is defined, other characteristics can be adjusted around it. In reality, the definition of functionality already encodes a position on trade-offs. It determines what kinds of error are tolerated, whose experience is prioritised and how much uncertainty is acceptable.

This becomes especially clear when systems are scaled or repeated. A functional behaviour that is tolerable once may be intolerable when encountered daily. A rejection that is acceptable for a single transaction becomes exclusion when persistent. A function that produces the same output every time may appear consistent, yet become unfit as contexts evolve.

Understanding functionality as a pressure rather than a foundation changes how systems are assessed. It shifts attention from whether outputs are produced to whether those outputs support decisions that remain defensible over time. It also explains why functional specifications that look complete on paper often unravel in practice.

Functionality is never just about what the system does. It is about what the system makes possible, what it forecloses and how it shapes the space in which other trade-offs are resolved. Recognising this is essential before turning to the quieter, but equally powerful, distortions introduced by performance pressure.

8.4 Performance: The pressure that quietly distorts everything else

Performance is rarely discussed in age assurance as a matter of judgement. It is more often framed as a constraint: systems must be fast enough, available enough and scalable enough to function in the environments in which they are deployed. These requirements are typically presented as self-evident, even unavoidable.

In practice, performance is one of the most consequential forces shaping how age assurance systems behave.

Latency, throughput, availability and scalability are not neutral properties. They exert continuous pressure on design and operation, narrowing what is feasible and redefining what is acceptable. Because performance expectations are often set early and treated as fixed, their influence is easy to overlook. Yet they quietly reshape functionality, security, privacy and acceptability in ways that are difficult to reverse once systems are live.

One reason performance has this effect is that it operates at scale. An extra second of delay in a high-volume system is not experienced as an isolated inconvenience; it compounds across users, transactions and time. As usage grows, tolerance for delay shrinks and pressure mounts to simplify interactions, reduce checks and eliminate anything that slows the critical path.

Under these conditions, nuance becomes expensive. Graduated responses, contextual prompts, extended explanations and human review all introduce latency and variability. They are often the first elements to be constrained or removed when performance targets are threatened. What remains is a streamlined flow optimised for speed, even if that speed is achieved by narrowing the space for discretion or understanding.

Performance pressure also changes how uncertainty is handled. Systems designed to respond quickly tend to prefer decisive outputs. Ambiguity, inconclusive results and provisional states complicate throughput and are difficult to manage at scale. Over time, thresholds are tightened, retries limited and intermediate states collapsed into binary outcomes. The system becomes faster and more predictable, but less expressive.

Performance pressure also changes how uncertainty is handled and with it, how accuracy is expressed in practice.

Age assurance systems do not simply produce correct or incorrect outcomes. They produce classifications under uncertainty. How that uncertainty is treated is inseparable from performance expectations.

Systems required to respond quickly and at scale tend to prefer decisive outputs. Inconclusive states, wide confidence intervals or graduated outcomes complicate throughput. They require additional interaction, explanation or escalation, all of which introduce delay and variability. As a result, uncertainty is often compressed rather than resolved.

Over time, this compression reshapes operational accuracy. Thresholds are adjusted to reduce indecision. Confidence bands are narrowed or collapsed. Retry opportunities are limited. Intermediate outcomes are converted into binary decisions. None of these changes alter the underlying method, yet each one changes how often errors occur, where they occur and who experiences them.

What is presented as improved performance is therefore often a redistribution of error rather than a reduction of it. Decisions become faster and more predictable, but less expressive. Accuracy becomes something measured within constrained operational boundaries, rather than across the full range of real-world variation.

These effects are rarely framed as trade-offs. They are justified as efficiency improvements or necessities of scale. Yet each adjustment encodes a judgement about how much uncertainty is acceptable, how much delay is tolerable and which users are expected to absorb misclassification when certainty cannot be achieved.

This is why accuracy metrics that appear stable in controlled settings often behave differently once embedded in live systems. Performance pressure does not merely sit alongside accuracy; it actively conditions how accuracy is realised, interpreted and relied upon.

The relationship between performance and privacy is particularly instructive here. Caching results, persisting classifications and retaining derived signals all improve responsiveness and reduce computational load. They also stabilise apparent accuracy by avoiding repeated reassessment. From a performance perspective, this is attractive.

From a privacy perspective, it creates persistence. Classifications outlive the conditions under which they were generated. Uncertainty that was present at the moment of decision is no longer visible. What remains is a durable outcome, increasingly detached from its original context.

What begins as a short-term optimisation can, over time, produce long-lived traces that were never central to the age decision itself. These traces may be retained "just in case", justified by auditability or troubleshooting and quietly normalised as part of the system's operation.

Because performance gains are immediate and visible, while privacy costs are delayed and diffuse, the balance tends to drift in one direction. By the time retention practices are questioned, they are often deeply embedded in infrastructure and workflow.

Performance pressure also interacts with acceptability in subtle ways. Users are generally sensitive to delay, particularly in contexts where age assurance interrupts an otherwise smooth interaction. A system that is technically accurate but slow will often be perceived as broken. Complaints focus on responsiveness rather than correctness.

In response, performance tuning intensifies. Interfaces are simplified, explanations shortened, fallback options deferred or removed. The system becomes faster, but also less forgiving. Users who do not fit the dominant pattern experience more abrupt failure, even as average completion times improve.

It is important to note that many of these adjustments occur after deployment. Early pilots may tolerate slower responses and manual intervention. As systems scale, expectations change. Performance becomes a headline metric, often monitored continuously. At that stage, revisiting foundational trade-offs is difficult. Changes are framed as fixes rather than as rebalancing exercises.

This is why "fast enough" is never a purely technical determination. It reflects judgements about acceptable friction, acceptable error and acceptable exclusion. It determines whether systems privilege decisiveness over nuance, efficiency over contestability and reuse over minimisation.

When performance is treated as a background requirement rather than as a shaping force, these judgements remain implicit. Systems appear to degrade other characteristics "unexpectedly", when in reality they are expressing the priorities embedded in their performance constraints.

Recognising performance as a pressure rather than a metric clarifies why age assurance systems often drift away from their original intent as they scale. It also explains why attempts to improve performance late in the lifecycle frequently have disproportionate effects on privacy and acceptability.

8.5 Security: When defensiveness becomes fragility

Security is often treated as the most straightforward of the age assurance characteristics. Threats exist. Systems must resist them. The stronger the defence, the safer the outcome. In this framing, security appears as a unidirectional good: more checks, tighter controls, stronger binding.

In practice, security behaves less like a shield and more like a force that reshapes the entire system.

Age assurance systems operate in environments where adversarial behaviour is expected. Some users will attempt to circumvent controls. Others will assist them, intentionally or otherwise. These realities make security unavoidable. Yet the way security is implemented and the assumptions it encodes about behaviour often has consequences that are poorly anticipated at design time.

One common pattern is the tendency to equate security with accumulation. Additional proofs, repeated challenges, stricter thresholds and layered verification are introduced in response to perceived risk. Each addition appears sensible in isolation. Together, they increase friction, narrow acceptable pathways and reduce tolerance for variation.

This does not merely inconvenience users. It changes who can succeed.

As security tightens, legitimate users who are atypical (because of age, disability, environment, device quality or circumstance) are more likely to fail. They experience the system not as protective, but as punitive or arbitrary. Meanwhile, determined adversaries adapt. They learn which controls matter, which can be bypassed and where assistance can be sourced. The system becomes harder to use for the compliant and more interesting for the persistent.

Security failures in age assurance are rarely clean breaches. They are more often behavioural and interactional. Users share techniques. Frontline staff intervene informally. Systems are configured to "let people through" to maintain flow. Controls that were designed as safeguards become negotiated obstacles.

None of this implies poor intent. It reflects the reality that security measures operate within social systems. People respond to friction, especially when it is repeated or unexplained. Over time, security that is experienced as excessive undermines its own effectiveness by driving workarounds.

Another source of fragility arises from the assumption that threats are static. Security designs often imagine a stable adversary model: a known set of attacks, countered by known defences. In age assurance, this assumption rarely holds. Adversarial behaviour evolves in response to the system itself. Changes to thresholds, timing or interaction flows create new incentives and new vulnerabilities.

As a result, security does not converge on a stable equilibrium. It oscillates. Measures are introduced, adapted around, tightened again and sometimes relaxed to restore usability. Each adjustment shifts the balance between protection and exclusion. Without explicit recognition of this dynamic, security changes are experienced as reactive rather than deliberate.

Security also interacts deeply with performance and acceptability. Stronger controls often slow systems down. They introduce retries, secondary checks or additional data capture. Under performance pressure, these controls are then streamlined, deferred or selectively applied. What emerges is not a uniformly secure system, but a patchwork of defences whose effectiveness varies by context.

From the user's perspective, this inconsistency erodes trust. A system that behaves differently depending on timing, load or perceived risk is difficult to understand. Decisions feel opaque. When outcomes are contested, explanations are hard to provide because the security logic itself has become conditional and adaptive.

This is why security cannot be treated as something that sits outside user experience. It actively shapes it. Every security measure is also an interaction design choice. It communicates expectations about trust, suspicion and compliance. When those expectations are misaligned with context, security measures can produce resentment rather than reassurance.

Understanding security as a trade-off rather than a maximisation problem changes the conversation. It allows security to be discussed alongside inclusion, usability and proportionality, rather than in opposition to them. It also makes clear that "more secure" is not synonymous with "more robust".

In age assurance, robust systems are not those with the most defences, but those whose security posture remains intelligible, adaptable and proportionate as contexts shift and behaviour changes. Recognising this requires abandoning the idea that security can be perfected and accepting instead that it must be balanced, revisited and governed – like every other characteristic.

8.6 Privacy: Not a constraint, but a trade-off made visible

Privacy is often spoken about as if it sits outside the system: an external constraint that limits what designers would otherwise prefer to do. In this framing, privacy appears as a brake on certainty, performance or security as something that must be "balanced against" effectiveness, rather than something that actively reflects how effectiveness has been pursued.

In practice, privacy is not external to age assurance systems. It is the surface on which other trade-offs become legible.

Decisions about privacy are rarely made in isolation. They emerge from earlier choices about functionality, performance and security. How much certainty is demanded, how quickly results must be produced, how strongly misuse must be resisted – all of these decisions shape what data is collected, how long it is kept and how widely it can be reused. Privacy does not simply constrain those choices; it records them.

This is why privacy discussions in age assurance often feel contentious. They are not arguments about a single characteristic, but about the cumulative consequences of many earlier decisions that were framed differently at the time they were made.

One reason privacy is misunderstood is that data minimisation is often treated as binary. Either a system collects personal data or it does not. Either retention is short or it is long. Either identifiers persist or they do not. This framing obscures the reality that privacy harm in age assurance tends to accumulate through configuration rather than through any single act of collection.

A system may collect only a small amount of data at each interaction yet retain it indefinitely. It may avoid explicit identifiers yet enable effective linkability through consistent tokens or metadata. It may delete raw inputs quickly, yet preserve derived artefacts that can be reused, correlated or reinterpreted later. Each of these choices appears modest. Together, they define the system's privacy footprint.

Reuse is particularly instructive. From a functional and performance perspective, reuse is attractive. It reduces friction, improves responsiveness and increases consistency. From a security perspective, it can support auditability and investigation. From a privacy perspective, it creates persistence.

The moment an age-related outcome is reused beyond its immediate decision context, it begins to outlive the assumptions under which it was generated. The original uncertainty, environmental conditions and user circumstances fade from view. What remains is a durable signal that can be relied upon in ways never explicitly contemplated.

Privacy concerns often crystallise at this point, not because something new has been collected, but because something old is being relied upon repeatedly. The harm is not in the initial interaction, but in the quiet extension of its consequences.

Another source of privacy tension lies in audit and accountability. Age assurance systems are frequently expected to justify their decisions after the fact, particularly where serious harm is alleged. This expectation encourages logging, retention and traceability. Each of these improves the ability to explain outcomes, but each also expands the amount of information held and the duration for which it remains sensitive.

In some cases, this pressure is driven by exceptional circumstances. Where a child is exposed to experiences they should not have had access to, it is entirely reasonable for investigators to ask how that access occurred. Questions about system behaviour, decision pathways and reliance on age assurance outputs are legitimate. The difficulty arises when the possibility of such inquiries is allowed to dictate routine data retention for all users.

Designing systems to support reconstruction of rare, high-impact events can create a disproportionate data dependency. If accountability requires the ability to reproduce originating material, contextual signals or interaction histories long after the fact, then those artefacts must be retained not just for the exceptional case, but for everyone, all the time. Privacy risk is therefore scaled to the population, while the investigative benefit applies only to a vanishingly small number of scenarios.

Here again, privacy is not opposing accountability. It is making visible a trade-off between preparedness for exceptional scrutiny and the ongoing exposure created by retaining data "just in case". Deciding how much evidence is enough and how long it should persist is not a technical question. It is a judgement about proportionality, likelihood and the distribution of risk across an entire user population.

What makes privacy particularly revealing in age assurance is that its effects are unevenly experienced. Some users encounter systems rarely; others encounter them repeatedly. Some have alternatives; others do not. The cumulative impact of retention, linkage and reuse therefore varies across populations, even when systems behave consistently.

This unevenness is easy to miss when privacy is treated as a static property of the system rather than as a lived experience over time. A design that appears privacy-preserving in a single interaction may feel intrusive when repeated daily. A retention period that seems short in isolation may feel permanent when outcomes are relied upon across contexts.

When privacy is framed purely as a constraint, these dynamics are obscured. Systems are described as compliant or non-compliant, privacy-preserving or privacy-invasive. This binary language makes it harder to see how small, defensible choices accumulate into significant exposure.

When privacy is understood as a trade-off made visible, the conversation changes. Attention shifts to how long consequences last, how far outputs travel and how much contextual meaning is lost as signals persist. Privacy becomes a way of interrogating the system's memory: what it remembers, what it forgets and what it allows to follow a person beyond the moment of decision.

This perspective does not elevate privacy above other characteristics. It situates it among them, as the place where tensions between certainty, speed, security and tolerance are recorded in durable form. It also explains why privacy debates so often surface late, after systems are embedded and difficult to change. By then, privacy is no longer abstract. It is experienced.

8.7 Demographic consistency: When performance depends on who is using the system

Performance in age assurance systems is often discussed in terms of overall accuracy: how frequently a system produces the correct outcome across a population. While this measure is useful, it is incomplete. A system can perform well on average while performing poorly, sometimes predictably, for particular groups of people.

This is the problem of demographic consistency.

Demographic consistency refers to the degree to which an age assurance system produces comparable outcomes across different user groups, such as age ranges, genders, skin tones, abilities or other relevant characteristics. When performance varies significantly between groups, the system's effectiveness is uneven, regardless of how strong its headline metrics appear.

This unevenness is often discussed under the heading of "bias", but not all bias arises in the same way. Some bias is inherent: it reflects design decisions, training data gaps or flawed assumptions about the populations a system will encounter. These issues, while serious, are at least conceptually tractable. They can be investigated, corrected and mitigated through better data, testing and design.

Other forms of bias are more difficult, because they arise not from design negligence, but from physical and environmental constraints. Systems that rely on captured visual data (whether for biometric binding, liveness checks or analytical estimation) are affected by the properties of light itself. Darker surfaces reflect less light. In suboptimal lighting conditions, this can reduce the fidelity of captured data, even when systems are functioning exactly as designed.

The result is a form of natural bias: not a failure of intent or modelling, but a predictable loss of signal quality that disproportionately affects people with darker skin. In practice, this often manifests as increased uncertainty, higher rejection rates or more frequent escalation to fallback mechanisms for particular groups. From the user's perspective, this does not feel like a technical limitation. It feels like the system is working against them on grounds of race or skin colour.

From an operational standpoint, demographic inconsistency creates concrete failure modes. Groups that experience higher rates of friction or rejection disengage more often, require assistance more frequently and are escalated disproportionately into manual review or appeal. What appears as a marginal performance issue at system level becomes a structural burden in deployment.

Crucially, these effects are easy to miss if performance is assessed only in aggregate. Average accuracy smooths over unevenness. Disparities appear as isolated complaints rather than as patterns. By the time clustering is recognised in the form of support queues, appeal volumes or staff intervention, trust may already have eroded.

Demographic consistency also interacts strongly with acceptability. Users who repeatedly encounter friction, delay or challenge are less likely to view a system as legitimate, even if they ultimately succeed. Over time, these users adapt their behaviour by avoiding services, relying on assistance or seeking ways around controls. These adaptations, in turn, further distort system signals and make performance harder to interpret.

It is important to recognise that demographic consistency is not determined solely by the underlying method or model. System configuration, thresholds, environmental assumptions, fallback design and user support all influence how differences manifest in practice. Two deployments using the same technology can produce very different demographic outcomes depending on how uncertainty is handled and where escalation occurs.

This is why demographic consistency must be treated as a system-level performance characteristic rather than as a one-off fairness check. What matters is not the elimination of all variation, but whether differences in error rates, escalation or exclusion remain within bounds that are reasonable for the context in which the system is used.

Parity, in this sense, is not absolute. It is contextual. Some variation may be unavoidable given physical constraints, user diversity or environmental conditions. The failure lies not in the existence of variation, but in failing to observe it, understand it or account for its consequences.

When demographic consistency is made visible, it strengthens rather than weakens decision-making. Trade-offs can be discussed honestly. Mitigations can be targeted. Fallback and support can be designed where they are actually needed, rather than assumed to be evenly distributed. Confidence in outcomes becomes grounded in evidence rather than assumption.

8.8 Acceptability: The characteristic that decides whether anything else matters

Acceptability is often treated as secondary to more concrete concerns. Functionality can be specified, performance measured, security tested and privacy assessed. Acceptability, by contrast, is sometimes framed as subjective, cultural or outside the system's core purpose.

In practice, acceptability determines whether any of the other characteristics have effect.

Age assurance systems do not operate in a vacuum. They operate in social environments, where people respond to friction, repetition and perceived unfairness in predictable ways. When systems are experienced as tolerable, users comply even when outcomes are not ideal. When systems are experienced as unreasonable, behaviour changes – often quietly and incrementally.

Acceptability failures rarely announce themselves as outright rejection. They emerge through avoidance, gaming and abandonment. Users seek alternative pathways. They delay or defer interactions. They ask for assistance, share techniques or rely on intermediaries. Frontline staff compensate with discretion, informal workarounds or selective enforcement.

From the system's perspective, everything may still appear to function. Outputs are generated. Decisions are logged. Metrics remain stable. Yet the system's effectiveness is increasingly sustained by human effort rather than by design.

This is why acceptability cannot be reduced to satisfaction or preference. It is not about whether users like a system. It is about whether they tolerate it enough to engage with it repeatedly and honestly. A system that is barely acceptable once may be intolerable when encountered daily. A system that is tolerable for one group may be exclusionary for another.

Acceptability is also where the interaction between characteristics becomes most visible. Performance pressure that reduces explanation may be acceptable in low-stakes contexts but deeply resented where consequences are serious. Security measures that are justified as protective may feel accusatory when applied repeatedly. Privacy practices that appear minimal in isolation may feel invasive when outcomes persist and follow users across interactions.

These experiences do not require malicious intent to produce resistance. They reflect normal human responses to systems that feel misaligned with context.

One reason acceptability is often underestimated is that it is unevenly distributed. Users who pass easily may never notice friction that others encounter repeatedly. Those who are excluded or delayed experience the system very differently. Over time, this unevenness produces patterns: the same people are stopped, challenged or escalated, while others flow through unnoticed.

From a design perspective, this can be hard to see. Aggregate metrics obscure distribution. Completion rates look healthy. Dropout appears modest. Only when behaviour is examined longitudinally does the cost of unacceptability become apparent.

Another source of acceptability tension lies in explanation and recourse. Users are more willing to tolerate adverse outcomes when they understand why they occurred and what can be done next. Systems optimised for speed and automation often provide limited explanation. Decisions appear final even when they are not intended to be.

When recourse exists but is difficult to access, users experience it as symbolic rather than real. Frustration accumulates. Staff are drawn into conflict management roles. Over time, trust in the system erodes, even if the underlying decisions are broadly reasonable.

Acceptability also feeds back into security. Systems that are not tolerated invite gaming. Users who feel unfairly treated are more likely to test boundaries, seek shortcuts or rely on others to help them circumvent controls. What begins as a user experience issue becomes a security concern, not because defences are weak, but because legitimacy has been undermined.

This dynamic explains why acceptability failures often surface as operational problems rather than as design critiques. Organisations respond with additional controls, tighter thresholds or stricter enforcement, further increasing friction. The cycle reinforces itself.

Recognising acceptability as a structural pressure changes how these patterns are interpreted. It shifts focus from blaming users for non-compliance to examining whether the system's demands remain reasonable in context. It also highlights that ignoring acceptability does not eliminate cost; it relocates it.

Users pay through frustration and exclusion. Staff pay through conflict and discretion. Organisations pay through complexity and reputational risk. The system continues to function, but its sustainability is compromised.

Acceptability is therefore not an optional extra or a finishing touch. It is the characteristic that determines whether all other trade-offs hold in practice. A system that is technically sound but socially intolerable will not remain effective for long.

8.9 Where trade-offs actually live: Configuration, practice and drift

By this point, the pattern should be clear. Trade-offs in age assurance are not abstract tensions resolved once at design time. They are practical decisions made repeatedly, often quietly, as systems are configured, operated and adapted to reality.

When people look for the source of trade-offs, they tend to look at architecture diagrams, policy statements or high-level descriptions of methods. These artefacts matter, but they rarely capture the decisions that shape day-to-day behaviour. The most consequential trade-offs are embedded in configuration, defaults and operational practice.

Thresholds determine what counts as "old enough" in practice, not in law. Retry limits determine how much uncertainty a user is allowed before being excluded. Timeouts determine how patient the system is prepared to be. Escalation paths determine who absorbs ambiguity; the user, a human reviewer or the organisation itself. Retention settings determine how long the consequences of a single interaction persist.

Each of these choices appears technical. Each is defensible in isolation. Together, they define how risk, friction and error are distributed.

Defaults are particularly powerful because they are rarely revisited. They encode assumptions about normal behaviour and typical conditions. Once deployed, they become the system's personality. Users who pass cleanly may never notice them; users who fail repeatedly experience the system as rigid and unforgiving. Both experiences are produced by the same configuration.

Operational practice adds another layer. Systems are rarely used exactly as described. Staff intervene. Shortcuts emerge. Informal guidance develops. Over time, these practices stabilise into how the system actually works, even if they are undocumented. This is not failure; it is how socio-technical systems survive contact with reality.

The difficulty arises when practice drifts away from declared intent without being acknowledged. Trade-offs that were supposed to be rare become routine. Temporary measures become permanent. Outputs designed for one purpose are reused for another. The system continues to function, but its behaviour no longer matches its description.

This drift is rarely sudden. Systems operate in environments that change continuously. Volumes increase. Usage becomes repetitive. User behaviour adapts. Adversarial pressure evolves. What was once acceptable becomes burdensome. What was once proportionate becomes exclusionary. The balance encoded in configuration shifts, even if nothing appears to "break".

This is why yesterday's acceptable balance so often becomes today's failure.

Rebalancing is therefore unavoidable. The question is whether it happens deliberately or by accident. When it is implicit, it occurs through piecemeal fixes and local adjustments, without a shared understanding of what is being traded off or why. When it is explicit, assumptions are revisited, consequences acknowledged and decisions recorded. Tension remains, but surprise is reduced.

Recognising where trade-offs live and how they move changes how systems are discussed. It shifts attention away from abstract capability and toward concrete behaviour. It also explains why failure, fallback and appeal are not exceptional states, but mechanisms through which systems respond when existing balances no longer fit reality.

8.10 Owning trade-offs as a governance obligation

By this point, one conclusion should be difficult to avoid: trade-offs in age assurance are not anomalies to be corrected, nor imperfections to be engineered away. They are the substance of the system.

Every age assurance deployment embodies judgements about uncertainty, risk, friction and harm. Those judgements determine who is excluded, who is delayed, who is asked to provide more evidence and whose experience is smoothed for the sake of efficiency. Whether these judgements are made explicitly or implicitly does not change their effects. It changes only who is accountable for them.

This is why trade-offs are ultimately a governance responsibility.

When trade-offs are denied or obscured, systems appear to make decisions on their own. Outcomes are attributed to "the technology", "the model" or "the process", rather than to the choices that shaped them. This diffusion of responsibility undermines trust. It makes it harder to explain outcomes, harder to correct misalignment and harder to respond when harms are identified.

Transparency matters more than optimisation in this context. A system that openly acknowledges its limits, assumptions and priorities is easier to contest, adapt and improve than one that claims technical inevitability. Being able to say *why* a system behaves as it does is more important than claiming that it behaves as well as possible.

This is also where the role of standards and frameworks is often misunderstood. They do not remove trade-offs. They do not decide balances. They provide a shared language for describing pressures, assumptions and consequences. They make it possible to talk about trade-offs without reducing them to slogans or metrics.

Compliance, on its own, is not a substitute for judgement. Saying "we complied" does not explain which risks were accepted, which harms were tolerated or whose interests were prioritised. Responsible deployment requires those questions to be asked and revisited, not deferred behind formal adherence.

Owning trade-offs means accepting that age assurance involves choices that cannot be made once and forgotten. It means recognising when contexts have shifted, when balances no longer hold and when previously acceptable outcomes have become problematic. It also means accepting that some disagreements cannot be resolved technically, because they are disagreements about values, not mechanisms.

This does not weaken age assurance. It grounds it.

Systems that acknowledge trade-offs are better prepared for scrutiny. They are less surprised by failure, less defensive when challenged and more capable of adaptation. Systems that deny trade-offs tend to encounter those same tensions later, under pressure, when options are narrower and trust is already strained.

Understanding trade-offs is therefore not an abstract exercise. It is the precondition for talking honestly about failure – and for designing systems that can respond to it without pretending it should never occur.

Chapter 9 – Failure Is Normal: Breakdown, Fallback and Appeal

9.1 Why age assurance must be designed for breakdown, not perfection

Age assurance is possible. It can work well. In many contexts it already does.

What undermines age assurance systems is not that they fail, but that they are often designed and discussed as if they should never do so. This creates unrealistic expectations – of systems, of operators and of users – and makes ordinary operational breakdowns appear as evidence of incompetence or bad faith rather than as normal aspects of complex decision-making.

Age assurance systems translate diverse, imperfect signals into outcomes that are necessarily simpler than the reality they represent. This is not a weakness of the approach; it is the nature of the task.

Earlier chapters have already established why this matters. Chapter 6 showed that age assurance systems are assemblages of interacting components, not singular mechanisms. Chapter 7 demonstrated that context of use shifts over time and across settings, reshaping how systems behave. Chapter 8 made clear that all systems embody trade-offs between objectives that cannot be maximised simultaneously.

Taken together, these insights point to a more constructive conclusion: effective age assurance is not about achieving perfection, but about anticipating where systems will be stressed and designing for those moments.

Uncertainty cannot be eliminated from age assurance, but it can be handled responsibly. Age is not directly observable; it must always be inferred, estimated, verified or implied through proxies. These proxies vary in availability, quality and relevance depending on who the user is and where the system is deployed. Systems that acknowledge this variability are more robust than those that assume uniform conditions.

Thresholds further reinforce this reality. Age assurance almost always involves drawing policy lines – above or below, permitted or restricted. These lines are imposed on continuous human development. People close to a threshold will always be harder to classify than those far from it. This does not indicate poor design; it reflects the fact that policy categories do not align neatly with human variation.

As systems scale, these borderline cases become more visible. As systems are reused, the same individuals encounter them repeatedly. What begins as an occasional challenge becomes an expected part of operation. Systems that anticipate this behave differently from those that do not.

Scale also introduces ordinary operational pressures. Volume increases. Dependencies fluctuate. Performance degrades unevenly. User behaviour adapts to friction and repetition. None of this prevents age assurance from working. It simply means that systems must function under conditions that are less controlled than those assumed during design or early deployment.

This is where the idea of "designing out failure" becomes misleading. It implies that breakdown is primarily a technical defect to be eliminated, rather than a predictable consequence of operating in dynamic, real-world environments. Efforts to remove one type of breakdown often expose another. Tightening controls may increase exclusion. Simplifying interactions may reduce contestability. Increasing automation may reduce transparency.

In practice, these are not failures of age assurance as a concept. They are signals that systems are encountering the limits of their original assumptions.

Well-designed age assurance systems do not deny these limits. They recognise where uncertainty will surface and provide structured ways to manage it. They allow ambiguity to be expressed rather than forced into brittle outcomes. They treat occasional breakdown not as embarrassment, but as information.

Reframing breakdown in this way shifts the central design question. Instead of asking how to prevent systems from ever failing, the more productive question becomes: *how should the system behave when its assumptions no longer hold?*

9.2 Contra-indicators: When evidence conflicts instead of fails

A large proportion of operational difficulty arises not when evidence is missing or incorrect, but when multiple pieces of evidence point in different directions. These situations are best understood as contra-indicators.

A contra-indicator occurs when available signals, inputs or contextual information are internally inconsistent, ambiguous or in tension with one another. The system is not broken and no single component has necessarily failed. Instead, the system is confronted with evidence that cannot be cleanly resolved into a single confident outcome.

Examples are familiar, even if rarely named. An age estimation result conflicts with observed user behaviour. A credential appears valid but is presented in an unexpected context. Repeated retries produce oscillating results. Environmental conditions degrade confidence without clearly invalidating the process. Human assistance changes the assumptions under which a check was designed to operate.

In each case, the problem is not lack of data. It is too much data pointing in incompatible directions.

Contra-indicators matter because they expose a common but risky design temptation: to force ambiguity into certainty. Systems are often configured to "decide anyway", to average signals, prioritise one input over others or silently downgrade confidence without making that choice visible. While this may keep processes moving, it also hides judgement inside automation.

When contra-indicators are not explicitly recognised, several predictable outcomes follow. Risk is displaced rather than managed. Decisions appear consistent while becoming less meaningful. Edge cases accumulate into patterns that no one owns. Staff overrides increase, but without a shared understanding of why they are needed. Appeals become adversarial because the system cannot explain itself.

Recognising contra-indicators changes how failure is understood. It shifts the question from "what went wrong?" to "what could not be resolved automatically?" This reframing makes space for proportional responses: requesting additional evidence, narrowing the scope of a decision, invoking a fallback or deferring judgement altogether.

Importantly, contra-indicators are not exceptional. In complex, real-world environments they are normal. Users behave unpredictably. Contexts shift. Systems interact in ways that designers cannot fully anticipate. Treating all ambiguity as error encourages brittle systems that break under pressure.

Designing for contra-indicators does not mean designing for worst-case adversaries. It means accepting that not all uncertainty can or should be resolved at the point of automation. Clear escalation paths documented fallback behaviours and meaningful appeal mechanisms are not signs of weakness; they are signs that a system understands its own limits.

Contra-indicators also have governance implications. Decisions about how they are handled, ignored, overridden, escalated or recorded are policy decisions, even when implemented as configuration. If these choices are undocumented, accountability dissolves. If they are acknowledged and described, responsibility becomes traceable.

For readers trying to understand why age assurance systems so often appear to work until they suddenly do not, contra-indicators offer an important clue. Many systems fail not because they encounter bad inputs, but because they encounter conflicting truths and were never designed to admit that some questions do not have a single, automatic answer.

9.3 What breakdown looks like in practice

When age assurance systems encounter strain, they rarely stop working altogether. More often, they continue to operate – but in ways that feel slower, less certain or less coherent than intended. Understanding breakdown in age assurance therefore begins not with dramatic collapse, but with recognising patterns that appear ordinary, even familiar, to those who interact with these systems regularly.

In practice, breakdown most often presents as friction rather than failure.

A user is asked to repeat a step that seemed to succeed moments earlier. A decision takes longer than expected. An outcome differs from a previous attempt without obvious explanation. A process quietly shifts from automated to assisted. None of these events necessarily signals that the system is "broken". In fact, many of them are signs that the system is attempting to cope with uncertainty or variation.

These experiences are common precisely because age assurance systems are designed to operate across diverse users, devices and environments. Inputs fluctuate. Conditions change. Signals degrade. Systems respond by retrying, recalculating or escalating. From a system perspective, this behaviour is adaptive. From a user's perspective, it can feel inconsistent or opaque.

Because these moments do not resemble traditional system failures organisations often do not recognise them as such. Instead, they are categorised as user error, misuse or non-compliance. The system is assumed to be functioning as intended; the difficulty is assumed to lie elsewhere.

This distinction matters. When breakdown is mislabelled, responses tend to focus on correcting user behaviour rather than examining system behaviour. Additional instructions are added. Warnings are strengthened. Controls are tightened. Over time, the system becomes more rigid, even as the underlying sources of friction remain.

Another common manifestation of breakdown is delay. Decisions that were designed to be near-instantaneous stretch into seconds or minutes. Queues form. Timeouts occur. Users are asked to wait, retry or return later. In low-frequency contexts, these delays may be tolerable. In high-frequency or time-sensitive contexts, they become disruptive.

Delays are often treated as purely performance issues, but they have broader effects. They change how users behave, how staff intervene and how decisions are perceived. A delayed decision can feel like a denied one. Repeated delays can feel like exclusion. Over time, users adapt by avoiding the system where possible or by seeking assistance that bypasses formal processes.

Breakdown also appears as contradictory outcomes. A user may receive different results from the same system under slightly different conditions. One component may indicate eligibility while another expresses uncertainty. From a technical perspective, these variations may be explainable. From a human perspective, they undermine confidence.

When outcomes appear inconsistent, trust shifts away from the system and toward whatever informal mechanisms seem to restore predictability – a helpful staff member, a familiar workaround or a personal judgement call. These adaptations are not failures of professionalism. They are attempts to restore coherence where the system no longer provides it.

Perhaps the most revealing sign of breakdown is manual intervention. At some point, a person steps in to interpret, override, assist or decide. This may be framed as exceptional support, customer service or operational flexibility. In practice, it often becomes routine.

Manual intervention is frequently treated as evidence that the system is humane or pragmatic. In many cases, it is. But it also indicates that the system has reached the limits of its automated assumptions. Where and how these interventions occur and who is empowered to make them tells us more about how the system actually works than its formal description ever could.

What is striking is how familiar these patterns are across different deployments. They are not signs of poor implementation. They are expressions of what happens when systems designed for generality encounter specific human situations.

Because breakdown often takes these everyday forms, it is easy to overlook. Systems continue to function. Decisions continue to be made. Metrics may remain within acceptable ranges. Yet the lived experience of the system shifts.

This is why organisations so often misinterpret breakdown as misuse. From an operational dashboard, the system appears healthy. From the ground, it feels strained. The gap between these perspectives widens until it becomes visible through complaints, avoidance behaviour or reliance on informal practices.

Recognising breakdown in these terms does not mean treating age assurance as fragile. It means acknowledging that real-world operation involves continual adjustment. Systems that are designed with this understanding respond differently. They treat friction, delay and intervention as signals to be understood rather than problems to be hidden.

9.4 Fail-Safe behaviour: What responsible systems do when assurance breaks down

Age assurance systems are often discussed in terms of how well they work when everything goes according to plan. Far less attention is paid to how they behave when that plan no longer holds. Yet in practice, the credibility of an age assurance system is determined as much by how it fails as by how it succeeds.

This is the principle of fail-safe behaviour.

Fail-safe does not mean that a system must always deny access when uncertainty arises, nor that it must always defer to human judgement. It means that when an age assurance process cannot produce a reliable, context-appropriate outcome, the system transitions into a state that minimises harm and preserves accountability.

What constitutes "safe" depends on context. In some cases, safety may mean restricting access until confidence can be restored. In others, it may mean allowing access while flagging increased risk, narrowing functionality or escalating for review. The defining feature is not the direction of the decision, but the fact that uncertainty is recognised and handled deliberately, rather than being forced into a false sense of certainty.

Many real-world failures occur because systems are not designed to admit uncertainty. When signals conflict, binding assumptions break down or environmental conditions degrade performance, systems often continue to operate as if nothing has changed. Decisions are still made, but their meaning quietly erodes.

This produces two dangerous patterns. Some systems fail *open* without acknowledgement, granting access in situations where assurance no longer holds. Others fail *closed* indiscriminately, excluding users without explanation or recourse. Both outcomes may appear defensible in isolation, but both undermine trust when they occur silently or unpredictably.

Fail-safe behaviour requires systems to surface their own limits. Contra-indicators must be recognised rather than averaged away. Fallback paths must be explicit rather than improvised. Appeals must be available not as exceptions, but as part of the normal lifecycle of a decision. Human intervention, where required, must be supported rather than treated as a workaround.

Importantly, fail-safe behaviour is a system property, not a single feature. It emerges from the interaction of binding, configuration, escalation rules, logging and governance. A system with accurate methods but no meaningful fallback is not fail-safe. A system with appeal rights but no visibility into how decisions were made is not fail-safe. A system that shifts risk onto users or frontline staff without acknowledging that shift is not fail-safe.

Fail-safe design also clarifies responsibility. When systems behave predictably under stress, it becomes clear who is accountable for each outcome and why. When they do not, responsibility diffuses. Organisations find themselves defending outcomes they did not intend and cannot fully explain.

There is no universal fail-safe posture for age assurance. Proportionality, context of use and societal risk all matter. What matters is that failure modes are anticipated, articulated and governed, not discovered accidentally after harm has occurred.

9.5 Functional breakdown: When the system cannot decide

One of the most important and least acknowledged forms of breakdown in age assurance occurs when a system is unable to reach a clear decision. Not because it is malfunctioning, but because the evidence available to it does not support a decisive outcome.

This kind of breakdown is functional rather than technical. The system is operating as designed, processing inputs and applying rules, yet it cannot confidently resolve the question it has been asked. In real-world deployments, this situation arises frequently, even though many systems are not designed to recognise it explicitly.

The roots of functional breakdown lie in the way age assurance outcomes are framed. As Chapter 3 established, age assurance is not about determining a person's "true age", but about supporting age-related eligibility decisions. Those decisions are usually expressed in simple categories (allowed or not allowed, above or below a threshold) even though the evidence feeding into them is rarely so clear.

Borderline ages are the most familiar source of this tension. Individuals close to a threshold often produce signals that plausibly support more than one outcome. Small changes in conditions such as lighting, behaviour, device quality, confidence or context can shift the system's interpretation. From a human perspective, this ambiguity is expected. From a system perspective, it is often treated as unacceptable.

Functional breakdown also emerges when different components within a system disagree. One part of the system may suggest eligibility based on one form of evidence, while another signals uncertainty or risk based on a different input. Each component may be behaving correctly within its own scope, yet the system as a whole lacks a coherent way to reconcile the inconsistency.

A third source of functional breakdown is over-narrow outcome design. When systems are built to produce only a small set of rigid outcomes, they leave no room to express uncertainty. The system must decide, even when the available information does not justify confidence. In these cases, indecision is not permitted, so it is hidden.

The common response to functional breakdown is to force a decision. Systems default to denial, escalate automatically or apply conservative thresholds that resolve ambiguity by excluding users. These responses create the appearance of decisiveness, but they do not resolve the underlying uncertainty. They merely displace it.

This displacement has consequences. Users experience exclusion without explanation. Staff encounter decisions that feel unjustified but difficult to challenge. Organisations see complaints that are hard to diagnose because, formally, the system behaved "correctly".

Recognising "cannot decide" as a legitimate state changes this dynamic. It reframes functional breakdown as information rather than error. It acknowledges that, in some cases, the system has reached the limits of what it can infer from the evidence available to it.

This recognition does not imply that systems should be indecisive or permissive by default. It implies that systems should be able to express uncertainty honestly and provide structured ways to address it. That may involve deferral, alternative routes, human involvement or other responses that reflect the context and stakes of the decision.

When systems lack this capability, functional breakdown tends to reappear elsewhere. It shows up as repeated attempts, inconsistent outcomes or reliance on informal judgement. The system appears decisive on the surface, but ambiguity resurfaces operationally.

Functional breakdown therefore reveals something important about earlier design choices. Decisions about thresholds, confidence margins, retry limits and escalation paths determine whether uncertainty is surfaced or suppressed. These decisions are rarely revisited once a system is deployed, even as contexts change.

Linking back to Chapter 3, this highlights the importance of outcome framing. Systems designed around rigid, binary outcomes struggle to accommodate the reality of uncertain evidence. Systems that allow for intermediate or unresolved states are better able to manage ambiguity without forcing it onto users or operators.

Understanding functional breakdown is a prerequisite for understanding other forms of strain. When systems cannot decide, they often compensate by retrying, escalating or delaying – behaviours that manifest as performance issues. They may also encourage workarounds or circumvention, with implications for security and acceptability.

9.6 Performance breakdown: When the system cannot keep up

Age assurance systems are often evaluated in terms of whether they reach the "right" decision. In everyday operation, however, an equally important question is whether they can reach that decision *in time*. Performance breakdown occurs when systems remain functionally capable but struggle to operate at the pace, volume or reliability demanded by their context of use.

This form of breakdown is rarely dramatic. Systems do not usually fail outright. Instead, they slow down. Responses take longer. Requests queue. Retries become common. What was designed as a brief interruption becomes an extended interaction. Over time, these delays shape how the system is experienced and how it is used.

Performance pressures are particularly visible at scale. As usage increases, small inefficiencies compound. Dependencies that were rarely stressed during early deployment become critical. Network latency, device variation and concurrency begin to matter in ways they did not before. Even when individual components perform within acceptable bounds, their interaction under load produces uneven behaviour.

From a system perspective, these are operational realities. From a user perspective, they are experienced as friction. Waiting feels like uncertainty. Delay feels like denial. Repetition feels like exclusion. Users adapt accordingly, often in ways that were never anticipated by designers.

Performance breakdown also has a subtle but significant effect on decision-making. When systems are under pressure, there is an implicit incentive to move people through quickly. Queues create urgency. Backlogs demand clearing. In response, systems may be configured to simplify checks, narrow acceptable inputs or reduce opportunities for reconsideration.

These adjustments are rarely described as trade-offs, but that is exactly what they are. To preserve throughput, systems may rely more heavily on cached decisions, retain information longer than originally intended or prioritise speed over precision. Each of these shifts affects privacy, accuracy and acceptability, often without explicit acknowledgement.

Performance pressure also reshapes human behaviour. Staff faced with long queues or frustrated users may intervene earlier or more decisively. Informal shortcuts emerge. Discretion is exercised to keep things moving. What begins as pragmatic assistance can become routine practice.

None of this implies poor design or bad faith. It reflects the fact that performance breakdown forces systems and organisations to reveal their priorities. When time is scarce, some values are protected more vigorously than others. Which ones those are becomes visible only under stress.

Importantly, performance breakdown is not evenly distributed. Some users experience it more acutely than others. People with slower devices, less stable connections, accessibility needs or limited time are disproportionately affected. For them, delay is not a minor inconvenience but a barrier to access.

This is where performance breakdown intersects with acceptability and privacy. Users who encounter repeated delays may abandon the process altogether. Others may seek assistance that involves sharing more information than they would prefer. Over time, performance-related friction erodes willingness to cooperate.

Because performance breakdown does not look like a clear failure, it is often addressed tactically rather than strategically. Capacity is added. Thresholds are adjusted. Instructions are shortened. These responses may relieve immediate pressure but can also entrench new assumptions about acceptable behaviour and data use.

Seen in this way, performance breakdown is not just about speed or capacity. It is about how systems behave when the demand placed upon them exceeds the conditions under which they were originally designed. It reveals how trade-offs shift silently and how operational pressure can reshape the character of an age assurance system without any formal change in policy.

9.7 Security breakdown: When the system is used against itself

Security breakdown in age assurance is often imagined in dramatic terms: deliberate attacks, hostile actors or sophisticated attempts to defeat technical safeguards. In practice, most security strain emerges in far quieter and more ordinary ways. It arises not because systems are under siege, but because they are being used repeatedly by real people adapting to real constraints.

Age assurance systems shape behaviour. Over time, users learn how they work, where they are strict, where they are forgiving and where they can be assisted. This learning is not inherently malicious. It is a natural response to friction, repetition and uncertainty. As systems become familiar, behaviour evolves to minimise effort, avoid delay and reduce disruption.

Many of the practices that later appear as "security issues" begin as coping strategies. Users help one another navigate complex steps. Parents or supervisors intervene on behalf of children. Staff explain shortcuts that are not formally documented. None of these actions are intended to undermine the system. They are attempts to make it usable in context.

As usage continues, these behaviours spread. What was once exceptional becomes routine. Workarounds become normalised. Informal guidance circulates. The system continues to operate, but not in the way its designers originally imagined.

This is where security breakdown takes shape. Safeguards that rely on isolation, independence or one-off interaction are gradually weakened by shared practice. Checks that assume individual effort are softened by collective assistance. Controls that depend on friction lose effectiveness as users adapt around them.

Importantly, these dynamics are often accelerated by earlier forms of breakdown. Performance delays encourage users to retry, seek help or bypass steps. Functional ambiguity encourages staff discretion. Acceptability strain reduces willingness to comply strictly. Security breakdown is therefore rarely a standalone problem; it is the cumulative effect of how systems respond to uncertainty elsewhere.

A common response is to increase security pressure. Additional checks are added. Tolerances are narrowed. Controls become more rigid. In isolation, these measures may appear sensible. In practice, they often intensify the very behaviours they are meant to prevent.

Increased friction encourages greater reliance on assistance. More complex processes increase the value of shared knowledge. Stricter enforcement pushes adaptation rather than compliance. Over time, the system and its users enter a cycle of tightening and circumvention, each responding to the other.

When this happens, it is tempting to attribute security breakdown to “bad users”. This framing is comforting because it externalises responsibility. It suggests that the system would function well if only users behaved properly.

Yet this explanation rarely withstands scrutiny. Behavioural adaptation is not an aberration; it is feedback. It reflects how people experience the system and how it fits into their lives. Treating adaptation as hostility misses an opportunity to understand where assumptions no longer align with reality.

Security breakdown, in this sense, is not primarily about adversaries. It is about how systems interact with human behaviour over time. It reveals which safeguards depend on user isolation, which rely on inconvenience and which degrade under repetition.

This does not mean that security concerns are unimportant or that misuse should be ignored. It means that sustainable security in age assurance cannot be achieved solely by adding controls. It depends on understanding how those controls shape behaviour and how behaviour, in turn, reshapes the system.

Recognising security breakdown as an emergent property of use rather than an external threat reframes responsibility. It shifts attention from blaming users to examining how design, configuration and context encourage certain practices. It also highlights the connection between security and acceptability: systems that people experience as unreasonable are rarely experienced as legitimate.

9.8 Acceptability breakdown: When people stop cooperating

Acceptability breakdown occurs when people (users, staff or intermediaries) no longer engage with an age assurance system in the way it was intended. This does not usually happen suddenly or dramatically. More often, it emerges gradually, as small frictions accumulate and cooperation becomes conditional, reluctant or selective.

Unlike other forms of breakdown, acceptability failure does not sit neatly within a single system component. It is relational. It reflects how the system is experienced over time and whether people perceive it as reasonable, proportionate and respectful of their circumstances. When acceptability weakens, the system may continue to function technically, but its social foundations begin to erode.

One of the earliest signs of acceptability breakdown is abandonment. Users begin to disengage before completing the process. They delay interaction, seek alternatives or avoid contexts where the system is encountered. In some settings, this avoidance is subtle; in others, it becomes visible through declining participation or increased reliance on exemptions and exceptions.

Another manifestation is superficial compliance. Users go through the motions without genuine engagement, doing only what is necessary to obtain an outcome while minimising effort or exposure. This behaviour may satisfy formal requirements but undermines the assumptions on which the system was designed. Signals become less reliable. Interactions become transactional rather than cooperative.

Workarounds are a further expression of acceptability strain. When formal processes feel unreasonable or burdensome, informal practices emerge to smooth the experience. Assistance is shared. Steps are skipped. Discretion is exercised. These practices are often tolerated, even encouraged, because they keep the system moving. Over time, they become part of "how things are done".

Staff overrides are perhaps the most visible sign of acceptability breakdown. Frontline staff intervene to resolve situations that the system cannot handle gracefully. They make judgement calls, interpret rules flexibly or override outcomes to avoid conflict or harm. These interventions are usually well-intentioned. They reflect a desire to treat people fairly in situations where the system's response feels inadequate.

However, as overrides become routine, they change the system's character. Decisions shift from documented processes to individual discretion. Outcomes vary depending on who is present and how much time or confidence they have. Accountability becomes blurred. The system still operates, but not in a way that is transparent or predictable.

Acceptability breakdown is particularly destabilising because it undermines all other characteristics at once. Functional accuracy becomes harder to assess when users disengage or comply superficially. Performance metrics lose meaning when avoidance and retries distort demand. Security assumptions fail when cooperation is replaced by adaptation. Privacy protections weaken when users seek assistance that involves sharing more information than intended.

This interconnectedness explains why acceptability cannot be treated as an optional or secondary concern. Systems that perform well on paper can still fail in practice if people no longer see value in cooperating with them. Conversely, systems that are perceived as reasonable and respectful can often tolerate technical imperfections without losing legitimacy.

The trade-offs discussed in Chapter 8 are central here. Choices that prioritise certainty, efficiency or control at the expense of user experience may appear justifiable in isolation. Over time, however, they accumulate acceptability debt. Each small friction makes cooperation slightly less likely. Each unexplained decision reduces goodwill. Eventually, people stop giving the system the benefit of the doubt.

Importantly, acceptability breakdown is rarely caused by a single design flaw. It emerges from the interaction of many small decisions: configuration choices, messaging, thresholds, retry limits, escalation paths. Individually, these choices may seem reasonable. Collectively, they shape whether people feel the system is worth engaging with.

Recognising acceptability breakdown therefore requires looking beyond individual interactions to patterns of behaviour over time. It involves paying attention to avoidance, workarounds and overrides not as failures of discipline, but as signals that the system's assumptions no longer align with lived reality.

When cooperation weakens, systems often respond by tightening controls or reducing flexibility. This response may restore order temporarily, but it usually deepens the underlying problem. Acceptability cannot be enforced. It must be sustained.

9.9 Fallback as a design choice, not a last resort

Fallback is often described as something that happens when an age assurance system fails. In practice, fallback is better understood as something the system *chooses* to do when its primary assumptions no longer hold.

This distinction matters. When fallback is treated as a last resort, it is designed defensively: minimally specified, lightly resourced and rarely revisited. When fallback is recognised as a design choice, it becomes a deliberate expression of how the system handles uncertainty, ambiguity and human variation.

In real deployments, fallback paths are activated far more often than design documents tend to suggest. They are triggered by borderline cases, performance pressure, accessibility constraints, conflicting signals or simple misunderstanding. Over time, fallback becomes familiar to staff and users alike. In some contexts, it becomes the dominant way the system actually operates.

This is not a sign that the primary system is defective. It is a sign that real-world use surfaces conditions that could not be fully anticipated. The question is not whether fallback will be used, but how it is structured and who it serves.

Every fallback mechanism advantages some users over others. Some fallback paths require additional time. Others require access to alternative evidence, confidence in dealing with authority or the presence of a supportive intermediary. Some rely on human discretion; others on repeated interaction. These differences matter, because they determine who is helped when the system cannot decide cleanly.

In this sense, fallback design quietly redistributes the trade-offs discussed in Chapter 8. A system that prioritises privacy in its primary flow may shift burden to fallback by requiring more disclosure at the point of escalation. A system that prioritises automation may place greater responsibility on staff discretion when automation fails. A system that prioritises speed may reserve fallback for those able to wait or return later.

Because fallback is often framed as exceptional, these redistributions are rarely examined explicitly. They emerge operationally, through practice rather than policy. Over time, the fallback path becomes the place where difficult cases accumulate and where the system's values are enacted most clearly.

There is a further reason fallback deserves attention. When fallback becomes routine, it effectively *is* the system. Decisions made in fallback shape outcomes more than those made in the primary flow. Yet fallback is often less visible, less documented and less governed.

This invisibility carries risk. Responsibility migrates from formal processes to individuals. Staff are asked to exercise judgement without clear guidance or protection. Users receive different outcomes depending on who they encounter and when.

Accountability becomes diffuse, even as the system continues to operate.

Treating fallback as a design choice does not mean prescribing how it should work. It means recognising that fallback is part of normal operation, not an admission of failure. It deserves the same level of attention as primary system behaviour, because it is where uncertainty is resolved in practice.

Seen this way, fallback is not about fixing mistakes. It is about how systems behave when certainty runs out. It reveals which forms of uncertainty are tolerated, which are escalated and which are quietly absorbed by people rather than processes.

This reframing leads naturally to a broader question. If fallback decisions carry real consequences and if they are activated under conditions of uncertainty, then the ability to question and challenge those decisions becomes critical.

9.10 Appeal, contestability and legitimacy

Appeal mechanisms in age assurance systems are often discussed in narrow terms: as ways to correct mistakes, resolve disputes or satisfy external expectations. While they can serve these functions, their deeper significance lies elsewhere. Appeals are not primarily about fixing errors. They are about sustaining legitimacy in the presence of uncertainty.

Concerns about freedom of expression and lawful access are not abstract or hypothetical in age assurance systems. Any mechanism that conditions access creates the possibility of unjustified exclusion, particularly when decisions are automated, opaque or difficult to challenge. The legitimacy of age assurance therefore depends not on preventing access, but on preventing *unwarranted* denial. Systems that cannot explain their decisions, provide meaningful appeal or reverse outcomes in a timely way risk functioning as de facto access controls rather than decision-support mechanisms. Where exclusion cannot be contested, trust erodes regardless of the system's stated purpose.

Age assurance systems make consequential decisions under conditions that are inherently imperfect. Even when systems function as intended, they will sometimes produce outcomes that feel wrong to those affected. In these moments, what matters most is not whether the system can defend its decision, but whether it allows that decision to be questioned.

Contestability is the ability to challenge an outcome meaningfully. It does not require that every challenge succeed, nor that every decision be reversible. It requires that the system recognises the possibility of being wrong and that it provides a visible, credible path for reconsideration.

This recognition has powerful effects, even when appeals are rarely used. The existence of an appeal mechanism changes how decisions are perceived. Users are more willing to accept adverse outcomes when they believe the system is open to challenge. Staff behave differently when decisions are not absolute. Organisations learn more when disagreement is surfaced rather than suppressed.

Appeal also functions as a signal of humility. It acknowledges that no system – however carefully designed – has perfect knowledge of every situation. This acknowledgement is not a weakness. It is a condition for trust.

When appeal is absent, minimised or purely symbolic, the consequences are rarely confined to the cases in question. Frustration migrates. Users disengage or avoid the system where possible. Staff absorb conflict informally. Decisions that cannot be challenged are tested elsewhere, through circumvention or escalation. Risk does not disappear; it reappears in less manageable forms.

Importantly, appeals are not only for users. They also provide protection and clarity for operators. When staff know that decisions can be reviewed, they are less likely to rely on ad hoc discretion or informal overrides. When organisations can see patterns in appeals, they gain insight into where systems are under strain or assumptions no longer hold.

This learning function is often overlooked. Appeals reveal not just individual disagreement, but systemic misalignment. They show where thresholds are too rigid, where communication fails or where fallback places undue burden on certain groups. Without appeal, these signals are muted or lost.

Contestability therefore supports legitimacy in two directions. It reassures users that the system is not arbitrary. It reassures operators that responsibility does not rest solely on individual judgement at the point of decision.

As with fallback, appeal mechanisms tend to become more important as systems scale and mature. Early deployments may see few challenges. Over time, as systems are encountered repeatedly and expectations solidify, the absence of meaningful appeal becomes more conspicuous. What once seemed efficient begins to feel inflexible. What once seemed decisive begins to feel unaccountable.

Removing or constraining appeal is sometimes justified in the name of efficiency or consistency. Yet this often increases risk elsewhere. Systems that cannot be challenged must be trusted absolutely – a standard that age assurance systems cannot realistically meet. When that trust is not forthcoming, cooperation weakens.

Appeal does not eliminate trade-offs. It does not guarantee fairness in every case. What it does is create space for disagreement without destabilising the system. It provides a pressure-release mechanism that allows uncertainty to be acknowledged rather than denied.

Seen in this light, appeal and contestability are not optional extras or compliance artefacts. They are structural features of legitimate age assurance. They allow systems to operate confidently without claiming infallibility.

9.11 What breakdown teaches us about responsibility

When age assurance systems operate smoothly, responsibility often appears diffuse. Decisions are attributed to technology, policy, configuration or process. Outcomes are explained as the natural result of how the system works. In these moments, it can be difficult to see where responsibility truly lies.

Breakdown changes that.

When a system cannot decide, when performance falters, when security assumptions no longer hold or when people stop cooperating, someone must respond. A decision must be explained. An exception must be made. A complaint must be handled. It is at these moments – not during routine operation – that responsibility becomes visible.

This is why breakdown is so informative. It exposes the points at which abstract design choices meet real human consequences. It reveals who is empowered to act, who bears the burden of uncertainty and who is expected to absorb the cost of imperfection. These distributions of responsibility are often implicit until something goes wrong.

In many organisations, responsibility only appears after breakdown. Roles that seemed clear in policy become ambiguous in practice. Authority and accountability drift apart. Frontline staff are asked to resolve situations without clear guidance or protection. Users encounter decisions that feel final, yet unsupported by explanation or recourse.

None of this implies bad intent. It reflects the fact that responsibility in complex systems is often assumed rather than articulated. Systems are designed to function, not to fail. When failure occurs, the absence of explicit responsibility becomes apparent.

Treating breakdown as exceptional encourages this pattern. Failures are handled case by case. Explanations are improvised. Learning is informal. Over time, similar failures recur because their underlying causes are never examined collectively.

Treating breakdown as normal changes the dynamic. It allows failure to be recognised as a source of insight rather than embarrassment. Patterns can be observed rather than hidden. Questions about design, configuration and governance can be revisited with evidence rather than speculation.

This is where responsibility shifts from individuals to institutions. Instead of asking who made a mistake, the more productive question becomes: *what assumptions led to this outcome and who is responsible for reviewing them?* Responsibility is no longer about blame, but about stewardship.

Stewardship involves owning the trade-offs discussed in Chapter 8 and owning the breakdowns described in this chapter. It requires acknowledging that systems evolve, contexts shift and behaviour adapts. It also requires recognising that legitimacy depends not on the absence of failure, but on how failure is handled and learned from.

Hiding breakdown undermines trust. Users sense when systems are brittle or defensive. Staff recognise when they are being asked to compensate for design gaps. Over time, confidence erodes not because systems are imperfect, but because imperfection is denied.

Learning from breakdown, by contrast, strengthens legitimacy. It demonstrates that the system is attentive, responsive and accountable. It shows that responsibility does not vanish when certainty does.

Chapter 10 – Trust and Confidence in Age Assurance

10.1 Why trust cannot simply be engineered

It is tempting to think of trust as something that can be designed into a system. If the technology is accurate enough, secure enough or certified against the right criteria, trust is expected to follow. This assumption is understandable, particularly in technical fields where performance can be measured, optimised and compared. Yet in age assurance, this intuition repeatedly proves misleading.

Trust is not a property of systems. It is a judgement made by people.

People decide whether to trust an age assurance system not by inspecting its architecture or reviewing its documentation, but by encountering it in moments that matter: when access is denied without explanation, when a process feels intrusive or confusing, when an appeal goes unanswered or when outcomes appear inconsistent over time. These encounters accumulate. They form impressions that are social and contextual, shaped by expectation, experience and comparison with alternatives.

This is why technical correctness, even when demonstrable, does not guarantee trust. A system may operate exactly as specified and still be experienced as arbitrary or unfair. Conversely, a system that is openly imperfect can retain legitimacy if it behaves predictably, explains itself clearly and responds reasonably when challenged. Trust attaches less to what systems *are* than to how they *behave*.

Age assurance heightens this dynamic because it sits at a sensitive intersection of uncertainty and consequence. Decisions are often binary, yet inputs are probabilistic and contextual. Outcomes affect access, dignity, autonomy and, in some cases, safety. Small errors can feel disproportionate. Even correct decisions can be resented if they are poorly handled. As a result, trust in age assurance systems is unusually fragile. It accumulates slowly through repeated, uneventful interactions and collapses quickly when expectations are violated.

This fragility is often misunderstood. Organisations sometimes interpret a loss of trust as evidence that the technology has failed or that users are misinformed. In reality, trust is more often responding to governance signals: how responsibility is exercised, whether decisions are contestable and whether the organisation appears willing to stand behind outcomes when they are questioned.

One of the consequences of this misunderstanding is an over-reliance on declarative signals of trustworthiness. Accuracy claims, certifications, compliance statements and technical assurances are treated as substitutes for trust, rather than as inputs into it. They are expected to do the work of legitimacy. When they fail to do so, confusion follows. From the organisation's perspective, the system is "working as designed". From the user's perspective, something feels wrong and the available explanations do not address that feeling.

This gap cannot be closed by more declarations. Trust does not increase linearly with the volume of assurances provided. In fact, excessive emphasis on technical claims can sometimes heighten suspicion, particularly when they are disconnected from lived experience. People are adept at sensing when explanations are offered to defend a system rather than to help them understand it.

What builds trust instead is consistency over time. Not consistency in outcomes, which age assurance cannot always guarantee, but consistency in how uncertainty is handled. Do similar situations lead to similar responses? Are explanations stable or do they shift depending on who asks? Are failures acknowledged openly or quietly normalised? These patterns are noticed, even if they are not articulated.

Trust is also shaped by comparison. Age assurance systems rarely operate in isolation. Users encounter them alongside other systems, both within and beyond the same organisation. Differences in tone, clarity and responsiveness are immediately apparent. A system that feels heavy-handed or opaque does not need to be egregiously wrong to lose trust; it only needs to feel less reasonable than the alternatives people have experienced elsewhere.

Crucially, trust is not only a user-facing phenomenon. It is also internal. Staff trust systems when they understand how decisions are made, feel supported when handling exceptions and believe that responsibility is shared rather than displaced. When internal trust erodes, external trust often follows. Frontline workarounds proliferate. Explanations become inconsistent. The system's public face begins to fracture.

All of this points to a simple but uncomfortable conclusion: trust cannot be engineered into existence. It emerges from behaviour over time and it is withdrawn when that behaviour no longer aligns with expectations. Technical performance matters, but it is only one ingredient. Governance – the ordinary, ongoing exercise of judgement, explanation and responsibility – is what gives that performance meaning in practice.

This does not mean that trust is uncontrollable or purely subjective. It means that it is relational rather than mechanical. Organisations influence trust through how they configure systems, how they respond to failure, how they communicate limits and how they treat those affected by decisions. These influences are cumulative. They cannot be switched on at the point of deployment, nor restored instantly once lost.

Understanding this is the first step in making governance unavoidable. If trust were simply a function of accuracy or compliance, it could be delegated to technology or outsourced to certification. Because it is not, accountability remains stubbornly present, even when organisations would prefer it to fade into the background.

10.2 Accountability: The question that never goes away

If trust is a judgement formed over time, accountability is the question that surfaces when that judgement is tested. It is the question that appears when something goes wrong, when an outcome is contested or when expectations collide with experience. Who is responsible for this decision? Who can explain it? Who can change it? Who bears the consequences?

In age assurance, this question never fully disappears. It can be deferred, obscured or redirected, but it does not go away.

Part of the difficulty lies in the way accountability is often confused with related but distinct ideas. Responsibility, accountability and control are frequently treated as interchangeable, yet they operate differently in practice. Responsibility is about roles and duties: who is meant to do what. Control is about capability: who has the technical or operational means to influence an outcome. Accountability, by contrast, is about answerability: who must stand behind a decision when it is questioned.

These distinctions matter because age assurance systems routinely separate control from accountability. The organisation that is answerable to users may have limited control over the underlying technology. The organisation that controls the technology may never interact with those affected by its decisions. Responsibility may be distributed across contracts and teams, yet accountability concentrates around moments of impact.

This is why accountability has a way of reasserting itself, regardless of how systems are structured.

A common attempt to resolve this tension is to point to delegation. An organisation relies on a third-party provider, adopts an off-the-shelf solution, uses a token or passkey or integrates a certified component. In doing so, it may feel that accountability has been transferred along with implementation. When challenged, explanations emphasise that the system meets required standards, that the provider is reputable or that the decision was automated according to predefined rules.

These explanations often fail, not because they are false, but because they do not answer the question being asked. The person affected is not seeking a description of procurement arrangements or compliance status. They are seeking recognition that a decision has been made about them, by someone and that this decision can be owned, explained and, if necessary, revisited.

From the outside, appeals to delegation can sound like evasion. From the inside, they may reflect genuine constraints. The technology behaves as specified. The contract limits intervention. The system is operating as approved. Yet accountability does not dissolve simply because intervention is difficult. In fact, it often becomes sharper.

This is one of the uncomfortable realities of age assurance: accountability persists even when control is limited. Organisations cannot automate it away, outsource it away or certify it away. They can only choose how to meet it.

Accountability also has a temporal dimension that is easy to overlook. Before a system is deployed, accountability is largely theoretical. Decisions are hypothetical, risks are modelled and responsibilities are assigned in anticipation of future events. After deployment, accountability becomes concrete. Specific people are affected. Specific decisions are questioned. Explanations are demanded in real time.

It is often only at this point that gaps become visible. Who can override a decision? Who can authorise an exception? Who can explain why this outcome occurred today, when a similar one did not occur last week? These questions rarely arise during design workshops or procurement processes. They arise in the aftermath of failure.

In many observed deployments, accountability emerges reactively rather than deliberately. A complaint escalates. A frontline worker improvises a solution. A manager steps in to resolve a dispute. These acts of accountability are real, but they are often unsupported. Authority is exercised without clear mandate. Responsibility is assumed without protection. Over time, this creates stress for individuals and fragility for the system.

What is striking is that accountability is frequently most visible where it is least formally recognised. Frontline staff become the face of decisions they did not design. Support teams absorb frustration for outcomes they cannot change. Managers are asked to justify behaviours that have evolved informally over time. The organisation, as a whole, appears inconsistent not because it lacks intention, but because accountability has not been aligned with control and responsibility in practice.

This misalignment has consequences for trust. When accountability feels improvised, explanations vary depending on who is asked. Decisions that are meant to be objective begin to look arbitrary. Users learn to escalate rather than engage. Staff learn to deflect rather than explain. The system's legitimacy weakens, even if its technical performance remains stable.

None of this is resolved by tighter contracts or clearer role descriptions alone. Accountability is not a clause that can be written once and relied upon indefinitely. It is enacted repeatedly, through how organisations respond when outcomes are challenged. It is visible in tone as much as in policy, in willingness to engage as much as in formal authority.

This is also where age assurance differs from many other technical systems. Because it deals with eligibility rather than optimisation, the moral weight of decisions is harder to ignore. Being denied access because a system cannot determine age confidently is not experienced in the same way as a recommendation being slightly off-target or a service being temporarily unavailable. The stakes are personal and so accountability is personal too.

Recognising this does not require organisations to promise outcomes they cannot guarantee. It requires acknowledging that decisions are being made in their name and that someone must be prepared to stand behind those decisions when they are questioned. This is not about blame. It is about answerability.

10.3 Practice statements: Making systems, claims and responsibility legible

In complex age assurance ecosystems, most failures of accountability do not arise because no one cares or because no controls exist. They arise because no single artefact clearly describes what a system actually does, under what assumptions and with whose responsibility.

This is the role of a practice statement.

A practice statement is not a marketing claim, a policy aspiration or a certification badge. It is a structured description of how an age assurance system or component operates in practice: the methods it uses, the configuration choices that matter, the contexts it is intended for and the limits within which its results should be interpreted.

Properly used, practice statements serve a simple but powerful purpose: they make systems legible. They allow different actors (age assurance providers, intermediaries, relying parties, auditors and regulators) to see the same system in the same way, rather than each projecting their own assumptions onto it.

This matters because age assurance is rarely delivered by a single organisation acting alone. Outcomes are shaped by chains of dependency: a method embedded in a service orchestrated through an intermediary, configured by a platform and relied upon by a downstream decision-maker. Without a shared description of how each part behaves, responsibility fragments long before anything goes wrong.

In practice, the absence of clear practice statements produces familiar patterns. Providers describe capabilities in general terms, assuming careful deployment. Relying parties configure systems to meet local pressures, assuming those choices are inconsequential. Intermediaries optimise for scale or convenience, assuming others will manage risk. When outcomes disappoint, each actor can point to something that was "technically true" while still missing the point.

Practice statements interrupt this drift.

They force systems to be described not only in terms of *what* they do, but *how* and *under which conditions*. They surface configuration choices that would otherwise remain invisible: retry limits, binding assumptions, fallback paths, data retention behaviour, human intervention points. They make explicit what is often left implicit and therefore unexamined.

Importantly, practice statements are not only for age assurance providers. Any actor whose choices materially affect age assurance outcomes has something to state. A relying party that sets thresholds, defines escalation rules or determines how long results persist is making age assurance decisions, whether it acknowledges them or not. Without its own practice statement, those decisions remain undocumented and effectively ungoverned.

This is why practice statements are a governance tool, not a paperwork exercise. They do not eliminate risk, but they reduce ambiguity about where risk is introduced and who is responsible for managing it. They create a basis for meaningful oversight, comparison and assurance, without pretending that one configuration will suit all contexts.

They also play a critical role in evidence and certification. Independent testing can only assess what has been declared. If a system's real behaviour lives in undocumented configuration or informal operational practice, no amount of certification can meaningfully speak to its outcomes. Practice statements anchor assurance to reality rather than to intention.

Crucially, practice statements are not static. As systems evolve, contexts change and threats adapt, they must be updated. A practice statement that no longer reflects operational reality is worse than none at all, because it creates false confidence. Maintaining alignment between stated practice and actual behaviour is an ongoing responsibility, not a one-off disclosure.

10.4 Purpose limitation and retention: When data outlives its justification

Discussions of privacy in age assurance systems often focus on data minimisation: collecting as little personal information as possible. While minimisation is essential, it is not sufficient. Many of the most serious and persistent privacy failures in real systems arise after collection, when data continues to exist long after its original purpose has been served.

This is the problem of purpose limitation and retention.

Purpose limitation asks a simple question: *why is this data being processed at all?*

Retention asks an equally important one: *how long does that justification remain valid?*

In age assurance, these questions are frequently answered implicitly rather than explicitly. Data is collected to support an eligibility decision, but retained to support something else: troubleshooting, audit, analytics, future investigation or hypothetical regulatory interest. Each extension of purpose feels reasonable in isolation. Together, they allow data to outlive the decision that justified its existence.

This drift is rarely malicious. It often emerges from a desire to be responsible. Organisations worry about being unable to explain decisions after the fact or about failing to assist authorities in rare but serious circumstances. In the absence of clear constraints, retention becomes precautionary. Data is kept *just in case*.

The problem is that precautionary retention quietly transforms the nature of the system.

An age assurance process designed to answer a narrow, time-bound question becomes a long-lived record about a person's behaviour, identity or inferred characteristics. Information that was proportionate for an instant decision becomes disproportionate once it persists. The risk profile of the system changes, even if no new functionality is added.

Over time, retained data attracts gravity. It is reused because it exists. It is repurposed because it is convenient. It is relied upon because it appears authoritative. Each reuse may be lawful or well-intentioned, but the cumulative effect is to turn a contextual safeguard into a surveillance artefact.

Retention also undermines trust in less visible ways. Users who believe that age assurance data will persist indefinitely behave differently. They avoid systems, misrepresent themselves or seek workarounds. The very presence of retained data changes the social dynamics the system depends on to function. A system that appears robust on paper becomes brittle in practice.

Importantly, retention is not only an age assurance provider issue. Relying parties, intermediaries and platforms all make retention decisions through logging, analytics, incident handling and escalation processes. If these actors do not articulate and govern their own retention practices, responsibility fragments. Each party retains "their part" of the data and no one retains accountability for the whole.

This is why purpose limitation and retention discipline are governance concerns, not implementation details. They require explicit decisions about what data is needed, for what purpose, for how long and equally explicit decisions about when that need ends. These decisions must be documented, reviewed and revisited as systems evolve.

Crucially, strong retention discipline does not weaken accountability. It strengthens it. A system that retains data indefinitely in order to explain itself later is often compensating for unclear decision logic or weak documentation elsewhere. Practice statements, configuration records and transparency reporting provide more reliable accountability than hoarded data ever can.

For age assurance systems to remain legitimate over time, data must expire along with its justification. When information outlives the decision it was collected to support, the system ceases to be proportionate even if nothing else changes.

10.5 Transparency and auditability: Making system behaviour observable over time

Trust in age assurance systems is often discussed as a matter of intention, reputation or formal assurance. In practice, trust depends on something more basic: whether system behaviour can be seen, examined and explained over time.

This is the role of transparency and auditability.

Transparency is frequently misunderstood as disclosure – publishing high-level descriptions, policies or claims about how a system works. While such disclosures may be necessary, they are not sufficient. A system can be transparent in theory while remaining opaque in operation.

Auditability goes further. It concerns whether a system's actual behaviour can be reconstructed, interrogated and understood after decisions have been made. It asks whether outcomes can be traced back to configuration, inputs and context, rather than explained away through generalities or intent.

In age assurance, this distinction matters because many of the most consequential decisions are made implicitly. Configuration settings determine thresholds, retries, fallbacks and escalation paths. Binding assumptions shape reuse and persistence. Contra-indicators trigger human intervention or silent downgrades. Data retention determines what evidence remains available later. If these behaviours are not observable, governance becomes speculative.

A common failure mode is retrospective confidence. Systems appear to function smoothly until challenged by a complaint, an incident, a regulator or the media. At that point organisations discover that they cannot reliably answer basic questions: how often fallbacks are used, when staff override automated decisions, how frequently contra-indicators occur or how configuration has changed over time.

The response is often to rely on narrative rather than evidence: "this should not happen often," "the system is designed to prevent that," "we believe this is an edge case." These statements may be sincerely held, but they do not constitute accountability.

True transparency requires systems to make their own limits visible. This does not mean logging everything indefinitely or exposing sensitive detail. It means designing systems so that meaningful aspects of behaviour, decision paths, escalation rates, override frequency or retention events can be observed and reviewed in proportion to risk.

Auditability also changes how failure is experienced. When systems can explain themselves, complaints become diagnostic rather than adversarial. Appeals focus on understanding rather than accusation. Learning becomes possible without waiting for crisis. Certification and oversight can assess real practice rather than inferred intent.

Importantly, transparency and auditability are not solely provider responsibilities. Relying parties, intermediaries and platforms all shape what can be seen through their own logging, reporting and review practices. If each actor observes only their fragment of the system, no one sees the whole. Accountability fractures along organisational boundaries.

This is why transparency must be treated as a system-level property. It depends on how components interact, how responsibilities are distributed and how evidence flows across organisational seams. Practice statements describe what should happen; transparency and auditability reveal what actually does.

There is no single correct level of transparency. What is proportionate depends on context of use, scale, risk and regulatory environment. The failure lies not in choosing a particular approach, but in assuming that trust can be sustained without visibility.

For age assurance systems to remain legitimate over time, they must be governable not only in principle, but in practice. That requires more than confidence that a system behaves well. It requires the ability to see when it does not and to respond before trust is lost.

10.6 Governance happens even when no one names it

Once accountability is understood as unavoidable, another assumption begins to unravel: the idea that systems can exist in a neutral or ungoverned state until governance is explicitly applied. In age assurance, this assumption is particularly persistent. Governance is often imagined as something formal like a framework, a committee or a policy document and in its absence, systems are described as merely "technical" or "operational".

In practice, there is no such thing as an ungoverned age assurance system.

Every age assurance system embodies decisions about risk, tolerance, priority and consequence. These decisions may not be labelled as governance and they may not be made in a single place or at a single moment, but they shape outcomes just as decisively as any formal policy. Defaults, configurations and routine practices quietly determine how the system behaves long before anyone speaks the language of governance.

Thresholds are set. Retry limits are chosen. Timeouts are configured. Certain signals are weighted more heavily than others. Some users are offered alternatives; others are not. These choices often feel technical, even mundane, yet they encode judgements about who should bear uncertainty and how strictly age-related rules should be enforced. Once deployed, they become the system's normal behaviour, rarely revisited unless something goes wrong.

This is governance by default.

Alongside these explicit configurations, a second layer of governance emerges through practice. Frontline staff learn how to handle borderline cases. Support teams develop informal scripts for explaining outcomes. Managers learn when to intervene and when to defer. Over time, these behaviours stabilise into routines.

They may never be written down, but they are widely understood within the organisation. New staff are trained into them. Deviations are quietly corrected.

This informal governance is not a failure. It is an inevitable response to the gap between designed systems and lived reality. Age assurance systems encounter ambiguity, distress and disagreement that cannot be fully anticipated. People adapt. They fill the gaps.

Problems arise not because informal governance exists, but because it is often invisible to those who assume the system is operating "as designed". Decisions that are in fact being made daily through habit and workaround are treated as if they were neutral consequences of technology. Responsibility becomes harder to trace precisely because governance has been displaced into the background.

This invisibility can be comforting. If outcomes are attributed to "the system", no one has to acknowledge the value judgements embedded in its operation. Defaults appear neutral. Exceptions appear anomalous. Over time, however, this fiction becomes harder to maintain. Patterns emerge. Certain groups are repeatedly escalated. Certain contexts generate disproportionate complaints. Staff rely increasingly on informal discretion.

A high-profile failure draws attention. A complaint escalates beyond the organisation. A regulator asks for explanation. Suddenly, decisions that were treated as technical are revealed as normative. Why was this threshold chosen? Why is this fallback available here but not there? Why do staff handle similar cases differently? The organisation scrambles to answer questions that governance would have anticipated, but did not.

This reactive emergence of governance is one of the most consistent features of age assurance deployments. It is not unique to poorly designed systems. Even thoughtful, well-resourced implementations can drift into it if governance is treated as something that happens later or somewhere else.

What becomes clear, with hindsight, is that the system was always governed. The question was never whether governance existed, but whether it was deliberate, visible and accountable.

This is where practice statements begin to matter, even if they are not yet named as such. In environments where governance is implicit, practice statements act as a moment of surfacing. They require organisations to articulate what has previously been left to assumption: how decisions are actually made, how uncertainty is handled and where responsibility sits when routine processes break down.

The act of writing such a statement often reveals the extent to which governance has already been occurring informally. Practices that were "just how things are done" must be described and justified. Exceptions that were handled quietly must be acknowledged. Boundaries that were assumed must be stated explicitly. In doing so, governance moves from habit to declaration.

This shift does not make systems rigid or over-controlled. On the contrary, it often makes them more honest. When governance is acknowledged organisations are better able to see where discretion is exercised, where judgement is required and where responsibility needs to be supported rather than denied.

The alternative is continuing to treat systems as ungoverned until failure forces recognition which tends to produce poor outcomes. Informal practices harden without scrutiny. Accountability concentrates on individuals rather than institutions. Trust erodes not because the system is malicious or incompetent, but because it appears unexamined.

Chapters 6 through 9 have already laid much of the groundwork for this realisation. Systems are not just collections of components;

they are patterns of interaction. Failure is not an anomaly; it is a normal condition. Human judgement does not disappear; it relocates. Governance is the thread that connects these observations.

Once this is seen, the idea of neutral operation becomes difficult to sustain. Every configuration choice, every routine practice, every unexamined default is a governance decision, whether or not it is recognised as such. The task is not to eliminate this reality, but to bring it into view.

Doing so raises a further question. If governance is already embedded in systems, often invisibly, how can it be made visible enough to support trust without collapsing into compliance theatre? How can organisations explain and justify behaviour without turning transparency into performance?

10.7 Transparency as infrastructure, not disclosure

Transparency is often invoked as the antidote to mistrust. When confidence falters, the instinctive response is to disclose more information: publish policies, reference standards, describe technologies or point to audits and certifications. These actions are not without value, but they frequently miss what transparency actually needs to accomplish in age assurance systems.

Transparency, in this context, is not primarily about revealing information. It is about enabling understanding.

An age assurance system can be highly transparent in a formal sense – extensively documented, publicly described, compliant with recognised standards – and still feel opaque to those who encounter it. Users may know that a process exists without understanding why it behaves as it does. Staff may be able to recite policy language without being able to explain individual outcomes. Regulators may be provided with reports that describe system properties without illuminating how decisions are experienced in practice.

This is the difference between disclosure and intelligibility.

Disclosure focuses on what is made visible. Intelligibility focuses on what can be grasped, questioned and reasoned about. In age assurance, the latter matters far more for trust.

When systems are intelligible, people can make sense of outcomes even when they disagree with them. They can understand why a particular decision occurred, what factors influenced it and what avenues exist for challenge or review. When systems are opaque, decisions feel arbitrary, even if they are technically correct. Confusion fills the gap left by explanation and suspicion grows.

This dynamic becomes especially pronounced in age assurance because decisions often appear simple on the surface while being complex underneath. An access denial may be the result of multiple interacting factors including uncertainty thresholds, contra indicators, environmental conditions, retry limits or contextual rules, yet the outcome is experienced as a blunt refusal. Without intelligible explanation, that refusal feels less like a judgement call and more like an impersonal veto.

Organisations sometimes respond to this by increasing the volume of information they provide. More documentation is published. More technical detail is shared. Yet volume does not guarantee clarity. In some cases, it has the opposite effect. Excessive disclosure can obscure responsibility by overwhelming those seeking understanding. When explanations become too technical, too legalistic or too generic, they cease to function as explanations at all.

What people are often looking for instead is reassurance that someone understands the system well enough to explain it plainly and is willing to do so honestly. This is why explanation matters more than exposure. An intelligible system is one where reasoning can be traced, not necessarily one where every component is visible.

Transparency, then, is better understood as infrastructure rather than performance. It is the set of conditions that make explanation possible and challenge legitimate. It includes the ability for staff to articulate how decisions are made without improvisation. It includes the existence of stable reference points against which behaviour can be assessed. It includes clarity about what the system is designed to do and what it is not.

This is where practice statements begin to play a subtle but important role. When treated as living accounts of system behaviour rather than static disclosures, they provide a shared narrative that supports intelligibility. They give organisations a way to say, in plain terms, how age assurance is intended to operate in practice, where discretion exists and how uncertainty is handled.

Such statements do not make systems simple, but they make them discussable. They allow questions to be asked against something concrete rather than abstract. They also make it easier to notice when behaviour diverges from declared practice, which is often the moment when trust is tested.

The absence of this kind of infrastructure has predictable effects. Explanations become inconsistent because they are assembled on the fly. Different parts of the organisation tell different stories about the same system. Users learn that outcomes depend on persistence rather than principle. Transparency exists on paper, but not in experience.

Over time, this erodes trust more effectively than any single failure. People do not expect perfection, but they do expect coherence. When a system cannot explain itself in a stable way, its claims to legitimacy weaken, regardless of how carefully it has been documented.

Reframing transparency in this way also helps to explain why it cannot be reduced to a compliance exercise. Compliance-driven transparency tends to focus on what must be disclosed, to whom and in what format. Infrastructure-driven transparency focuses on whether explanations can actually be given, challenged and sustained over time.

This distinction becomes increasingly important as systems evolve. As configurations change, vendors are replaced or contexts of use expand, the ability to explain behaviour depends less on static disclosures and more on whether the organisation has maintained a coherent understanding of its own system. Without that understanding, transparency degrades quietly, even if documentation remains formally up to date.

Seen in this light, transparency is not an optional add-on to governance. It is one of the ways governance becomes visible and accountable in practice. It does not eliminate disagreement or prevent failure, but it makes those moments navigable rather than corrosive.

10.8 Change is the core governance problem

If trust is formed over time and transparency enables understanding at a given moment, then change is the force that quietly undermines both. In age assurance systems, change is not an occasional disruption. It is the normal condition under which systems operate.

Age assurance systems are rarely built once and left alone. They evolve as software is updated, technology evolves, vendors revise their offerings, policies shift and as organisations respond to operational pressures. Thresholds are adjusted to reduce friction. New methods are introduced to improve coverage. Temporary exceptions become permanent accommodations. Contexts of use expand beyond those originally anticipated.

Each of these changes may appear modest in isolation. Taken together, they alter how the system behaves in ways that are not always immediately visible. Over time, the system that is actually experienced may differ substantially from the system that was originally designed, approved or explained.

This is often described as configuration drift, but the term understates what is happening. Drift suggests something accidental or purely technical. In practice, these changes are expressions of judgement. Decisions are made about which frictions are acceptable, which risks are tolerable and which failures are preferable to others. The fact that these decisions are incremental does not make them less consequential.

What makes change such a difficult governance problem is that it rarely announces itself. Systems continue to function. Performance metrics remain within acceptable ranges. No single modification appears dramatic enough to warrant reconsideration of the whole. Yet assumptions embedded in earlier explanations and assurances slowly become outdated.

A system that was once described as low-friction may become increasingly intrusive as checks are repeated more often. A method that was initially presented as a fallback may become the default through operational convenience. A configuration chosen for a narrow context may be reused elsewhere without reconsideration. In each case, behaviour shifts without a corresponding shift in how the system is understood or described.

This divergence matters because trust depends on coherence between expectation and experience. When systems change without that coherence being maintained, people begin to sense inconsistency even if they cannot immediately articulate it. Outcomes feel less predictable. Explanations feel less convincing. Appeals reference justifications that no longer quite fit.

From a governance perspective, the problem is not that systems change. It is that change is often treated as an operational concern rather than a governance one. Updates are approved because they improve efficiency or reduce error rates, without revisiting the assumptions about context, impact or responsibility that originally justified the system's design.

In this environment, accountability becomes blurred. When a decision is challenged, which version of the system is being defended? Which configuration assumptions apply? Which trade-offs were intended and which have emerged through gradual adjustment? Without a stable point of reference, explanations become fragile.

This is where practice statements, understood as living accounts of system behaviour, become particularly important. They provide a way of anchoring governance over time. Not by freezing systems in place, but by making change visible and discussable.

When a practice statement is treated seriously, change forces a question: does this adjustment alter how the system behaves in ways that matter for trust, accountability or user experience? If it does, the statement needs to evolve alongside the system. That evolution is itself a governance act. It requires someone to acknowledge that the system is no longer quite what it was and to take responsibility for explaining what it has become.

Where practice statements are static, ignored or treated as marketing artefacts, this anchoring function is lost. Change continues, but explanations lag behind. Over time, the gap widens between declared practice and lived reality. When failures occur organisations find themselves defending systems on the basis of assumptions that no longer hold.

This is why "approved once" governance is so fragile in age assurance. Approval often reflects a moment in time, a particular configuration, a particular context of use. As systems evolve, those approvals quietly lose their relevance unless governance evolves with them. Certification, audit and review processes can support this evolution, but they cannot substitute for it.

Change also interacts with human behaviour in predictable ways. As systems become more complex, staff rely increasingly on heuristics. Workarounds become normalised. Informal practices fill gaps left by outdated configurations. These adaptations may keep the system functioning, but they further distance it from its declared form.

Seen from the outside, the system still appears stable. Seen from within, it has become something different. Trust erodes not because change occurred, but because it occurred without acknowledgement.

Recognising change as the core governance problem reframes many familiar challenges. Inconsistency is no longer a failure of training. Confusion is no longer a communication issue. Complaints are no longer outliers. They are signals that the system has moved faster than its governance.

Addressing this does not require freezing systems or resisting improvement. It requires accepting that change is not neutral. Every adjustment reshapes the balance between efficiency, accuracy, privacy and inclusion. Every substitution redistributes risk and responsibility. Treating these moments as governance moments, rather than as purely technical updates, is what allows trust to be maintained over time.

This temporal dimension of governance leads naturally to the next question. If systems are constantly changing, how do organisations notice when those changes begin to matter? What signals indicate that assumptions are no longer holding or that trust is beginning to fray?

10.9 Monitoring, feedback and learning

When organisations talk about monitoring age assurance systems, they often mean something narrow and technical. Metrics are collected. Dashboards are reviewed. Performance is checked against expectations. These activities are important, but they capture only a small part of what governance actually needs to notice.

From a governance perspective, monitoring is not primarily about whether a system is functioning as specified. It is about whether the system is behaving in ways that remain legitimate over time.

This distinction matters because many of the most significant governance failures do not announce themselves through obvious technical degradation. Systems continue to meet accuracy targets. Availability remains high. Error rates appear stable. Yet something begins to feel off. Complaints increase in tone rather than volume. Staff express unease without being able to point to a specific fault. Users disengage quietly rather than escalating. Trust weakens without a clear trigger.

These signals are easy to miss precisely because they are not easily quantified. They do not sit neatly within operational dashboards. They appear at the edges of systems, where human judgement and organisational behaviour intersect.

In practice, what organisations most need to notice are patterns of friction rather than isolated failures. Repeated appeals from similar users. Consistent confusion at particular points in a journey. Informal workarounds that become routine. Discretion exercised more frequently than intended. These are not anomalies. They are indicators that the system's assumptions are being tested by reality.

Learning from these signals requires a shift in orientation. Instead of asking whether the system is performing correctly organisations must ask whether it is still behaving as they believe it is and whether that behaviour remains acceptable. This is a governance question, not an operational one.

One of the reasons this shift is difficult is that learning requires admitting imperfection. It requires acknowledging that earlier decisions may no longer be appropriate or that trade-offs once accepted now carry different consequences. For organisations invested in the idea that systems are "approved" or "compliant", this can feel destabilising. Monitoring becomes defensive rather than reflective. Signals that challenge assumptions are explained away rather than explored.

Yet in age assurance, learning is inseparable from legitimacy. Systems operate under uncertainty, in contexts that change, with users who adapt. Treating early design choices as settled facts rather than provisional judgements makes governance challenging. Over time, the gap between declared intent and lived experience widens.

This is where feedback loops become critical. Not feedback in the sense of satisfaction surveys or performance ratings, but feedback as a mechanism for surfacing disagreement, discomfort and misalignment. Appeals processes, complaints handling, staff escalation paths and external scrutiny all function as feedback, whether or not they are recognised as such.

Organisations that treat these mechanisms as irritations to be managed tend to miss what they reveal. Organisations that treat them as sources of learning are better able to adapt without crisis. The difference lies not in the existence of feedback, but in how it is interpreted.

Practice statements play a supporting role here as well. When an organisation has articulated how its system is intended to behave, feedback can be assessed against that articulation. Are appeals arising because the system is behaving as described but that behaviour is no longer acceptable? Or because the system is behaving differently than claimed? These are different governance problems and they require different responses.

Without such reference points, feedback tends to be handled case by case. Individual complaints are resolved. Individual workarounds are tolerated. The underlying pattern remains unexamined. Over time, this erodes coherence. The system continues to function, but its governance becomes increasingly reactive.

Learning, in this sense, is not about optimisation. It is about recalibration. It is the process by which organisations realign their understanding of the system with how it is actually operating and decide whether that alignment remains defensible. This process is ongoing. It does not end when a system reaches steady state, because steady state is itself temporary.

Seen from this perspective, monitoring is less about control and more about attentiveness. It requires organisations to pay attention to weak signals, to value qualitative insight alongside quantitative data and to resist the temptation to treat discomfort as noise. This kind of attentiveness is labour-intensive. It cannot be fully automated. It relies on people noticing, questioning and reflecting.

10.10 When governance fails (and how it looks)

Governance failure in age assurance rarely looks like a dramatic collapse. Systems do not usually stop working. Access controls do not suddenly disappear. Decisions continue to be made, often at scale and with apparent consistency. From a distance, everything can appear stable.

This is one of the reasons governance failure is so difficult to recognise in its early stages. It does not announce itself as failure. It presents instead as confusion, discomfort and quiet erosion of confidence.

One of the most common signs is the diffusion of responsibility. When decisions are questioned, explanations begin to fragment. Different parts of the organisation offer different accounts of how the system works and why a particular outcome occurred. Frontline staff defer to policy. Policy defers to technology.

Technology defers to vendors or certification. At no point is responsibility explicitly denied, but neither is it clearly owned.

To the person affected, this feels like being passed between abstractions. The decision exists, but no one appears able to stand behind it. Trust falters not because the outcome was necessarily wrong, but because accountability has become elusive.

Another familiar pattern is blame shifting. When failures attract attention organisations may focus on compliance status, contractual boundaries or technical limitations. The language used is often careful and accurate, yet it subtly relocates responsibility away from the organisation itself. Decisions are described as inevitable consequences of laws, rules, standards or automated processes, rather than as the result of human choices made during design and configuration.

This framing can be reassuring internally, but it rarely reassures those outside the organisation. It signals that responsibility is conditional, present only when outcomes align with expectations. When outcomes are contested, responsibility appears to retreat behind structures that are difficult to challenge.

Over-reliance on certification and formal assurance is a related symptom. Certifications and audits have an important role to play, but governance failure often occurs when they are treated as substitutes for ongoing responsibility rather than as supports for it. A system may be repeatedly described as "certified" or "compliant" even as its behaviour diverges from what users experience as acceptable.

In these cases, certification becomes a rhetorical shield. It answers questions about process, but not questions about impact. When people are told that a system is compliant but still experience it as exclusionary, confusing or unfair, trust erodes further. The problem is not the existence of certification, but the expectation that it should silence critique.

Another sign of governance failure is the emergence of outcomes that are defensible on paper but unacceptable in practice. Decisions align with policy language. Processes are followed correctly. Documentation is complete. Yet the result feels disproportionate, insensitive or detached from context. Appeals may be formally available, but practically inaccessible. Explanations may be accurate, but incomprehensible.

These situations are particularly corrosive because they expose a gap between procedural correctness and social legitimacy. Organisations may struggle to respond precisely because they have done everything "right" according to their own criteria. The discomfort arises not from error, but from misalignment between governance as documented and governance as experienced.

Governance failure also tends to concentrate burden on individuals. Frontline staff become informal governors, exercising discretion without guidance or protection. Support teams absorb frustration they cannot resolve. Managers intervene ad hoc to smooth over conflicts. These individuals are often acting responsibly, but they are doing so in the absence of structural support. Over time, this leads to burnout, inconsistency and risk-aversion.

From the outside, this can look like variability or unfairness. From the inside, it feels like carrying responsibility without authority. Both perspectives point to the same underlying issue: governance has not been aligned with how the system actually operates.

It is important to note that none of these patterns require malicious intent or negligence. Governance failure in age assurance is usually the result of accumulated decisions that were reasonable in isolation but never fully integrated. Defaults were accepted. Changes were made incrementally. Informal practices filled gaps. Over time, the system became harder to explain and harder to defend, even as it continued to function.

This is why governance failure often becomes visible only after trust has already been damaged. By the time a pattern is recognised as a problem, it has usually been present for some time. Responses then tend to be reactive and defensive, focused on restoring confidence quickly rather than understanding what has drifted.

Making governance failure recognisable earlier does not require heightened vigilance or harsher controls. It requires attentiveness to the kinds of signals described in the previous section and a willingness to treat discomfort as meaningful rather than inconvenient. It also requires humility: an acceptance that systems can remain technically sound while becoming socially resisted.

Recognising these patterns is not about assigning blame. It is about understanding how governance actually fails in practice, so that failure does not have to be spectacular in order to be taken seriously.

10.11 Governance as an ongoing commitment

By this point, the idea that governance is something that can be completed, signed off or settled should feel increasingly implausible. Age assurance systems do not reach a stable end state in which trust, accountability and legitimacy can be assumed to hold indefinitely. They operate in environments that change, with technologies that evolve and with social expectations that shift over time.

Governance, in this context, is not a structure that can be put in place and left to run. It is a form of ongoing work.

This work is often understated because it lacks the visible markers of progress that technical development offers. There is no final deployment milestone for governance, no moment when it can be declared finished. Instead, it consists of repeated acts of attention: revisiting assumptions, responding to challenge, updating explanations and acknowledging when systems have become something other than what they were originally understood to be.

One of the reasons this is difficult is that governance rarely feels efficient. It requires time, judgement and dialogue. It involves explaining decisions that are uncomfortable to defend and reconsidering trade-offs that were previously accepted. In organisations oriented towards delivery and optimisation, this labour can feel like friction rather than value.

Yet it is precisely this labour that sustains trust.

Trust is not maintained by asserting that systems are compliant or approved. It is maintained by demonstrating, again and again, that responsibility is taken seriously when decisions affect real people. This demonstration happens in how organisations handle disagreement, how they respond to failure and how willing they are to adapt when experience diverges from expectation.

Age assurance makes these dynamics especially visible. Because the systems deal with eligibility and access, the consequences of governance choices are immediate and personal. People notice when decisions feel unexamined. They notice when explanations are rehearsed rather than responsive. They notice when accountability appears to recede behind process.

In this sense, governance is not about control so much as stewardship. It is the practice of caring for how a system behaves over time, even as the conditions around it change. This includes caring for the people who operate the system, the people who are subject to it and the credibility of the organisation that relies on it.

Standards can support this work, but they cannot replace it. Frameworks, certifications and practice statements provide useful reference points, shared language and external scrutiny. They help organisations articulate intent and assess behaviour. What they cannot do is exercise judgement, notice emerging discomfort or take responsibility when outcomes are contested.

Practice statements, in particular, illustrate this distinction. When treated as static artefacts, they quickly lose relevance. When treated as living expressions of how governance is exercised in practice, they become tools for continuity. They help organisations remember what they have said about their systems and give them a basis for explaining how those statements evolve as reality changes.

Seen this way, governance is not a constraint imposed on age assurance systems. It is what makes their operation intelligible, defensible and sustainable. Without it, systems may continue to function, but their legitimacy erodes quietly, often unnoticed until it is difficult to restore.

There is a sobering clarity in this conclusion. Age assurance systems will always be governed, whether or not organisations choose to acknowledge that fact. The only real choice is whether governance is exercised deliberately, visibly and accountably or whether it is left to emerge through habit, workaround and crisis.

Chapter 11 – Procurement, Markets and the Problem of Who is Actually Involved

11.1 Approaching procurement

By the time age assurance systems are discussed in terms of procurement, it is often already unclear who the buyer is meant to be.

The language of procurement implies a straightforward exchange: one organisation identifies a need, evaluates options and selects a solution. Age assurance rarely fits this model. In practice, age assurance is more often encountered as something embedded, inherited, delegated or assumed and present in the environment long before a formal purchasing decision is made. This has profound implications for responsibility, accountability and trust.

This chapter explores why age assurance outcomes are shaped not only by what is used, but by who sits between whom. As assurance is layered across platforms, services and intermediaries, power concentrates, choice narrows and accountability becomes increasingly difficult to locate. These dynamics are not accidental. They arise from the structure of modern digital ecosystems and from the way assurance is distributed within them.

Understanding this allows governance to be approached more deliberately after deployment and helps position certification and assurance claims as foundations on which accountability and trust can be built, rather than as mechanisms expected to resolve every dispute on their own.

11.2 Why age assurance is rarely bought as a single thing

Age assurance is often discussed as though it were a discrete capability: something an organisation decides to introduce, evaluates options for and then procures. This framing is convenient, but it increasingly misrepresents how age assurance enters real systems. In practice, age assurance is rarely bought as a single thing because it is rarely encountered as a single thing.

For many organisations, age assurance arrives indirectly, embedded within other technical, commercial or regulatory arrangements. It may be part of a platform's access controls, bundled into an operating system's parental settings, enforced through an application marketplace's policies or inferred from an identity or credential service that serves multiple purposes at once. In these cases, age assurance is not selected in isolation; it is inherited as part of participation in a wider ecosystem.

This matters because procurement, as traditionally understood, assumes a moment of choice. Someone identifies a requirement, compares alternatives and makes a decision. Age assurance increasingly bypasses this moment. Organisations find themselves operating within environments where age-related decisions are already being made or where the parameters of those decisions are defined elsewhere. The question is no longer "which age assurance system should we buy?" but "what age assurance behaviour are we already subject to?"

Consider a service that depends on a distribution channel with age-based rules. The service may not run any age checks of its own, yet its access, visibility or functionality is constrained by age signals generated upstream. From the user's perspective, the service appears to be enforcing age restrictions. From the service provider's perspective, those restrictions are a condition of participation, not a design choice. Procurement, in the conventional sense, never occurred.

A similar dynamic arises where age assurance is embedded in identity, authentication or account infrastructure. An organisation may procure an identity service for reasons unrelated to age, only to find that age-related attributes, thresholds or inferences are part of the package. These signals may then be reused, implicitly or explicitly, to support age-related decisions elsewhere. Age assurance has entered the system sideways, as a secondary effect of another procurement decision.

In these situations, age assurance is not something that can be cleanly swapped out or reconsidered without revisiting the entire relationship on which it depends. It is entangled with other functions, incentives and obligations. The practical effect is that age assurance becomes part of the environment rather than a component within it.

This embeddedness complicates responsibility from the outset. When age assurance is procured directly, there is at least a notional point at which assumptions can be examined: what risks matter, what errors are acceptable, what happens when the system fails. When age assurance is inherited, these assumptions are already baked in. They may be documented elsewhere or not at all. They may reflect priorities that do not align neatly with the relying organisation's own context of use.

The absence of a clear procurement moment also affects how governance is perceived. If no one explicitly chose the age assurance mechanism, it can feel as though no one is fully responsible for it. Decisions appear to have been made, but not by anyone present. This is not a failure of diligence; it is a consequence of operating within layered systems where agency is distributed.

Importantly, this does not mean that organisations are passive. They still make choices: whether to participate in a given ecosystem, whether to rely on inherited signals, whether to add supplementary checks or mitigations. But these choices are constrained. They are made within boundaries set by others, often under conditions where alternatives are limited or costly.

This is why age assurance so often resists the language of vendor selection. The relevant question is not always "which provider?" but "which dependencies are we accepting?" An organisation may have little influence over how age is determined upstream yet remain accountable for how that determination affects users downstream. The procurement decision that matters most may not mention age at all.

These dynamics help explain why age assurance governance feels difficult even in organisations with strong procurement capabilities. The challenge is not simply evaluating claims or comparing offerings; it is recognising when age assurance is already present, already shaping outcomes and already constraining future options.

Seen this way, age assurance is less like a product that is bought and more like an infrastructure condition that is joined. Participation brings benefits such as reach, functionality and legitimacy, but it also brings inherited rules. Age assurance is one of those rules, often invisible until it becomes contested.

11.3 The expanding cast of actors

Once age assurance is no longer treated as a single thing that is bought, it becomes harder to describe who is actually involved. The apparent simplicity of an "age check" gives way to a more crowded picture, in which multiple organisations contribute, constrain or rely on age-related decisions without any one of them controlling the whole.

At one level, this is obvious. Someone defines the rules under which age matters. Someone produces an age-related signal. Someone applies that signal to a decision. Someone presents the outcome to a user. What is less obvious is how rarely these roles align within a single organisation and how often they overlap in partial and shifting ways.

An organisation may define policies about acceptable content or access without operating any age assurance technology itself. Another may operate technical systems that generate age-related indicators, but have no relationship with the end user affected by the decision. A third may aggregate signals from several sources, combining them into a single outcome, while a fourth relies on that outcome downstream, treating it as authoritative.

From the perspective of any one actor, the system can appear bounded and intelligible. Each organisation knows what it is responsible for, what inputs it receives and what outputs it produces. Yet no single actor sees the entire chain. Decisions taken upstream are experienced downstream without context. Constraints imposed at one layer are interpreted as facts at another.

This fragmentation is not accidental. It reflects how modern digital systems are built: modular, layered and interconnected. Age assurance fits into this structure not as a standalone service, but as a capability that can be invoked, reused and recombined across contexts. As a result, the number of actors involved in producing an age-related decision is often greater than it appears.

Crucially, these roles are not fixed. An organisation that sets rules in one context may be a relying party in another. A service that produces assurance signals for its own purposes may find those signals reused elsewhere. Boundaries shift as systems evolve, partnerships change and new uses emerge. Over time, responsibilities blur not because actors are careless, but because the system itself resists neat categorisation.

This matters for accountability because responsibility is often imagined as something that can be allocated cleanly: to a provider, a platform or a supplier. In actor-rich ecosystems, responsibility is instead distributed across interactions. Each actor contributes to the outcome, but none can fully own it in isolation.

The difficulty becomes apparent when things go wrong. A disputed decision may be traced back through several layers, each of which can point to another as the source of authority or evidence. From the user's perspective, this distinction is irrelevant; they experience a single outcome. From the system's perspective, the outcome is the product of multiple, loosely coupled judgements.

Importantly, the expanding cast of actors does not imply dysfunction. Many of these arrangements are efficient, scalable and commercially rational. They allow age assurance to be deployed widely without requiring every organisation to reinvent the same capabilities. The challenge is not the existence of multiple actors, but the lack of shared visibility across them.

Where roles overlap without being articulated, assumptions travel unnoticed. One actor may assume that another has considered certain risks, handled certain edge cases or provided certain safeguards. Downstream, those assumptions solidify into expectations that may not be justified. Accountability then becomes retrospective, assembled only after a problem has surfaced.

This is why actor diversity is such a persistent source of governance tension. The system works precisely because responsibilities are partitioned, yet trust is tested when those partitions become visible. Without a clear understanding of who is involved – and how their roles intersect – it is easy to misinterpret both failures and assurances.

Recognising the expanding cast of actors is therefore not about creating a taxonomy or assigning blame. It is about acknowledging that age assurance is produced collectively, even when it is experienced individually. Governance challenges arise not from bad actors, but from the gaps between them.

11.4 Delegated and inherited assurance

As the number of actors involved in age assurance grows, assurance itself begins to move. It is passed along chains of reliance, reused in contexts for which it was not originally designed and absorbed into systems that did not create it. Age assurance becomes delegated and inherited rather than deliberately constructed end to end.

This delegation often begins innocently. An organisation relies on an upstream service for reasons of scale, efficiency or necessity. That service provides signals that include, among other things, age-related information. Over time, those signals are treated as authoritative, not because they are perfect, but because they are available, convenient and already embedded in the flow of interaction. Assurance becomes part of the background infrastructure.

Inherited assurance has a particular quality: it feels settled. Because the decision logic is not locally owned, it can appear objective or external, even when it is the product of very specific assumptions made elsewhere. Downstream actors may not fully understand how age is determined, what uncertainty is tolerated or how edge cases are handled. What they receive is a result, not a rationale.

This matters because inherited assurance is often reused beyond its original scope. Signals generated for one purpose – eligibility, safety, compliance – may be repurposed for another. Each reuse subtly shifts the context of use, even if the technical interface remains unchanged. Over time, assurance travels further from the conditions under which it was originally justified.

Delegation also changes how responsibility is experienced. When an organisation actively chooses an age assurance method, it tends to feel ownership over its limits and consequences. When assurance is inherited, ownership becomes diffuse. The organisation may feel responsible for the outcome, yet unable to influence the mechanism that produced it. Responsibility is accepted without control.

This dynamic connects directly to the system-level view explored earlier. Age assurance is rarely a single component; it is a chain of interactions. Delegated assurance means that decisions are made at one point in the chain and enforced at another. The actor closest to the user is often the one least able to explain or modify the decision.

From a governance perspective, this is a fragile arrangement. Disputes surface where assurance is applied, not where it is generated. Questions about fairness, error or exclusion are directed at the organisation delivering the outcome, even when that organisation had little role in shaping the underlying logic. Appeals are therefore constrained by the boundaries of delegation.

Delegation also introduces asymmetry in how risk is distributed. Upstream actors may design systems to perform well across broad populations, optimising for scale and consistency. Downstream actors, operating in narrower contexts, experience the residual risk: the misclassifications, the edge cases, the mismatches between system behaviour and local expectations. Inherited assurance concentrates these effects where users are most visible.

None of this implies that delegation is misguided. On the contrary, it is often the only viable way to deploy age assurance at scale. The problem arises when delegation is treated as neutral, rather than as a governance choice with consequences. Inherited assurance carries with it inherited assumptions, inherited trade-offs and inherited blind spots.

Because these assumptions are rarely articulated at the point of inheritance, they tend to surface only when challenged. At that moment, it becomes clear that assurance has travelled without its justification. The question "why did this happen?" has no simple answer, because the answer is distributed across multiple decisions made at different times, by different actors, for different reasons.

This is where the connection to earlier chapters becomes apparent. In Chapter 6, age assurance was described as a system rather than a method. In Chapter 10, responsibility was shown to persist even when execution is delegated. Delegated and inherited assurance is the point where these ideas meet operational reality.

Understanding delegation helps explain why accountability becomes blurred long before deployment. It also helps explain why later attempts to impose clarity – through policy, documentation or certification – often struggle. They arrive after assurance has already been embedded and reused, not at the moment when its assumptions were formed.

As assurance continues to travel along chains of reliance, power begins to concentrate at certain points in the ecosystem.

11.5 Power asymmetry in layered ecosystems

Once age assurance is delegated and inherited across multiple layers, differences in power between actors become more pronounced. These differences are not primarily about technical capability or intent. They arise from position: where an actor sits in the chain of reliance, how many others depend on them and how easily relationships can be altered.

In layered ecosystems, power tends to accumulate upstream. Actors whose systems or policies are widely relied upon shape the conditions under which others operate. They define acceptable approaches, set default behaviours and establish the practical meaning of compliance. Downstream actors, by contrast, adapt. Their choices are constrained not because alternatives do not exist in theory, but because the cost of deviating from upstream expectations is often prohibitive.

This asymmetry is most visible where age assurance intersects with access to markets or audiences. Participation may depend on meeting certain age-related requirements, enforced through mechanisms the downstream actor does not control. Negotiation, where it exists at all, is uneven. For many organisations, the realistic option is to comply or withdraw, not to reshape the terms.

Standards and certification interact with this asymmetry in subtle ways. For actors at the centre of an ecosystem, they can be tools for structuring expectations and demonstrating legitimacy. For those at the edges, they may function primarily as entry conditions. The same assurance signal carries different weight depending on where an actor sits.

Power also shapes which trade-offs are considered acceptable. Decisions about friction, exclusion or error rates may be optimised for system-wide efficiency rather than local impact. Upstream actors are often insulated from the day-to-day consequences of these choices, while downstream actors absorb their effects. This is not indifference; it is distance.

Over time, asymmetry influences how problems are interpreted. When age assurance works well at scale, success is attributed to robust design. When it fails in specific contexts, failure is often localised: a particular service, implementation or user group is seen as the issue. Structural causes remain upstream, largely unchanged.

This dynamic helps explain why accountability feels misaligned. Authority to change systems sits with actors who may not experience the consequences of those changes. Responsibility for managing outcomes sits with actors who may lack the leverage to influence underlying assumptions. The gap between power and accountability widens as ecosystems grow.

Importantly, power asymmetry does not imply bad faith. Large-scale systems require consistency to function. Standardisation reduces complexity. Centralisation enables coordination. The problem arises when these necessities obscure the fact that trade-offs are still being made and that their effects are unevenly distributed.

For governance, this creates a persistent tension. Downstream actors are expected to stand behind outcomes they did not shape, while upstream actors are shielded from direct challenge by layers of abstraction. Trust is therefore tested at the weakest point in the chain, even when its causes lie elsewhere.

Recognising power asymmetry is a precondition for understanding why procurement and assurance claims behave as they do. It clarifies why certain actors frame age assurance in particular ways and why others accept those framings despite their limitations.

11.6 How assurance is framed when there are many actors

As age assurance moves through layered ecosystems, it must be made legible. Complex arrangements involving multiple actors, inherited assumptions and uneven power cannot easily be explained each time a decision is made or a dependency is formed. Instead, complexity is compressed into familiar forms: short phrases, signals of legitimacy and references that stand in for deeper explanation.

This is where framing becomes critical.

In multi-actor environments, assurance is rarely described in terms of how decisions are actually produced. Instead, it is framed in ways that reassure without fully specifying boundaries. References to alignment, compliance or delegation allow organisations to communicate that age assurance has been "handled" without reopening questions about who decided what or under which conditions.

These framings perform an important function. They allow ecosystems to operate at scale. Without them, every integration would require extensive negotiation and shared understanding. Markets depend on shorthand. However, the cost of shorthand is that ambiguity is preserved rather than resolved.

When an organisation states that it relies on upstream assurance, it signals legitimacy while quietly passing responsibility along the chain. When it refers to industry-standard approaches, it invokes collective authority without identifying whose standards, whose interpretations or whose trade-offs are in play. When it points to certification, it gestures toward external validation without explaining scope or limits.

For buyers and downstream actors, these framings are often sufficient at the point of procurement. They reduce uncertainty to a manageable level. They make participation possible without requiring full visibility. The problem is not that they are misleading, but that they are incomplete.

As assurance travels downstream, the ambiguity embedded in these framings travels with it. Each actor interprets the signal in light of their own context, often assuming more coverage or certainty than was intended. By the time an age-related decision reaches a user, the original framing has been abstracted several times over.

This abstraction becomes visible when outcomes are contested. Questions that appear straightforward – why was access denied, what evidence was used, who can change the decision – turn out to have answers distributed across multiple actors. The framing that once reassured now obscures.

Importantly, this is not a communication failure that can be fixed with better wording. It reflects a structural reality: no single actor can fully describe the system without overstepping their role or revealing dependencies they do not control. Framing therefore balances honesty with practicality, often erring toward simplicity.

These dynamics help explain why assurance claims are frequently asked to do more than they can. They are expected to resolve uncertainty, allocate responsibility and establish trust across organisational boundaries. When they fail to do so, disappointment is directed at the claim rather than at the structure that necessitated it.

11.7 Procurement with limits (and how choice is shaped)

Procurement in age assurance is not uniformly without choice, but it is rarely unconstrained. In some contexts, relying parties procure age assurance directly from providers, evaluate alternatives and retain a high degree of control over how systems are selected and configured. In others, age assurance is inherited through participation in wider ecosystems, where key parameters are set elsewhere and local choice is narrower.

What matters is not whether choice exists in principle, but how it is shaped in practice.

Even where multiple providers or approaches are theoretically available, practical considerations often narrow the field quickly. Integration effort, compatibility with existing systems, operational continuity, contractual commitments and user impact all influence what is viable. These factors do not eliminate choice, but they give it form. Some options become realistic whilst others remain hypothetical.

In ecosystem settings, this shaping is more pronounced. Age assurance may be bundled into platforms, devices or services that organisations depend on for reach or functionality. Alternatives may exist, but at the cost of losing access, breaking interoperability or departing from established expectations. In these cases, procurement is less about selecting between interchangeable options and more about deciding whether and how to participate.

This distinction matters for governance. Where organisations experience procurement as an active choice, ownership of system behaviour tends to feel clearer. Where assurance is inherited or strongly constrained, ownership can feel more diffuse, even though responsibility remains. The difference is not one of accountability, but of perceived agency.

Importantly, constrained choice does not mean passive acceptance. Organisations still make decisions: whether to rely on inherited assurance, whether to supplement it, whether to introduce additional safeguards or explanations. These decisions are made within boundaries, but they are decisions nonetheless. Governance operates in the space between what is fixed and what remains adjustable.

Misunderstandings arise when procurement is viewed from the outside as freely substitutable. Observers may assume that if an age assurance system causes problems, it can simply be replaced. From within the system, this is often unrealistic. Changing assurance arrangements can affect integration, user experience, compliance relationships and operational stability. The cost of change is not just financial; it is organisational.

Recognising how choice is shaped rather than assuming its absence helps explain why age assurance systems persist even as their limitations become visible. It is not that actors are unaware of trade-offs or unwilling to address them. It is that those trade-offs are embedded in broader arrangements that cannot be easily unwound.

This perspective also clarifies why accountability debates can become strained. Responsibility is rightly expected, but the mechanisms available to exercise it vary depending on how procurement choices were formed. Governance must therefore work with these realities, rather than against an idealised model of free selection.

Seen in this light, procurement in age assurance is best understood not as a binary of choice versus no choice, but as a spectrum of constraint. Where an organisation sits on that spectrum shapes how responsibility is exercised, how change is managed and how trust is sustained over time.

11.8 When things go wrong: Who is answerable?

Age assurance systems are often experienced as stable until they are not. It is in moments of failure such as a disputed denial, an unexpected exclusion, a confusing or inconsistent user journey that the underlying structure of responsibility becomes visible. By that point, however, responsibility has usually already been distributed and the question of who is answerable becomes harder rather than clearer.

Failures in age assurance rarely originate at a single point. An outcome may depend on an upstream signal, an intermediary interpretation, local configuration choices and a user interface designed elsewhere. Each element may have operated as intended within its own scope, yet the combined effect still produces harm or confusion for the individual affected.

In these situations, accountability tends to concentrate at the point of interaction. The organisation closest to the user receives the complaint, manages the appeal and absorbs the reputational impact. This is not necessarily because it exercised the greatest control, but because it is visible, accessible and directly connected to the risk experienced by the user.

This concentration is not accidental. In many regulatory and legal frameworks, primary responsibility follows proximity to risk rather than technical authorship. The actor that creates, enables or benefits from a risky activity is often expected to bear responsibility for its consequences, even where parts of the decision-making process are delegated or inherited. Reliance on others does not dissolve that responsibility, particularly in higher-risk environments where the consequences of error are more severe.

This creates an important distinction between *how assurance is produced* and *who remains answerable for its effects*. Upstream actors may design systems, generate signals or define policies, but they are often removed from the immediate context in which harm occurs. Downstream actors, by contrast, may have limited influence over upstream logic while remaining legally and socially accountable for outcomes experienced by users.

Delegation therefore creates a buffer for some actors and a concentration of exposure for others. Contracts, APIs, policies and standards mediate responsibility technically, but they do not necessarily mediate it legally or socially. Documentation and assurances may explain how a system operates, but they do not always satisfy the expectation that someone must take responsibility when things go wrong.

This leads to a familiar but uncomfortable pattern. Frontline staff are asked to explain decisions they cannot fully inspect. Support teams handle appeals without authority to alter underlying behaviour. Organisations stand behind outcomes they did not design, using language supplied by others to justify decisions whose rationale they cannot completely unpack.

As disputes unfold, attention often shifts from the substance of harm to questions of boundary and scope. Which actor's evidence applies? Which rules govern escalation? Which layer has authority to intervene? Responsibility fragments into partial explanations, even as the user's experience remains singular and concrete.

These moments expose a divergence between power and responsibility. The capacity to change system behaviour may sit upstream, while the obligation to respond to harm sits downstream. The more layered the ecosystem, the wider this gap becomes and the more pressure is placed on governance arrangements to compensate.

Importantly, this is not a story of negligence or indifference. Each actor is typically operating within the limits of its role and the constraints of its dependencies. The difficulty is structural: decision-making is distributed, but accountability expectations are not.

This is why failure handling is such a critical test of age assurance governance. In these moments, technical accuracy recedes in importance. What matters instead is clarity about who can act, who can explain and who can accept responsibility for change. Where these questions have not been addressed in advance, responses become defensive or reactive and trust erodes quickly.

The patterns described in Chapter 9 reappear here with greater intensity. Failure is not only about system behaviour; it is about the challenge of aligning authority, responsibility and risk across multiple actors. Appeals and complaints become pressure points where inherited assumptions and constrained procurement choices are exposed.

Over time, organisations adapt. Informal workarounds emerge. Discretion is exercised to soften rigid outcomes. These responses are often pragmatic and humane, but they are also signals that governance is compensating for structural misalignment rather than operating from a stable foundation.

Understanding who is answerable when things go wrong is therefore not about assigning blame after the fact. It is about recognising that accountability must be anchored to risk and consequence, not just to technical contribution. In ecosystems where age assurance is delegated or inherited, making that anchoring explicit is one of the most difficult and most necessary governance challenges.

11.9 What procurement decisions really lock in

Procurement decisions are often understood as choices between suppliers or solutions. In age assurance ecosystems, what is actually locked in runs much deeper. Long after contracts are signed or integrations completed, early decisions continue to shape how systems behave, how disputes are handled and what forms of accountability are possible.

One of the most significant commitments made through procurement is architectural. Decisions about where age assurance sits – at the device level, the platform level, the service boundary or the point of interaction – determine how visible and adaptable it will be. Once assurance is embedded at a particular layer, moving it is rarely trivial. It requires rethinking data flows, user journeys and responsibilities across multiple actors.

Procurement also locks in assurance models. Choices about whether age is treated as a one-time check, a persistent attribute or a repeated assessment shape user experience and risk exposure over time. These models carry assumptions about trust, behaviour and context that are difficult to revisit once systems are operational. What begins as a pragmatic choice becomes an organising principle.

Equally important is the form of evidence that procurement privileges. Decisions about which signals are acceptable, which indicators matter and which documentation is sufficient establish a baseline for legitimacy. Over time, these evidence forms become entrenched. Appeals and audits are framed around what can be produced within that evidentiary model, even if it no longer aligns well with lived experience.

Appeal paths themselves are often shaped indirectly by procurement. The question of who can review or override an age-related decision depends on where authority has been placed. If assurance is inherited from upstream systems, local actors may lack meaningful escalation routes. If responsibility is fragmented, appeals may circulate without resolution. These patterns are rarely designed deliberately; they emerge from the way systems are assembled.

What makes these lock-ins particularly powerful is that they are seldom revisited. Once systems are working "well enough," attention shifts elsewhere. The assumptions embedded in early procurement decisions fade into the background, becoming part of the operational landscape. Only when contexts change – new user groups, new expectations, new forms of harm – do these assumptions resurface as constraints.

At that point, governance options are already limited. Changing assurance models can require renegotiating relationships across ecosystems. Adjusting evidence standards may conflict with upstream requirements. Introducing new appeal mechanisms may expose gaps in authority that are difficult to close. The cost of change grows as systems become more deeply embedded.

This persistence helps explain why age assurance systems can feel resistant to reform even when their limitations are widely acknowledged. The issue is not lack of awareness, but accumulated commitment. Procurement decisions, especially those made indirectly or under constraint, set trajectories that are hard to alter.

Seen in this light, procurement is less a moment than a path. Each decision narrows future possibilities, shaping how responsibility and accountability can be exercised. Governance then operates within the contours set by those early choices, adapting rather than redesigning.

Recognising what procurement really locks in clarifies why accountability challenges persist across the lifecycle of age assurance systems. It also underscores why later mechanisms – including certification, testing and assurance – must contend with structures they did not create.

11.10 Rethinking "buying" in an ecosystem world

By the time the full structure of age assurance is visible – its inherited assumptions, layered actors, power asymmetries and locked-in commitments – the language of "buying" begins to feel inadequate. It suggests a level of agency and control that rarely exists in practice and it obscures the ways in which organisations become participants in assurance systems rather than owners of them.

In an ecosystem world, age assurance is less often purchased than *entered into*. Organisations join environments in which age-related decisions are already being made. They rely on signals generated elsewhere, delegate aspects of judgement to intermediaries and accept constraints as the price of access. Procurement still occurs, but it is only one moment within a broader pattern of participation and dependence.

This shift in perspective matters because it reframes responsibility. If age assurance is understood as something bought from a supplier, accountability can be imagined as transferable. If it is understood as something inherited through relationships, accountability becomes relational and ongoing. Organisations remain responsible not because they control every element, but because they have chosen to rely on systems that affect people.

It also reframes the role of standards and certification. In ecosystem contexts, they function less as simplifiers and more as boundary markers. They help clarify roles, articulate expectations and create shared reference points, but they do not collapse complexity into a single guarantee. Their value lies in making structures visible, not in pretending those structures do not exist.

Understanding who is involved – and how they are connected – becomes more important than understanding which product was selected. Questions of governance shift from vendor choice to role awareness: who sets rules, who generates signals, who interprets them and who must answer when outcomes are contested. Without this awareness, even well-intentioned assurance efforts risk addressing symptoms rather than causes.

This perspective also helps explain why accountability in age assurance so often feels blurred. It is not because responsibility has disappeared, but because it is distributed across systems designed to scale rather than to explain themselves. Trust is therefore tested not by technical performance alone, but by how well these distributions of responsibility are acknowledged and managed.

Reframing age assurance as participation rather than purchase does not resolve the challenges described in this chapter. It does, however, make them intelligible. It reveals why governance cannot be bolted on after deployment, why appeals and explanations struggle to find a foothold and why procurement decisions carry consequences long after their rationale has faded.

Chapter 12 – Certification, Testing and Assurance: Building Trust in Age Assurance Systems

12.1 Getting checked

By the time age assurance systems reach certification, they are no longer abstract ideas or technical possibilities. They are becoming relied upon. Decisions are being made, access is being granted or denied and responsibility is being exercised across organisational and jurisdictional boundaries. At this stage, trust is no longer optional. It must be supported, shared and sustained.

Certification, testing and assurance exist to make that trust possible.

This chapter explains why independent assurance matters in age assurance systems, how certification contributes to confidence and accountability and why well-designed assurance strengthens governance rather than replacing it. It presents certification not as a constraint, but as an enabling infrastructure: one that allows confidence to scale without collapsing into blind faith or informal belief.

12.2 Why age assurance needs independent assurance

Age assurance systems make claims that are both consequential and difficult to verify independently. They assert that a person is above or below an age threshold, that an interaction is appropriate to allow or restrict or that a decision has been made in a way that is proportionate, privacy-respecting and fair. These claims have real effects on access, participation and trust. Yet for almost all actors in the ecosystem, the internal workings of age assurance systems are not directly observable.

This creates a distinctive challenge. Unlike many technical services, age assurance operates at the boundary between systems and people. Decisions are often automated, probabilistic and context-dependent, while their consequences are immediate and personal. Relying parties must act on outcomes they did not generate. Regulators must oversee behaviours they cannot inspect transaction by transaction. Users must accept decisions without visibility into how they were produced. In this environment, confidence cannot rest solely on vendor assertion or informal reputation.

In age assurance, certification provides a mechanism by which claims about systems and components can be examined by parties who are not embedded in their commercial or operational success. Certification introduces a structured form of independence – particularly through accredited certification: not independence from context or policy, but independence from self-description. This matters because age assurance systems are often deployed into situations of asymmetrical power. Users have little choice but to comply. Relying parties may have limited alternatives. Regulators are asked to trust that systems behave as described at scale.

Certification changes this dynamic. By subjecting age assurance systems and components to independent testing and assessment against declared criteria, assurance creates confidence that does not rely on personal trust or informal networks. It allows relying parties to depend on systems responsibly, regulators to anchor oversight in shared evidence and users to have confidence that decisions affecting them are not arbitrary.

This role becomes more important as age assurance systems scale and interconnect. Early deployments may be limited in scope, operating within a single organisation or service. As systems expand across platforms, sectors and jurisdictions, the number of actors involved increases rapidly. Age assurance providers supply components. Intermediaries orchestrate flows and decisions. Relying parties integrate outcomes into their own services. Each layer introduces additional assumptions and dependencies.

Independent assurance provides a common reference point across these layers. It allows confidence to travel without requiring every actor to re-test or re-interpret every component themselves. In doing so, it supports interoperability not just at a technical level, but at a governance level. Actors can rely on each other's systems with a shared understanding of what has been examined, for what purpose and under which conditions of uncertainty.

Crucially, this applies not only to age assurance providers themselves, but to intermediaries and relying parties as well. Age assurance outcomes are often shaped as much by orchestration, configuration and use as by the underlying method. Independent assurance can therefore play a role in examining how components are combined, how decisions are triggered and how results are acted upon. This widens the scope of confidence from individual tools to the systems in which they operate.

In this sense, certification is not merely a badge attached to a product. It is part of the accountability infrastructure of the age assurance ecosystem. It supports clear allocation of responsibility by making it explicit what has been assured and what has not. When systems behave as expected, certification helps explain why confidence was reasonable. When they do not, it provides a structured basis for understanding what assumptions failed and where corrective action is needed.

Independent assurance also strengthens legitimacy. Age assurance is often deployed in sensitive contexts involving children, vulnerable users and contested social norms. Public confidence in these systems depends not just on technical performance, but on the perception that they are governed responsibly. Certification demonstrates that systems are not operating solely on the basis of private judgement but are subject to external scrutiny and shared standards.

Importantly, this does not require assurance to claim infallibility. On the contrary, the legitimacy of certification in age assurance rests on its willingness to be explicit about scope, conditions and limitations. Confidence is strengthened when systems are described honestly, rather than when they are presented as universally reliable. Independent assurance allows this honesty to be institutionalised rather than left to voluntary disclosure.

12.3 What certification actually contributes

Certification contributes to age assurance not by declaring systems perfect, but by changing the *quality* of how claims are made, examined and relied upon across the ecosystem. Its value lies less in any single outcome than in the discipline it introduces into design, deployment and governance.

At its core, certification brings structured scrutiny to age assurance systems, components and practice statements. Age assurance inevitably involves claims: about accuracy, privacy protection, resistance to misuse, fairness, reliability and suitability for particular contexts of use. Without certification, these claims are largely self-declared. They may be well intentioned and technically grounded, but they remain difficult for others to evaluate consistently.

Certification requires those claims to be made explicit, bounded and testable. It compels system providers, intermediaries and relying parties to articulate what their systems are designed to do, under what conditions and with what assumptions. This alone raises the standard of discourse. Vague assurances give way to declared characteristics. Implicit design choices become visible.

This process has a material effect on system quality. When age assurance systems are designed with independent assessment in mind, attention is paid earlier to documentation, configuration control, traceability and clarity of purpose. Decisions that might otherwise be left informal – such as how thresholds are set, how fallback is handled or how results are conveyed – must be recorded and justified. Certification therefore improves not only what is tested, but what is *designed*.

Certification also contributes disciplined evidence gathering. In age assurance, evidence is often fragmented: technical tests in one place, privacy assessments in another, operational metrics somewhere else again. Certification brings these strands together within a coherent assurance frame. Evidence is collected against declared purposes rather than as an unstructured accumulation of results.

This discipline matters because age assurance evidence is inherently contextual. Test results only have meaning when interpreted against assumptions about users, environments and threats. Certification creates a framework in which that interpretation is explicit. Evidence is not presented as universal truth, but as support for confidence within a defined scope.

A further contribution of certification is independent challenge. Independent assessors are positioned to question claims that may otherwise go unexamined, to probe edge cases and to surface tensions between objectives. This challenge is constructive rather than adversarial. Its purpose is not to block deployment, but to ensure that confidence is warranted.

In age assurance ecosystems, this independent challenge is particularly valuable because incentives are often misaligned. Providers are incentivised to emphasise strengths. Relying parties are incentivised to seek reassurance. Intermediaries are incentivised to smooth integration. Certification introduces a counterbalancing role whose legitimacy rests precisely on not sharing these incentives.

Certification also creates a common language across actors. One of the persistent difficulties in age assurance governance is that different participants talk past each other. Engineers focus on methods and metrics. Policymakers focus on outcomes and harms. Procurement teams focus on comparability and risk. Certification provides shared reference points through declared scopes, assurance statements and documented evidence which allow these conversations to converge.

This common language is especially important where age assurance systems are reused across sectors or jurisdictions. Certification does not eliminate contextual differences, but it allows them to be discussed explicitly rather than discovered through failure. Actors can understand not just whether something has been certified, but *how* and *for what purpose*.

In procurement and governance contexts, certification therefore plays an enabling role. It allows decisions to be grounded in shared artefacts rather than informal trust. It supports more nuanced conversations about suitability, risk and responsibility. Importantly, it allows confidence to be scaled without becoming blind.

Certification's contribution extends beyond age assurance providers themselves. Intermediaries that orchestrate flows, apply business rules or manage integrations can also be examined within assurance frameworks. Relying parties, whose configuration choices and operational practices materially affect outcomes, can likewise be brought into scope. This reflects the reality that age assurance behaviour emerges from systems, not isolated tools.

By supporting assurance across these roles, certification strengthens accountability. It clarifies who is responsible for which aspects of behaviour and on what basis confidence is claimed. When outcomes are questioned, certification provides a starting point for analysis rather than a shield against it.

Perhaps most importantly, certification contributes to confidence without complacency. It allows actors to rely on age assurance systems responsibly, knowing that claims have been examined independently, while still recognising that judgement and oversight remain necessary. Confidence grounded in certification is not fragile optimism; it is confidence supported by evidence, challenge and transparency.

In this way, certification does not compete with trust. It makes trust possible at scale.

12.4 Certification, regulation and earned recognition

Certification does not exist in opposition to regulation. Its value lies precisely in its symbiotic relationship with regulatory oversight. Together, certification and regulation form a governance system that is both more effective and more proportionate than either could be alone.

Age assurance is a domain where this relationship is particularly important. Systems are complex, behaviour is probabilistic and compliance is not binary. Some organisations are motivated to do the right thing but need structure, clarity and validation. Others may be unaware, under-prepared or still developing their practices. A smaller subset may be unwilling to comply at all. Treating all of these actors in the same way is neither efficient nor fair.

Through independent assessment and ongoing assurance, certification provides a mechanism for earned recognition. Organisations that invest in good practice, transparent documentation and disciplined operation can demonstrate this through certification. This, in turn, allows regulators to focus their attention where it is most needed, rather than expending equal effort across the entire market.

In age assurance ecosystems, earned recognition changes the dynamic of oversight. Regulators are not required to inspect every system at the same depth or frequency. Certification provides trusted signals that allow regulatory attention to be calibrated. Well-certified, well-monitored operators can be subject to lighter-touch oversight, while those without assurance or those whose behaviour raises concern, can receive closer scrutiny.

Certification helps regulators distinguish between organisations that are broadly compliant and engaged, those that are progressing toward compliance, those that lack awareness or capability and those that are actively resistant. This differentiation is essential in markets where the cost of full inspection is high and the number of actors is growing.

The economic implications of this division of labour are significant. Certification is typically funded by providers as a private cost. Regulation, by contrast, is funded by the public. When certification is used effectively, it shifts a substantial portion of assurance effort away from the taxpayer and toward those who benefit directly from participation in the market.

By encouraging organisations to demonstrate compliance through certification, regulatory systems can reduce the cost of compliance overall. Resources are not consumed by repeated, duplicative checks on well-governed operators. Instead, regulatory effort can be directed toward education, remediation or enforcement where it is most needed.

However, this only works because certification and regulation reinforce each other. Certification derives its authority from the regulatory environment in which it operates. It matters because organisations care about compliance, legitimacy and continued operation. Without the backdrop of regulation, certification would lose much of its force. It would become optional signalling rather than accountability infrastructure.

Conversely, regulation benefits from certification because it cannot, on its own, deliver the depth of scrutiny required for complex, technical systems like age assurance. Regulators do not design systems, operate platforms or configure components. Certification bodies are better positioned to examine technical and operational detail, provided they do so independently and transparently.

This complementary relationship is particularly important in age assurance, where compliance is not simply about following rules, but about how systems behave in practice. Certification allows regulators to rely on evidence generated through structured testing, assessment and monitoring, rather than relying solely on declarations or enforcement after harm has occurred.

Earned recognition also has an important behavioural effect. It creates a pathway to compliance, not just a threshold. Organisations that are developing their age assurance practices can engage with certification progressively, improving documentation, governance and operation over time. This supports learning and maturation rather than forcing a binary compliant/non-compliant divide.

At the same time, certification does not replace the need for enforcement. Some actors will not engage voluntarily. Some will ignore guidance, resist scrutiny or actively seek to evade requirements. Regulation is essential to address these cases.

12.5 Testing, assessment and assurance as complementary activities

Confidence in age assurance systems is not produced by any single activity. It emerges from the way testing, assessment and assurance work together to transform technical behaviour into something that others can reasonably rely upon. Understanding their distinct roles and why they are deliberately separated is essential to understanding how certification builds trust rather than diluting it.

Testing is the foundation. In age assurance, testing involves controlled observation of how systems and components behave under defined conditions. This may include examining how an age estimation component performs across demographic groups, how an age verification process handles invalid inputs or how an intermediary service enforces decision rules under load. Testing produces observable results. It answers the question: *what happens when the system behaves in this way, in this context, under these conditions?*

Crucially, testing in age assurance is not about proving correctness in an absolute sense. Age-related decisions are inherently probabilistic and context dependent. Testing therefore focuses on characterising behaviour rather than asserting infallibility. It provides structured insight into patterns of performance, error, resilience and failure.

Assessment sits alongside testing but serves a different purpose. Assessment is the application of expert judgement to test results and other evidence, interpreting them against declared purposes and expectations. In age assurance, assessment considers whether observed behaviour is appropriate for the claimed context of use, whether trade-offs have been managed transparently and whether assumptions are coherent.

Assessment recognises that evidence does not speak for itself. The same test result may be acceptable in one context and problematic in another. Assessment therefore links evidence to meaning. It evaluates not just what a system does, but whether that behaviour aligns with its declared role in an age assurance ecosystem.

Assurance is what allows the outcomes of testing and assessment to be relied upon by others. It provides confidence for declared purposes, communicated through practice statements and supporting artefacts. Assurance answers a different question again: *on what basis can others reasonably place confidence in this system or component, within defined bounds?*

The separation of these activities strengthens confidence rather than weakening it. When testing, assessment and assurance are conflated, confidence becomes opaque. Claims are harder to interrogate and disagreement becomes personalised rather than evidence based. By contrast, when each activity has a clear role, confidence becomes structured and transferable.

This structure is particularly important in age assurance because multiple actors rely on the same outputs for different reasons. A regulator may be concerned with fairness and accountability. A relying party may be concerned with operational reliability. An intermediary may be concerned with integration and consistency. Testing generates the evidence. Assessment interprets it in relation to these concerns. Assurance allows each actor to rely on that interpretation without needing to replicate the entire process themselves.

The complementary nature of these activities also supports independence. Testing can be designed to be repeatable and transparent. Assessment can be conducted by parties with relevant expertise but without operational responsibility for the system. Assurance can be issued by bodies whose role is to communicate confidence, not to develop or deploy systems. This separation reinforces legitimacy.

Importantly, this structure applies across the age assurance ecosystem, not just to core method providers. Intermediaries that orchestrate age assurance flows can be tested for how they enforce decisions, handle exceptions and manage dependencies. Relying parties can be assessed in terms of how they configure and use age assurance outcomes. Assurance can then be issued at appropriate levels, reflecting the reality that system behaviour is shaped by use as much as by design.

When testing, assessment and assurance are understood as complementary, certification ceases to be a blunt instrument. It becomes a precise one. Confidence is not asserted wholesale; it is constructed carefully, with each layer doing its part.

In age assurance, where trust must be justified repeatedly and at scale, this disciplined separation is not a bureaucratic choice. It is the reason certification can support confidence without overstating it.

12.6 The central role of declared scope and context

In age assurance, confidence is strongest when it is specific. Declared scope and context are not constraints to be worked around; they are the mechanisms that make assurance meaningful, comparable and accountable across the ecosystem.

Age assurance systems and components are designed for particular purposes: a defined age threshold, a particular channel of interaction, an expected level of repetition, supervision or risk. Their behaviour is shaped by these choices. Certification that does not make those choices explicit cannot support reliable confidence, because it leaves too much to assumption. By contrast, assurance that is grounded in declared scope and context allows confidence to be transferred responsibly, within understood bounds.

Declared scope performs several essential functions at once. It clarifies what has been examined. It defines the questions the assurance is intended to answer. It establishes the conditions under which evidence is relevant. In doing so, it turns confidence from a generalised sentiment into a usable reference point.

This specificity is especially important in age assurance because systems are often reused across contexts that appear similar but behave very differently in practice. An approach that is appropriate for supervised, low-frequency access may behave quite differently when used repeatedly, at scale or without human oversight. Declaring scope allows certification to say, with precision, *this is what confidence applies to*, rather than leaving others to infer applicability after the fact.

Context plays a complementary role. Age assurance does not operate in a vacuum. User behaviour, environmental conditions organisational incentives and threat models all shape outcomes. Declared context makes these influences visible. It allows assurance to acknowledge that behaviour is situated, without undermining confidence in what has been examined.

Far from weakening trust, this explicitness strengthens it. When relying parties and regulators understand the context in which assurance holds, they are better able to judge whether it transfers to their own use. Confidence becomes something that can be reasoned about, rather than something that must be taken on faith.

Declared scope and context also enable comparability. One of the recurring challenges in age assurance markets is the difficulty of comparing claims that are framed differently. Certification grounded in explicit scope allows like to be compared with like. Differences can be attributed to context rather than assumed to reflect quality or maturity. This supports healthier procurement and governance conversations, where decisions are based on suitability rather than headline claims.

Repeatability is another benefit. Assurance that declares its scope can be revisited over time. As systems change, evidence can be refreshed against the same declared frame, allowing drift to be detected and confidence to be maintained. Without declared scope, change is harder to assess because there is no stable reference point against which to judge it.

Most importantly, declared scope and context enable accountability. When confidence is bounded, responsibility becomes clearer. Actors can see what has been assured, what assumptions were made and where responsibility remains. This clarity is essential in age assurance ecosystems, where responsibility is distributed across providers, intermediaries and relying parties.

In practical terms, this means that certification is not limited to age assurance methods in isolation. Scope can include how components are configured, how decisions are triggered and how results are used. Context can include whether systems are deployed online or in person, whether access is supervised or automated and whether users interact repeatedly or occasionally. Making these dimensions explicit allows assurance to reflect how systems actually operate.

This approach also supports proportionality. Not all age assurance contexts require the same level of confidence. Declared scope allows assurance to be matched to risk, rather than defaulting to a one-size-fits-all model. Confidence can be calibrated to purpose and actors can make informed decisions about whether it is sufficient for their needs.

There is a further, often underappreciated, benefit. Explicit scope creates space for disagreement without undermining trust. When assurance is clear about its boundaries, actors can disagree about applicability or sufficiency without disputing the integrity of the certification itself. Debate shifts from whether a system is "certified" to whether a given certification is appropriate for a given use. This is a sign of maturity, not weakness.

In age assurance, where social expectations, regulatory approaches and technical capabilities continue to evolve, this flexibility is critical. Confidence that is transferable within bounds is more durable than confidence that pretends to be universal.

Declared scope and context also reinforce independence. By anchoring assurance to explicit claims and conditions, certification bodies are protected from being asked to underwrite outcomes they did not examine. This preserves the legitimacy of assurance over time. Confidence remains credible because it remains honest.

Seen in this light, scope is not a caveat to be buried in footnotes. It is the foundation on which trust is built. It enables confidence to scale without becoming brittle. It allows assurance to support governance rather than replace it.

For age assurance systems and components to function as trusted infrastructure, confidence must be both strong and bounded. Declared scope and context are what make that balance possible.

12.7 Components, systems and layered confidence

Age assurance does not operate as a single, self-contained mechanism. In practice, it is realised through systems composed of interacting components, often supplied, operated and governed by different actors. Certification supports trust in this complexity by enabling layered confidence: confidence that is built at appropriate levels, for appropriate purposes and then composed rather than assumed.

Component-level certification plays a foundational role in age assurance ecosystems. Individual components can be examined in depth against declared characteristics. Certification at this level allows specific capabilities to be understood, compared and reused. It provides clarity about what a component contributes, under what conditions and with what limitations.

This is particularly valuable in age assurance because components are frequently reused across multiple systems and contexts. An age assurance provider may supply the same component to different intermediaries or relying parties, each of whom integrates it differently. Component-level assurance allows confidence to travel with the component, without needing to be recreated from scratch in every deployment.

System-level certification addresses a different, equally important set of questions. Systems are not just collections of components; they are orchestrations of behaviour. Decisions emerge from how components are combined, configured and governed. System-level assurance examines these interactions: how age assurance results are triggered, how thresholds are applied, how fallback and appeal are handled and how outcomes are enforced.

By distinguishing clearly between component-level and system-level assurance, certification avoids two common failures. The first is assuming that a well-certified component guarantees a well-behaved system. The second is treating systems as opaque wholes that cannot be meaningfully decomposed. Layered confidence allows both precision and completeness.

This distinction also supports clearer allocation of responsibility. Component providers are accountable for the behaviour of what they supply. Intermediaries are accountable for how components are orchestrated. Relying parties are accountable for how outcomes are used. Certification that recognises these layers allows accountability to align with actual control, rather than being blurred by contractual or organisational boundaries.

Layered confidence is particularly important in platform and multi-actor environments. Large platforms may rely on external age assurance providers, integrate intermediary services and apply their own policies on top. Certification at multiple layers allows each actor to rely on assurance appropriately, without assuming responsibility for aspects they do not control.

This approach also supports evolution. Components can be updated or replaced without invalidating system-level confidence, provided changes are understood and assessed. Systems can adapt to new contexts without discarding all existing assurance. Layered certification makes confidence resilient to change rather than brittle.

Importantly, this is not a defensive argument for narrow assurance. It is a positive argument for clarity. When assurance is layered, confidence becomes more intelligible. Actors know what has been examined, at what level and why. Questions about trust can be directed to the right place.

In age assurance, where systems must operate across varied contexts and under public scrutiny, this clarity is essential. Users experience outcomes, not architectures. Regulators oversee systems, not components. Providers develop components, not end-to-end services. Layered confidence allows each perspective to be supported without collapsing them into a single, misleading claim.

Certification that recognises the distinction between components and systems therefore strengthens trust rather than complicating it. It reflects the reality of how age assurance actually works. It allows confidence to be built incrementally, responsibly and transparently.

As age assurance ecosystems continue to grow in complexity, this ability to compose confidence from well-understood parts will become increasingly important. Layered assurance is not a compromise. It is the mechanism that allows trust to scale.

12.8 Evidence as a foundation for confidence

Confidence in age assurance systems cannot rest on assertion alone. It must be supported by evidence that is visible, interpretable and capable of being challenged. Certification plays a central role in creating this evidence discipline, not by claiming to eliminate uncertainty, but by providing a shared foundation on which confidence can be built and sustained.

In age assurance, evidence serves a distinctive purpose. Systems are expected to make decisions that affect access, participation and protection, often at scale and under conditions of uncertainty. Evidence allows those decisions to be examined not only for technical performance, but for alignment with declared purposes and expectations. It transforms trust from a matter of belief into a matter of reasoned reliance.

Certification structures how evidence is produced and used. It requires evidence to be gathered against declared characteristics and contexts, rather than as an unstructured collection of metrics. This discipline matters because age assurance evidence is inherently multifaceted. Accuracy figures, error distributions, privacy controls, security measures and user experience considerations all interact. Certification provides a framework in which these different forms of evidence can be considered together, rather than in isolation.

Evidence also functions as a shared reference point across actors. Age assurance ecosystems involve providers, intermediaries, relying parties and regulators, each with different concerns and incentives. Certification allows evidence to be communicated in a way that is intelligible and usable across these perspectives. Disagreements can then be grounded in what has been observed and documented, rather than in competing narratives.

This is particularly important where confidence is contested. Age assurance systems often operate in socially sensitive domains. Public debate may be intense and trust fragile. Evidence produced within a recognised assurance framework allows critique and defence to be conducted on common ground. It supports accountability without requiring unanimity.

Evidence also enables learning. Age assurance systems are rarely perfect at first deployment. Patterns of error, exclusion or misuse may only become visible through systematic observation. Certification encourages evidence to be collected and retained in ways that support reflection over time. This allows systems to improve in response to observed behaviour rather than anecdote or assumption.

Importantly, certification does not treat evidence as static. Evidence is contextual and time bound. Test results reflect specific conditions and assumptions. Certification makes this explicit, allowing evidence to be understood as a snapshot rather than a permanent verdict. Confidence is strengthened when this temporality is acknowledged rather than obscured.

Evidence discipline also supports proportionality. Not all age assurance contexts require the same depth or breadth of evidence. Certification frameworks allow evidence requirements to be aligned with risk and impact. This avoids both under-assurance, where confidence is ungrounded and over-assurance, where burdensome evidence is demanded without corresponding benefit.

The role of evidence extends beyond age assurance providers themselves. Intermediaries that configure and operate systems generate evidence through their practices. Relying parties influence outcomes through their use of results. Certification can encompass these dimensions, recognising that evidence about system behaviour often emerges from operation as much as from design.

By anchoring confidence in evidence, certification strengthens trust without demanding blind acceptance. Actors can rely on age assurance systems knowing that claims are supported, examined and open to scrutiny. When confidence is questioned, evidence provides a basis for explanation and response rather than defensiveness.

In age assurance, where legitimacy depends on both effectiveness and fairness, this evidence-based approach is indispensable. Certification does not replace judgement, but it ensures that judgement is informed. Confidence built on evidence is not only more robust; it is more deserving of trust.

12.9 Ongoing assurance and the maintenance of trust

Trust in age assurance systems is not established once and then fixed. It is maintained over time through continued attention to how systems behave as they evolve, scale and interact with changing environments. Ongoing assurance plays a central role in sustaining this trust, transforming certification from a one-off event into a living element of governance.

Certification cycles are necessarily time-bounded, but the meaning of a certificate is not preserved by time alone. In age assurance systems, practice, configuration, context of use and threat models can change far more quickly than formal reassessment schedules. As a result, certificates often expire in meaning before they expire in date. This does not make certification ineffective; it clarifies its role. Certification provides a structured snapshot of confidence under declared conditions, not a durable guarantee of future behaviour. Where certification is treated as static assurance rather than provisional evidence, it risks creating misplaced confidence precisely when systems are drifting most.

Age assurance systems change for many reasons. Models are updated, thresholds adjusted, interfaces redesigned and dependencies replaced. User behaviour shifts. New risks emerge. None of this is a sign of failure. It is the normal condition of systems that operate in dynamic social and technical contexts. What matters is whether confidence evolves alongside these changes.

Ongoing assurance strengthens trust by recognising time as a core dimension of confidence. Surveillance, monitoring and periodic reassessment allow assurance to reflect how systems actually operate in practice, rather than how they were expected to operate at a particular moment. This does not undermine initial certification; it builds on it.

For age assurance systems and components, this ongoing perspective is especially valuable. Behaviour that appears acceptable in early testing may change as systems are used at scale or in new contexts. Patterns of exclusion or misuse may only become visible over time. Ongoing assurance provides a structured way to surface these developments and respond to them constructively.

Importantly, ongoing assurance supports responsible change. Systems that are subject to regular review can adapt with confidence, knowing that changes will be examined and understood rather than feared. This encourages improvement rather than stagnation. Confidence becomes something that grows through learning, rather than something that is protected by resisting change.

Surveillance and review also reinforce accountability across the ecosystem. Providers remain responsible for the behaviour of components they update. Intermediaries remain responsible for how systems are operated. Relying parties remain responsible for how outcomes are applied. Ongoing assurance ensures that these responsibilities do not fade once initial certification is achieved.

This temporal dimension of assurance is particularly important for adaptive and data-driven age assurance approaches. Models that learn from data or that are sensitive to environmental conditions require confidence that extends beyond initial performance. Ongoing evidence allows confidence to be refreshed as behaviour evolves, maintaining legitimacy in the face of adaptation.

From a governance perspective, ongoing assurance provides continuity. Regulators and oversight bodies can rely on a stable assurance framework even as specific systems change. Users can have confidence that systems affecting them remain under scrutiny. Assurance becomes a durable infrastructure rather than a temporary signal.

Crucially, ongoing assurance does not imply constant suspicion or instability. It reflects a mature understanding of how trust is maintained in complex systems. Confidence is strengthened when it is supported by attention over time, rather than weakened by the acknowledgement that systems evolve.

In age assurance ecosystems, where trust must endure across repeated interactions and changing contexts, ongoing assurance is not an optional enhancement. It is what allows certification to remain meaningful long after the initial assessment. Trust that is maintained is trust that can be relied upon.

12.10 Certification in multi-actor and platform ecosystems

Age assurance increasingly operates within multi-actor ecosystems rather than as isolated services. Platforms rely on age assurance providers. Providers rely on infrastructure, data sources and intermediaries. Relying parties integrate age assurance outcomes into their own services and decision-making processes. Responsibility is distributed, but trust must still be coherent.

In these environments, certification plays a particularly important role. It provides assurance anchors that allow confidence to be shared responsibly across organisational and technical boundaries. Without independent assurance, trust in multi-actor age assurance ecosystems would be fragile, fragmented and difficult to sustain.

One of the central challenges in platform ecosystems is that no single actor has full visibility or control. Relying parties often cannot inspect the internal workings of age assurance components. Providers may not control how their outputs are used. Intermediaries may orchestrate flows without owning the underlying methods. Certification creates a way for these actors to rely on each other without requiring unrealistic transparency or duplicated effort.

Shared assurance artefacts – certification statements, declared scopes, supporting evidence – allow actors to align their expectations. They provide a common basis for confidence that does not depend on personal trust or informal relationships. This is particularly important where actors may not have direct contractual relationships but are nonetheless interdependent.

Certification also supports accountability across layers. In a multi-actor ecosystem, failures are often systemic rather than attributable to a single component. Independent assurance helps disentangle where responsibility sits by making clear what has been examined at each level. Providers can be held accountable for the behaviour of their components. Intermediaries can be examined for how they orchestrate and configure systems. Relying parties can be assessed in terms of how they apply age assurance outcomes in practice.

This layered accountability is essential for trust. Without it, responsibility tends to diffuse. Problems become harder to address and confidence erodes not because systems are ineffective, but because no one appears clearly responsible. Certification counteracts this tendency by anchoring responsibility in declared, examinable roles.

The role of certification in platform ecosystems is also closely tied to power asymmetry. Large platforms may exert significant influence over smaller providers or users. Independent assurance provides a counterbalance by establishing shared standards of scrutiny that do not depend on market power. It allows confidence to be grounded in evidence rather than dominance.

For regulators and oversight bodies, certification enables more effective supervision of complex ecosystems. Rather than attempting to inspect every interaction directly, they can rely on assurance frameworks that distribute scrutiny appropriately. This does not remove the need for oversight, but it makes it more tractable and proportionate.

From the perspective of users, certification in multi-actor ecosystems supports legitimacy. Decisions that affect access or participation are easier to accept when they are known to be part of a system subject to independent scrutiny. Even when outcomes are contested, the presence of assurance helps demonstrate that decisions are not arbitrary or unchecked.

Importantly, certification does not require ecosystems to be static. On the contrary, shared assurance frameworks allow ecosystems to evolve while maintaining trust. New actors can enter, components can be replaced and integrations can change without undermining confidence, provided assurance is maintained at appropriate levels.

In age assurance, where systems increasingly operate across platforms, sectors and jurisdictions, this role is indispensable. Independent assurance allows trust to scale beyond individual relationships and become a property of the ecosystem itself. Without it, confidence would remain local, provisional and difficult to defend.

Certification, in this sense, is not merely supportive infrastructure. It is what allows multi-actor age assurance ecosystems to function as coherent, governable systems rather than as loose collections of services.

12.11 Using certification well

Certification is most effective when it is used as infrastructure for judgement, not as a substitute for it. In age assurance ecosystems, its value lies in how it supports responsible decision-making across actors, rather than in any promise of certainty or finality.

Used well, certification provides a stable reference point in an environment characterised by uncertainty, trade-offs and evolving expectations. It allows actors to rely on age assurance systems with confidence that claims have been independently examined, while still recognising that responsibility for outcomes remains with those who deploy and use them.

For age assurance providers, certification supports clarity. It creates a disciplined way to describe systems, articulate assumptions and present evidence. This strengthens credibility and allows providers to engage constructively with scrutiny rather than defensively. Confidence becomes something that can be demonstrated, not merely asserted.

For intermediaries, certification supports coherence. It allows complex orchestration and integration decisions to be grounded in shared assurance artefacts. Intermediaries can rely on certified components while remaining accountable for how they are combined and operated. This enables confidence without overreach.

For relying parties, certification supports responsible reliance. It provides a basis for trusting age assurance outcomes without requiring deep technical inspection of every component. Importantly, it also clarifies where reliance must be supplemented by judgement for example, when deploying systems into new contexts or at different scales.

For regulators and oversight bodies, certification supports proportional governance. It allows scrutiny to be distributed across the ecosystem, anchored in independent assessment rather than ad hoc inspection. This makes oversight more effective, more scalable and more transparent.

Using certification well also means understanding what it is not. It is not an endorsement of all uses. It is not a transfer of responsibility. It is not a guarantee of future behaviour. Treating it as such weakens trust rather than strengthening it.

By contrast, when certification is treated as evidence that is contextual, bounded and open to re-examination it strengthens accountability. Decisions can be justified. Disagreements can be reasoned. Change can be managed without destabilising confidence.

Standards-based certification also supports maturity over time. As age assurance practices evolve, certification frameworks provide continuity. They allow confidence to be refreshed as systems adapt, rather than reset from scratch. This cumulative quality is essential for building durable trust in systems that will be relied upon repeatedly.

Perhaps most importantly, certification enables confidence without naivety. It allows age assurance to function as trusted infrastructure rather than as a collection of isolated tools or private assurances. Trust becomes something that is supported by shared evidence, independent scrutiny and clear allocation of responsibility.

In age assurance, where decisions are consequential and trust must be earned repeatedly, certification is not a peripheral concern. Used well, it is one of the central mechanisms by which confidence, accountability and legitimacy are sustained across the ecosystem.

Chapter 13 – Change, Monitoring and Learning Over Time

13.1 Why age assurance systems never stand still

Age assurance systems are often described using the language of completion. They are designed, implemented, tested, certified and then relied upon. This sequence is deeply embedded in how technology is procured, governed and discussed and it gives reassurance that complexity can be bounded. Once the work is done, confidence can follow.

Yet this way of framing does not reflect how age assurance systems actually exist once they are deployed. In practice, they operate within environments that are constantly changing, shaped by forces that no single actor controls and no initial design can fully anticipate. The most important feature of these systems is therefore not their stability, but their exposure to change.

Change begins with people. Users are not static inputs to a system; they are active participants who adapt to what they encounter. Over time, people learn how age checks work, how strict they feel, where they are flexible and where they are not. They adjust their behaviour accordingly. Sometimes this adaptation is deliberate and strategic. More often it is simply practical: a response to friction, confusion or inconvenience. The result is that the system as experienced by users gradually diverges from the system as imagined by designers.

Alongside this, technology itself evolves. Software updates are applied. Performance is optimised. Models are retrained or replaced. Dependencies are upgraded, deprecated or outsourced. These changes are rarely controversial. They are part of routine maintenance and improvement. But each one subtly alters the conditions under which earlier assumptions were made. A system that behaves acceptably under one configuration may behave differently under another, even when the changes appear minor.

Policy expectations also move. New concerns come into focus. Public debate reshapes what is considered acceptable or proportionate. Regulators refine their interpretations. What once felt sufficient may later appear inadequate or overly intrusive. Even where formal requirements remain unchanged, the social meaning of age assurance shifts over time.

Organisations change as well. Teams are restructured, responsibilities migrate and institutional memory fades. Decisions that were once carefully reasoned become inherited defaults. Knowledge that was once tacitly shared is lost when people move on. The system continues to operate, but the context that once made sense of its design slowly dissolves.

None of this implies instability or failure. It is simply how socio-technical systems behave over time. The illusion lies in believing that stability is a natural resting state, rather than a temporary alignment between assumptions and reality.

This is why designing for stasis is a mistake. Systems that are assumed to be static are treated as complete. Attention drifts elsewhere. Monitoring becomes perfunctory. Change, when it occurs, is framed as deviation rather than evolution. In these conditions, the system continues to move, but without guidance or reflection. Confidence persists not because the system remains well aligned, but because misalignment has not yet become visible.

By contrast, systems designed with change in mind behave differently. They treat deployment not as an endpoint, but as the beginning of a new phase. They recognise that the environment will shift and that this shift does not invalidate the system's purpose. Instead, it creates a responsibility to remain attentive.

Normalising change from the outset is therefore reassuring rather than alarming. It removes the pressure to pretend that systems can be final. It acknowledges that uncertainty is not a flaw to be eliminated, but a condition to be managed. When change is expected, it can be discussed openly. When it is denied, it accumulates silently.

This reframing also changes how responsibility is understood. If systems are assumed to stand still, then responsibility appears to diminish over time. Once the correct choices have been made and the right assurances obtained, oversight can relax. If systems are understood as evolving, responsibility persists. Confidence must be maintained, not inherited.

Seen this way, change is not the enemy of trust. It is the context in which trust is sustained. Age assurance systems do not lose legitimacy because they evolve. They lose legitimacy when evolution is ignored.

This chapter starts from that premise. The sections that follow do not ask how to prevent change, but how to remain oriented as it occurs. They explore what changes in practice, how monitoring supports confidence, how learning stabilises systems over time and why maturity lies not in closure, but in stewardship.

Age assurance systems never stand still. The question is not whether they will change, but whether those responsible for them will remain engaged as they do.

13.2 What changes in practice (and why it matters)

Once age assurance systems are in operation, change rarely announces itself as change. It arrives as adjustment. A configuration is tweaked to reduce friction. A threshold is nudged to address an edge case. A fallback path is reordered to improve completion rates. A dependency is replaced because a supplier has changed terms or a component is no longer supported. Each decision is defensible, often necessary and usually taken with good intent.

What matters is not that these changes occur, but how easily their significance is underestimated.

Configuration sits close to the surface of age assurance systems. It determines how strict a check feels, when escalation occurs and which users encounter additional scrutiny. Small changes in configuration can alter outcomes disproportionately, particularly for users near decision boundaries. A system that appears functionally identical before and after a change may nonetheless produce meaningfully different experiences for those who pass through it.

Thresholds are especially sensitive. They are often treated as technical parameters, but in practice they encode judgements about risk, tolerance and inclusion. Adjusting a threshold can quietly rebalance false positives and false negatives, shifting who is challenged and who is waved through. These shifts may be statistically modest yet socially significant, especially when they affect already marginal groups.

Fallback paths introduce another layer of complexity. Age assurance systems rarely rely on a single method. When one path fails, another is invoked. Over time, the ordering and availability of these paths may change. What was once an exceptional route becomes routine. What was intended as a safety net becomes a primary channel. As this happens, the effective character of the system evolves, even if its formal description does not.

Dependencies compound this effect. Modern age assurance systems rely on external services, libraries and infrastructures. Changes in these dependencies can alter latency, reliability or behaviour in ways that are only partially visible to system owners. When a dependency changes, the system changes with it, often without a clear moment of decision or review.

Crucially, much of this change occurs incrementally and informally. Operational teams respond to pressures as they arise. A temporary workaround becomes standard practice. An exception becomes a pattern. Decisions made to resolve immediate issues are rarely revisited once the problem appears to have been addressed. Over time, these accumulated adjustments reshape how the system behaves in practice.

Documentation struggles to keep pace. Design documents describe how the system was intended to work. Certification artefacts capture how it was configured and tested at a particular moment. As changes accrue, these artefacts become less reliable guides to lived behaviour. The system continues to operate, but the story told about it becomes increasingly detached from reality.

This gap matters because age assurance systems derive their legitimacy from alignment: between declared purpose, tested behaviour and actual use. When configuration drift is unacknowledged, confidence rests on outdated assumptions. The system may still "work" in a narrow sense, but it no longer behaves as expected by those relying on it.

Earlier chapters in this book explored how context of use and trade-offs shape system design. What becomes visible over time is that context itself is not static. It is continually renegotiated through operational decisions. Each adjustment implicitly answers questions about risk, fairness and proportionality, whether or not those questions are explicitly asked.

Understanding what changes in practice therefore requires looking beyond formal system descriptions. It requires attention to how decisions are made day to day, how pressures are resolved and how exceptions are handled. These are not peripheral concerns. They are where the system's real character is formed.

Recognising this does not imply that change should be avoided. It means that change should be understood. When adjustments are acknowledged and reflected upon, they can improve systems. When they pass unnoticed, they quietly alter the basis on which trust was originally established.

Age assurance systems do not drift because people are careless. They drift because change is normal and attention is finite. The task of responsible stewardship is not to prevent evolution, but to notice when evolution is occurring and to understand what it is doing.

13.3 Monitoring as the maintenance of confidence

If change is inevitable, then confidence cannot be assumed to persist on its own. It has to be maintained. Monitoring is the means by which this maintenance occurs.

In age assurance, monitoring is often misunderstood as a technical or managerial function: the collection of data, the tracking of performance or the detection of failures. While these activities may be part of monitoring, they do not capture its deeper purpose. Monitoring, in this context, is about checking whether the assumptions that once justified the system still hold as the system evolves.

Those assumptions are rarely written down explicitly. They are embedded in design choices, configurations and operating practices. They include beliefs about how users will behave, where friction will be acceptable, which risks are tolerable and how often exceptional cases will occur. As conditions change, these assumptions may quietly become outdated.

Monitoring brings these shifts into view. It does so not by seeking precise measurements, but by paying attention to patterns. A rise in incomplete journeys may indicate increasing friction. A growing reliance on fallback paths may suggest that primary methods are no longer functioning as intended. Recurring complaints may point to a misalignment between declared purpose and lived experience.

What matters is not any single signal, but how signals combine over time. Monitoring is therefore interpretive rather than mechanical. It requires judgement to decide which changes are meaningful, which are transient and which reflect deeper shifts in behaviour or context.

This kind of attention is often uncomfortable, because it resists simple answers. It does not produce clear thresholds that declare success or failure. Instead, it raises questions: Why are users behaving differently? Why is a particular group experiencing more friction? Why are staff relying on workarounds more frequently? These questions do not always have immediate solutions, but they are essential to maintaining confidence.

Framing monitoring in this way also clarifies what it is not. It is not surveillance of users. It is not a tool for enforcement or discipline. When monitoring becomes punitive or extractive, it undermines trust rather than supporting it. Users experience it as scrutiny, not care. Staff experience it as oversight, not support.

By contrast, monitoring that is oriented toward understanding system behaviour is protective. It makes visible the points at which systems are struggling to meet their own intentions. It creates space to respond before problems become entrenched. It demonstrates, both internally and externally, that the system is being actively stewarded rather than passively relied upon.

Monitoring also plays a crucial role in sustaining external trust. Regulators, partners and the public are rarely reassured by claims that systems are "finished" or "fully compliant." Confidence grows when it is clear that systems are being watched with care, that concerns are noticed rather than dismissed and that learning is ongoing.

Importantly, monitoring does not require perfect visibility. It requires attentiveness. It requires organisations to remain curious about how their systems are actually functioning, rather than assuming that what was true at launch remains true indefinitely.

Seen in this light, monitoring is not an admission that something is wrong. It is a recognition that confidence is temporal. It must be renewed as conditions change. Without monitoring, systems continue to operate, but confidence slowly detaches from reality. With it, trust is actively maintained.

The sections that follow build on this understanding. Monitoring creates the conditions for learning. Learning enables adaptation. And adaptation, when governed responsibly, allows systems to evolve without losing legitimacy.

13.4 Learning from use, not just design

No matter how carefully an age assurance system is designed, its most important lessons are learned only after it begins operating in the world. Design captures intent. Use reveals reality.

Before deployment, systems are imagined through models, scenarios and test cases. Designers anticipate how users will interact, where failure may occur and how safeguards will function. Certification and assurance test these expectations under defined conditions. This work is essential, but it is necessarily bounded. It reflects what is known at the time, not what will be discovered through sustained use.

Live operation exposes dynamics that design cannot fully predict. Users encounter systems in moments of frustration, urgency or uncertainty. Staff apply discretion in ways that were never formally specified. Edge cases appear not as isolated anomalies, but as recurring experiences for particular groups. Over time, patterns emerge that challenge the assumptions embedded in the original design.

Feedback from users is often the first signal that something is misaligned. Confusion about what is being asked, discomfort with certain interactions or a sense of unfairness in outcomes may all point to deeper issues. These signals are easy to dismiss as subjective or anecdotal, yet they often surface problems that formal testing cannot detect.

Feedback from staff provides another perspective. Those who operate systems day to day develop a practical understanding of where processes work and where they strain. They see which cases consume disproportionate effort, which decisions are repeatedly contested and where informal workarounds become necessary. This operational knowledge is rarely captured in design documents, but it is central to how systems actually function.

Appeals and complaints add further depth. They reveal how decisions are experienced, not just how they are made. They expose the emotional and practical consequences of error, delay or exclusion. Patterns in appeals often highlight where thresholds, explanations or fallback paths are misaligned with user expectations or societal norms.

Incidents, when they occur, provide the sharpest form of feedback. They reveal how systems behave under stress, how responsibilities are exercised and where assumptions break down. While incidents are disruptive, they also offer clarity. They show what matters when conditions are no longer ideal.

Learning from this feedback requires openness about imperfection. It requires organisations to accept that initial designs were provisional, not definitive. This can be uncomfortable, particularly in environments where confidence is equated with certainty. Yet resisting learning in order to preserve an image of correctness ultimately weakens systems.

When learning is embraced, systems stabilise over time. Not because they stop changing, but because they become better aligned with their environment. Adjustments are informed by evidence rather than speculation. Trade-offs are revisited with greater understanding. Confidence grows not from claims of completeness, but from demonstrated responsiveness.

Learning also reshapes how success is understood. Rather than asking whether a system conforms perfectly to its original design, the question becomes whether it continues to meet its purpose under evolving conditions. This shift does not lower standards; it makes them more realistic.

Importantly, learning is not a one-off activity triggered by failure. It is an ongoing process embedded in operation. It depends on curiosity, humility and the willingness to revisit assumptions. Systems that learn remain legitimate because they remain connected to the realities they govern.

In this sense, learning does not destabilise age assurance systems. It anchors them. It transforms monitoring from observation into understanding and adaptation from reaction into stewardship.

13.5 Change control as a governance activity

As age assurance systems evolve, the question is not whether change will occur, but how that change is understood and owned. This is where governance becomes visible.

Change in age assurance is often framed as technical adjustment: a configuration update, a revised dependency, a performance optimisation. Yet these changes do not operate in a neutral space. They affect who is challenged, who is excluded, how decisions are explained and where discretion is exercised. In that sense, change is never purely technical. It reshapes outcomes and therefore responsibility.

For this reason, change control is best understood as a governance activity rather than an engineering one. It is the means by which organisations remain accountable for how systems behave as they evolve.

This does not require treating every adjustment as a major policy decision. That would be unworkable. What it requires is an appreciation that small changes accumulate and that their combined effect can materially alter the character of a system. A threshold adjusted today, a fallback reordered next month, a dependency replaced quietly the month after – each change may seem minor, yet together they can produce behaviour that no longer reflects the system's stated purpose or the conditions under which assurance was originally granted.

Governance provides a way to remain oriented as this accumulation occurs. It creates space to ask questions that technical processes alone do not prompt: Why is this change being made? What assumption does it modify? Who is affected by it? How does it interact with earlier decisions? These questions are not about slowing change, but about making it legible.

Without this orientation, change tends to drift. Decisions are taken to resolve immediate pressures, then forgotten. The system continues to function, but the reasoning that once justified its operation is lost. Accountability becomes diffuse. When concerns later arise, it is no longer clear which decisions mattered or who is responsible for their effects.

Governance does not eliminate this risk entirely, but it reduces it by keeping change visible. It encourages organisations to treat configuration and operational decisions as part of the system's public behaviour, not as internal housekeeping. In doing so, it preserves the link between design intent, lived behaviour and assurance.

This perspective also reshapes how responsibility is experienced by those operating systems. When change is governed, staff are supported in raising concerns, questioning assumptions and reflecting on consequences. Change becomes something to be discussed rather than something to be quietly implemented. This reduces the temptation to rely on informal workarounds that solve short-term problems while creating long-term fragility.

The relationship between governance and confidence is therefore direct. Stakeholders are more likely to trust systems whose evolution is acknowledged and overseen than systems whose changes are opaque. Transparency about change signals care. It demonstrates that those responsible are paying attention not only to whether systems function, but to how they function over time.

This section also connects back to earlier discussions of assurance. Certification and testing provide confidence under defined conditions. Governance ensures that, as those conditions shift, confidence is revisited rather than assumed. In this way, governance does not compete with assurance; it sustains it.

Change control, understood as governance, is not about preventing evolution. It is about ensuring that evolution remains aligned with purpose, responsibility and trust. It allows systems to adapt without losing their legitimacy and organisations to remain accountable even as circumstances change.

13.6 Assurance over time

Chapter 12 located certification, testing and assurance within the realities of uncertainty, context and judgement. What becomes clear when systems are viewed over time is that assurance does not end at the moment it is granted. It changes character.

At the point of certification, assurance speaks to a specific configuration, under defined conditions, at a particular moment. This is not a limitation; it is the nature of evidence. What creates risk is not that assurance is time-bound, but that it is sometimes treated as timeless.

As age assurance systems evolve, the relationship between assurance and confidence must evolve with them. Assurance over time does not attempt to preserve systems in their certified state. Instead, it preserves the *meaning* of assurance by ensuring that confidence remains anchored to current behaviour rather than past evaluation.

This shift is subtle but important. Static assurance invites complacency. It encourages reliance on artefacts that describe how a system once functioned, even as operational reality moves on. Dynamic assurance, by contrast, accepts that systems will change and asks how confidence can be maintained as they do.

In practice, this means recognising that assurance degrades if it is not revisited. Test results become less predictive as configurations drift. Documentation becomes less representative as dependencies change. Certification statements retain their formal validity, but their practical relevance diminishes unless they are interpreted in light of what has changed since they were issued.

Seen in this way, ongoing review and reassessment are not burdens imposed on otherwise complete systems. They are what keeps assurance honest.

This perspective also reframes how assurance is communicated. Rather than presenting certification as a guarantee, assurance over time presents it as evidence within a living system. It acknowledges its scope, its assumptions and its temporal limits. Far from undermining confidence, this transparency strengthens it. Stakeholders are more likely to trust systems whose limitations are acknowledged than systems that imply permanence where none exists.

There is sometimes concern that ongoing assurance resembles surveillance or continual scrutiny. In practice, the opposite is true. Assurance that adapts over time reduces the need for reactive intervention. When systems are reviewed deliberately, surprises are fewer. Issues are identified earlier. Confidence is maintained through continuity rather than crisis.

Importantly, assurance over time also supports adaptation. When change is expected and reviewed organisations are less tempted to freeze systems in outdated forms simply to preserve certification status. They can evolve responsibly, knowing that confidence will be revisited rather than revoked. This encourages improvement rather than stagnation.

This approach aligns naturally with the idea of stewardship introduced earlier in the chapter. Stewardship implies care over time, not one-off validation. Assurance becomes part of that care: a structured way of asking whether systems still behave as intended, still reflect their declared purpose and still justify the confidence placed in them.

Time-bound assurance is therefore not a weakness. It is a form of honesty about uncertainty and change. It accepts that no assessment can speak forever and that legitimacy is sustained through attention rather than declaration.

As the next section explores, problems arise not because systems change, but because change goes unobserved. Assurance over time does not eliminate risk, but it ensures that risk remains visible – and visibility is the foundation of trust.

13.7 When change goes wrong

Most problems in age assurance systems do not arise because change occurred. They arise because change happened without being noticed, understood or owned.

When systems evolve quietly, confidence often persists longer than it should. Certification remains valid on paper. Processes continue to function. Complaints are handled individually rather than collectively. From the outside, nothing appears to be wrong. Yet beneath this surface stability, assumptions may be drifting away from reality.

This is how misalignment develops. Configuration changes accumulate. Fallback paths become more prominent than originally intended. Systems are used in contexts that were never reviewed. Thresholds that once reflected careful judgement are inherited without reconsideration. Over time, the system that is actually operating no longer resembles the system that was designed, described or assured.

Because this drift is gradual, it is rarely experienced as failure. Instead, it manifests as friction, inconsistency or unease. Users encounter decisions that feel arbitrary or opaque. Staff rely increasingly on informal judgement. Appeals become more frequent but are treated as isolated exceptions. Each signal is manageable on its own. Together, they point to a deeper problem that remains unacknowledged.

By the time issues are formally recognised, they often appear sudden and disproportionate. Confidence erodes quickly. Questions are asked about why problems were not anticipated, why safeguards failed or why assurance did not prevent the outcome. In reality, the warning signs were present, but they were not connected.

This is why unobserved change is more dangerous than deliberate adaptation. When change is recognised, it can be assessed. When it is invisible, it reshapes systems without accountability.

Problems can also arise when changes are made with a narrow focus. Adjustments intended to optimise performance or reduce friction may inadvertently shift risk elsewhere. A decision that improves outcomes for most users may disproportionately affect a minority. Without attention to these trade-offs, improvement in one dimension can quietly undermine legitimacy in another.

Importantly, none of this implies negligence or bad faith. These patterns emerge precisely because systems are complex and responsibility is distributed. People act reasonably within their local context, solving the problems they can see. The risk lies not in those actions, but in the absence of a broader view that connects them over time.

Recovery is possible and often straightforward, when monitoring exists. Where patterns have been noticed organisations can retrace decisions, understand how drift occurred and make informed adjustments. Confidence can be rebuilt because there is a narrative that explains what happened and why.

Where monitoring has been absent, recovery is harder. Without shared understanding, responses become defensive. Explanations focus on formal compliance rather than lived experience. Change is resisted rather than guided. Trust, once lost, is slower to return.

The lesson is not that age assurance systems are fragile. It is that they require attention. Problems arise not from evolution, but from neglect. Systems that are watched, questioned and discussed remain resilient even when they encounter difficulty.

Change going wrong is therefore not a failure of design, assurance or intent. It is a failure of orientation. When systems are allowed to drift out of view, their legitimacy erodes quietly. When they remain visible, even mistakes can be addressed with credibility.

13.8 Maturity as the capacity to learn

Maturity in age assurance is not marked by certainty. It is marked by attentiveness.

Immature systems seek closure. They aspire to be finished: fully designed, fully assured, fully compliant. Once this state is declared, attention moves elsewhere. Change is treated as disruption, learning as correction and monitoring as a sign that something has gone wrong.

Mature systems take a different view. They assume that conditions will change, that assumptions will be challenged and that no configuration will remain optimal indefinitely. Rather than seeking finality, they invest in the capacity to notice, reflect and adapt.

This capacity to learn is not an outcome that can be achieved and then set aside. It is an organisational and cultural capability that must be sustained. It depends on curiosity about how systems behave in practice, humility about what design and testing can achieve and openness to revisiting decisions as contexts evolve.

When learning is embedded in this way, confidence grows through responsiveness rather than rigidity. Stakeholders are reassured not because systems claim to be perfect, but because they demonstrate care. Users experience systems that are willing to adjust rather than defend themselves. Regulators encounter organisations that engage rather than deflect. Assurance remains meaningful because it is treated as part of an ongoing conversation, not a concluding statement.

Seen from this perspective, learning does not undermine authority. It strengthens it. A system that can explain how it has changed, why it has changed and what has been learned commands more trust than a system that insists nothing has changed at all.

This also clarifies the role of standards and assurance. They do not exist to close systems or declare them complete. They exist to provide shared reference points as systems evolve: common language, structured evidence and points of comparison that support judgement over time. They make learning legible, rather than replacing it.

Across this book, age assurance has been presented not as a single method or technology, but as a system shaped by context, trade-offs, governance and responsibility. Chapter 13 brings these threads together by showing how those considerations persist after deployment. Design choices continue to matter. Trade-offs continue to shift. Governance continues to shape outcomes. Assurance continues to require interpretation.

Learning is what holds these elements together across time.

The future of age assurance will not be defined solely by new techniques or tighter rules. It will be shaped by whether systems are treated as static solutions or as evolving practices. Those who expect change, monitor its effects and learn from experience will be better placed to sustain legitimacy in environments that continue to move.

Maturity, in this sense, is not the absence of uncertainty. It is the ability to live with it responsibly.

Chapter 14 – The Future of Age Assurance (and Why It Will Never Be Finished)

14.1 Why age assurance has no final form

Age assurance is often discussed as if it were moving toward completion: a future moment in which the right methods are agreed, the right standards are in place, and the right balance has finally been struck. This framing is intuitive, particularly in technical and regulatory contexts where progress is often equated with settlement.

Age assurance does not behave that way. This is not because the field is immature, nor because the necessary tools have yet to be developed. It is because age assurance exists to operationalise judgements that are themselves unstable. It translates social, legal and ethical expectations into system behaviour, knowing that those expectations will continue to change. As long as this remains true, age assurance cannot converge on a single, final form.

One reason for this is that age assurance is increasingly shaped not only by questions of access and restriction, but by expectations about how services should behave for different age groups. As digital services are designed with children and young people in mind, the role of age assurance begins to shift.

Historically, age assurance has often been framed as a gate: a mechanism for permitting or denying access, enforcing thresholds or satisfying legal constraints. In that framing, maturity might plausibly be imagined as stronger gates, clearer thresholds or more reliable decisions.

Age-appropriate design challenges this assumption.

When services are designed to be accessed by children, age assurance is no longer only about deciding *whether* access should be granted. It becomes part of a broader question about *what kind of experience* should be provided at different stages of development. The function of age assurance shifts away from simple permissions toward enabling differentiated, proportionate and supportive interactions.

This shift has important consequences. It means that age assurance is no longer a discrete decision point that can be "solved" in isolation. It becomes embedded in design choices about content, interaction, defaults, safeguards and escalation. As expectations about age-appropriate behaviour evolve, so too does the role age assurance is asked to play.

These expectations are not fixed. Societal views about childhood, autonomy, protection and participation change over time. New concerns emerge about harm, inclusion or exclusion. Legal frameworks respond unevenly, reflecting cultural context and political judgement. Technical systems are then asked to give practical effect to these evolving balances.

No technical architecture can stabilise this process. Systems can express current judgement with increasing precision, but they cannot fix the values on which that judgement rests. Each attempt to resolve one set of concerns introduces new questions about proportionality, responsibility and experience.

This is why age assurance repeatedly appears to reinvent itself. New approaches do not replace old ones cleanly; they coexist, overlap and reframe familiar debates. What changes is not the existence of tension, but where it is expressed sometimes at the point of access, sometimes in design defaults, sometimes in ongoing interaction rather than initial decision.

The absence of a final form is therefore not a failure of age assurance. It is a consequence of its purpose. Age assurance exists to remain responsive to changing understandings of risk, capability and responsibility, particularly where children are concerned. Any system that claims to have settled these questions permanently is, by definition, already misaligned with the future.

Recognising this is clarifying rather than pessimistic. It removes the pressure to chase definitive solutions and replaces it with a more realistic orientation: one that treats age assurance as a continuing design and governance challenge rather than a problem to be solved once and for all.

In this sense, age assurance is not unfinished because it is incomplete. It is unfinished because its task continues to evolve. Stability, where it exists, is always conditional. Responsibility does not end with deployment, certification or compliance. It persists as expectations, contexts and experiences change.

This understanding provides the foundation for the rest of the chapter. If age assurance has no final form, then the important questions are not about what will replace current approaches, but about what changes over time, what endures beneath that change, and how governance, standards and confidence can remain meaningful without promising closure.

14.2 Why there will be no "end state" for age assurance

The idea that age assurance might one day be "finished" is deeply intuitive. It reflects how many technical and regulatory problems are framed: as journeys from uncertainty to resolution, from experimentation to settlement. In that framing, complexity is temporary, disagreement is transitional and maturity is marked by closure.

Age assurance does not follow that pattern.

This is not because the field is underdeveloped or because the right solution has yet to be discovered. It is because age assurance exists to operationalise judgements that are themselves dynamic. It translates social, legal and ethical expectations into system behaviour, knowing that those expectations will continue to evolve. As long as that remains true, there can be no final architecture, no definitive method and no permanent settlement. This is the concept of age awareness.

At its core, age awareness is tied to how societies understand age, risk and responsibility. These understandings are not fixed. They change as social norms shift, as new harms become visible and as views about autonomy, protection and inclusion are contested and renegotiated. What counts as an acceptable safeguard in one period may later be seen as intrusive. What once felt proportionate may come to feel insufficient. These changes are not anomalies; they are the normal movement of social judgement.

Legal frameworks respond to this movement unevenly. Law often lags social change, sometimes deliberately, sometimes reluctantly. Different jurisdictions codify different balances, reflecting political priorities, cultural history and institutional trust. Age assurance systems are then asked to give practical effect to these balances, even as they remain contested and provisional.

Technical systems cannot close this gap. They can express current judgement with increasing precision, but they cannot stabilise the values that judgement rests upon. When those values change, the systems built to reflect them must change as well. Each attempt at technical resolution therefore creates new questions rather than ending the conversation.

This dynamic is often misunderstood as instability or failure. In reality, it is responsiveness. Age assurance is not meant to freeze social decisions in time. It is meant to support them as they are made, revised and sometimes reversed. The absence of an end state is not a sign that the field is unfinished; it is evidence that it remains connected to the society it serves.

Another reason there can be no end state is that age assurance continually generates new effects. Introducing any form of control reshapes behaviour. Users adapt. Organisations adjust incentives. New edge cases appear. Groups that were previously unaffected become visible. Each intervention alters the environment into which the next intervention must fit.

This is not a design flaw. It is a characteristic of systems that operate at scale in human environments. Every solution answers a question that did not previously exist and in doing so, brings new considerations into view. As harms evolve, so too do expectations about what protection should look like and who should bear its costs.

Attempts to define an end state often underestimate this generative quality. They assume that once the "right" balance is found, it can be maintained. Experience suggests otherwise. What feels settled is usually a moment of alignment between assumptions and reality – one that persists only until conditions shift.

Importantly, recognising the absence of an end state does not mean embracing constant upheaval. Age assurance systems are not perpetually unstable, nor are they endlessly provisional. They can be robust, reliable and widely trusted within the contexts for which they are designed. What they cannot be is permanently final.

This distinction matters. Treating age assurance as unfinished in principle allows stability to be understood as conditional rather than absolute. It encourages responsibility to be seen as ongoing rather than discharged. It frames revision as a normal part of governance rather than as an admission of failure.

The expectation of finality, by contrast, creates its own risks. It encourages overclaim, premature closure and resistance to learning. When systems are presented as settled, emerging concerns are more easily dismissed as anomalies or misuse rather than signals of change. The longer this dismissal persists, the more abrupt and destabilising the eventual reckoning tends to be.

Understanding that there will be no end state is therefore not pessimistic. It is clarifying. It removes the pressure to chase certainty and replaces it with a more realistic orientation: one that values readiness, adaptability and restraint.

In this sense, the future of age assurance is not a destination to be reached but a condition to be navigated. Its unfinished nature is not a weakness to be corrected, but the reason it can remain legitimate as society continues to change.

14.3 What actually changes over time

Discussions about the future of age assurance often give disproportionate attention to visible change. New approaches appear. Interfaces evolve. Responsibility shifts between actors. Assurance moves into new settings or becomes embedded into existing ones. These developments are real and they matter. But they are only part of what changes over time.

To understand how age assurance evolves, it is necessary to distinguish between surface change and structural continuity. Many of the most consequential dynamics in age assurance do not disappear when methods are updated or systems are redesigned. They persist beneath successive waves of innovation, shaping outcomes in ways that are remarkably consistent.

At the surface, age assurance changes in form. How assurance is requested, delivered and experienced evolves with broader patterns of interaction. What once required deliberate engagement may later be folded into routine processes. The points at which users encounter checks move. The degree to which assurance is visible or invisible shifts. These changes influence perception, friction and acceptance, even when the underlying purpose remains the same.

Where assurance sits within larger systems also changes. Responsibilities migrate between organisations. What was once handled locally becomes centralised or vice versa. Assurance may move closer to the user, further away or be mediated through additional layers. Each relocation alters lines of accountability and shapes how failure is experienced and addressed.

These changes can be significant. They affect who is empowered to make decisions, who bears risk and who absorbs the cost of error. Yet they rarely resolve the deeper questions that define the field.

What persists is uncertainty. No matter how assurance is implemented, results remain probabilistic rather than absolute. Borderline cases continue to exist. Contextual judgement cannot be fully eliminated. Decisions still involve trade-offs between competing objectives and those trade-offs are rarely visible to all parties in the same way.

Incentives also remain strikingly stable. Users continue to respond to systems in ways that minimise effort or maximise access. Organisations continue to balance compliance obligations against operational cost, reputational exposure and user satisfaction. Providers continue to optimise for the metrics that matter most to their survival. These behaviours are not aberrations; they are predictable responses to structural conditions.

As a result, many debates that are presented as new are in fact replays of older ones. Questions about proportionality, exclusion, fairness, error tolerance and appeal recur with each change in form. They may be framed differently or raised by different stakeholders, but their substance remains familiar.

This repetition is sometimes mistaken for stagnation. In reality, it reflects the fact that age assurance addresses enduring tensions rather than transient problems. The field revisits similar questions because the underlying constraints have not changed, even as the environment has.

Recognising this continuity has practical value. It tempers the expectation that new approaches will finally settle long-standing concerns. It also provides perspective when familiar anxieties resurface. Rather than asking why progress has failed, it becomes possible to ask how current conditions reshape old challenges and what can be learned from past responses.

At the same time, continuity should not be mistaken for inevitability. While uncertainty, incentives and adaptation persist, how they manifest does change. The distribution of impact shifts. Some groups gain influence while others lose it. New forms of harm become visible and older ones recede. The balance between friction and access is recalibrated, sometimes deliberately, sometimes implicitly.

What changes, then, is not the existence of tension, but where it is felt most strongly. Age assurance does not move from problem to solution; it moves from one configuration of trade-offs to another. Each configuration reflects the priorities, assumptions and constraints of its moment.

Understanding this helps orient expectations about the future. It suggests that attention should be paid less to novelty and more to pattern. The question is not whether age assurance will look different, but which familiar dynamics will reassert themselves under new conditions.

This perspective also explains why claims of radical transformation often disappoint. When surface change is mistaken for structural resolution, the persistence of old problems can feel like failure. When continuity is anticipated, those same problems can be approached with greater realism and patience.

In this sense, the future of age assurance is best understood not as a sequence of breakthroughs, but as a series of adjustments around a stable core of unresolved tensions. Appreciating what actually changes – and what does not – is essential to engaging with that future without either complacency or alarm.

This understanding sets the stage for the uneven landscape ahead: a future in which some forms of convergence occur alongside persistent fragmentation and in which coexistence, rather than uniformity, becomes the dominant condition.

14.4 Convergence, fragmentation and coexistence

If age assurance were driven solely by technical efficiency, it might plausibly converge on a small number of dominant approaches. In practice, its future is shaped by a wider set of forces, many of which pull in different directions. The result is not steady convergence or persistent fragmentation, but a combination of both – alongside long-term coexistence.

Some convergence is already visible and will continue. Shared concepts emerge as experience accumulates. Common language develops around objectives, risks and safeguards. Expectations align sufficiently to allow systems to be compared, discussed and evaluated across organisational and jurisdictional boundaries. This kind of convergence supports communication and coordination, even where agreement remains partial.

Standards contribute to this process by offering reference points rather than prescriptions. They allow actors with different priorities to speak a common language, even when they disagree about outcomes. Over time, this reduces unnecessary misunderstanding and makes differences more explicit rather than less.

Yet convergence has clear limits. Age assurance operates in environments shaped by legal tradition, cultural expectation and institutional trust. These factors vary widely and change slowly. What is considered acceptable, proportionate or legitimate in one setting may be rejected in another, even when the technical means are identical.

Fragmentation persists because it reflects real differences in context rather than a failure of coordination. Jurisdictions adopt different thresholds. Sectors apply different risk tolerances. Organisations make different trade-offs depending on their role, scale and exposure. These variations are not noise to be eliminated; they are signals of plural values.

At the same time, large ecosystems exert a gravitational pull toward standardisation. Scale rewards uniformity. Interoperability reduces friction. Shared infrastructure simplifies procurement and oversight. As age assurance becomes embedded into broader systems, these pressures increase.

Local solutions do not disappear under this pressure. They coexist. Some persist because they better reflect local needs or constraints. Others survive because they serve niches that larger systems do not address. Still others remain because replacing them would introduce costs or risks that outweigh the benefits of alignment.

Interoperability initiatives often sit at the intersection of these forces. They promise connection without uniformity, allowing different approaches to interact without collapsing into a single model. In practice, interoperability reduces some forms of fragmentation while leaving others intact. It aligns interfaces more than values.

This partial resolution can be frustrating for those seeking clarity or closure. Yet it is a realistic reflection of how plural systems evolve. Coexistence is not a transitional state on the way to uniformity; it is the durable condition of a field that serves diverse purposes under different constraints.

Importantly, coexistence does not imply incoherence. Systems can differ while remaining intelligible to one another. Governance can operate across diversity without imposing sameness. Standards and frameworks make this possible by clarifying what is being claimed, under what conditions and with what limitations.

Understanding this landscape helps recalibrate expectations about the future. The presence of multiple approaches does not mean that the field lacks direction. It means that direction is negotiated rather than dictated.

Attempts to force convergence beyond what context allows tend to produce resistance, workaround or superficial compliance. They may simplify oversight in the short term, but they often undermine legitimacy in the longer term by ignoring the reasons diversity exists.

A more resilient future for age assurance accepts unevenness as a fact rather than a flaw. It recognises that stability comes not from eliminating difference, but from managing it openly. Convergence where it supports shared understanding. Fragmentation where it reflects genuine variation. Coexistence as the normal state.

Seen this way, pluralism is not a failure to agree. It is evidence that age assurance remains responsive to the environments in which it operates.

14.5 The ongoing role of standards and certification

As age assurance continues to evolve, standards and certification will remain central to how trust is built, challenged and maintained. Their role, however, is often misunderstood. They are sometimes treated as mechanisms for closure – as tools that settle debate, eliminate uncertainty or guarantee outcomes. In reality, their enduring value lies elsewhere.

Standards do not resolve complexity. They provide structure within it.

In a field characterised by plural approaches and shifting contexts, standards offer a shared vocabulary. They make it possible for different actors to describe what they are doing, what they are claiming and under what conditions those claims hold. This shared frame enables comparison, scrutiny and dialogue, even when agreement on outcomes remains elusive.

Crucially, standards will continue to lag practice – and this is appropriate. Age assurance develops through deployment, feedback and adaptation. Lessons about what matters, where risks emerge and how trade-offs play out are learned in operation, not in abstraction. Standards that attempt to move ahead of practice risk codifying assumptions before they have been tested or narrowing interpretation prematurely.

By consolidating experience rather than predicting it, standards help stabilise understanding without freezing it. They capture what has been learned so far, while leaving room for revision as conditions change. This restraint is not a weakness. It is what allows standards to remain relevant over time.

Certification plays a complementary role. Where standards provide language and structure, certification provides bounded confidence. It allows claims to be assessed against defined criteria under specified conditions. In doing so, it supports trust without pretending to eliminate uncertainty.

This bounded nature is essential. Certification does not assert that a system will behave correctly in all circumstances, nor that it is immune to change. It signals that, at a particular point in time, under particular assumptions, certain properties have been demonstrated. This distinction is often overlooked, yet it is what makes certification compatible with learning and adaptation rather than opposed to it.

As explored in Chapter 12, certification can be misused when it is treated as a guarantee rather than as evidence. The future of age assurance will continue to test this boundary. There will be pressure to over-interpret certification as permanence, especially as systems scale and responsibility becomes more diffuse. Resisting that pressure is part of responsible governance.

Chapter 13 reinforces why this matters. Systems change after deployment. Assumptions drift. Configurations evolve. Without ongoing monitoring and learning, certification risks becoming disconnected from lived behaviour. In this context, standards and certification are not endpoints, but anchors – points of reference that help organisations navigate change without losing sight of declared intent.

Standards also play a subtle but important political role. They provide a forum in which disagreement can be expressed in structured form. They allow competing priorities to be articulated, negotiated and, at times, deferred. In doing so, they support governance across diversity rather than enforcing uniformity.

This function becomes more important, not less, as the field matures. As age assurance becomes more embedded in everyday systems, the need for common reference points increases. Not because everyone agrees, but because disagreement must be intelligible to be managed.

The future will therefore not reduce the importance of standards and certification. It will deepen it. But their contribution should be understood correctly. They do not promise finality. They support continuity. They do not eliminate uncertainty. They make it visible and discussable.

In a domain that will never be finished, this is precisely the role that enduring governance tools must play.

14.6 Why confidence will always be contextual

One of the most persistent hopes attached to the future of age assurance is that confidence will eventually become generalisable: that systems will reach a level of maturity where trust can be assumed, transferred or standardised across contexts. Experience suggests otherwise.

Confidence in age assurance is not a property that systems possess in isolation. It is a relationship between a system, its declared purpose, its operating conditions and the expectations of those affected by its decisions. Change any one of these and confidence must be reassessed.

This is not a limitation of current approaches. It is a structural feature of age assurance itself.

Age-related decisions are inherently contextual. The consequences of error differ widely depending on what is at stake. The tolerance for friction varies depending on who is affected and why. What feels acceptable in one setting may feel disproportionate in another, even if the underlying technical process is identical. Confidence cannot be detached from these judgements and treated as a universal attribute.

Claims that assurance can be made "future-proof" often obscure this reality. They suggest durability independent of circumstance, as though technical robustness alone could insulate systems from changing expectations. In practice, such claims tend to disappoint. When contexts shift – legally, socially or operationally – confidence erodes not because systems have failed, but because their assumptions no longer align with current values.

This misalignment is often experienced as a loss of trust. Yet it is better understood as a signal that the conditions under which confidence was granted have changed. Treating this as failure encourages defensiveness and overclaim. Treating it as a normal feature of responsible governance encourages recalibration instead.

Confidence therefore remains tied to declared use and stated conditions. It depends on clarity about what a system is intended to do, what risks it is designed to manage and what trade-offs it embodies. When these declarations are explicit, confidence can be maintained even as circumstances evolve, because reassessment is expected rather than resisted.

Humility plays a crucial role here. Systems that acknowledge their limits tend to retain trust longer than those that promise too much. By making assumptions visible, they invite scrutiny rather than deflect it. By recognising uncertainty, they avoid the shock that follows unmet certainty.

This does not mean confidence is fragile or fleeting. On the contrary, contextual confidence can be remarkably durable when it is well-governed. It persists because it is continuously earned, not because it is assumed to be permanent.

The future of age assurance will not eliminate the need for judgement about confidence. It will make that judgement more frequent, more distributed and more visible. Systems will operate across multiple contexts, sometimes simultaneously. Confidence will need to be articulated, bounded and revisited, rather than declared once and left untouched.

Understanding this helps recalibrate expectations. It shifts attention away from searching for universally trusted solutions and toward building practices that support informed confidence over time. It reinforces the book's central theme: that trust in age assurance is not produced by certainty, but by clarity, accountability and restraint.

In this light, the persistence of contextual confidence is not a problem to be solved. It is the mechanism through which age assurance remains legitimate as conditions change.

14.7 Risks of overconfidence and premature lock-in

One of the quieter risks shaping the future of age assurance is not technical failure, but success.

When systems appear to work, when complaints are manageable, audits are passed and obligations are met, confidence naturally grows. Over time, that confidence can harden into certainty. Assumptions become embedded. Design choices are treated as settled facts rather than contingent responses to particular conditions.

This is how overconfidence emerges: not through neglect, but through familiarity.

Early success tends to narrow attention. Once a system is seen as effective, scrutiny shifts away from its underlying assumptions and toward maintaining throughput, consistency and compliance. Questions about alternative approaches feel unnecessary. Signals that do not fit existing explanations are more easily dismissed as outliers or misuse.

This dynamic is especially pronounced as systems scale. What works well in limited deployment acquires momentum through repetition. Processes are optimised. Interfaces are streamlined. Dependencies accumulate. Each improvement makes the system more efficient – and more resistant to reconsideration.

Lock-in rarely occurs through explicit decision. It emerges gradually as change becomes costly. Architectural choices constrain future options. Contracts and procurement frameworks reduce flexibility. Organisational knowledge aligns around existing models. Reversing course begins to feel disruptive rather than prudent.

The risk is not that systems stop functioning. It is that they stop being questioned.

Scale amplifies this effect. As reach increases, so does the impact of small design assumptions. Edge cases become common experiences. Informal workarounds harden into standard practice. What was once a tolerable limitation becomes a systemic pattern. Yet the visibility of these effects often lags behind their emergence.

Overconfidence makes this lag harder to detect. When systems are treated as settled, signals of misalignment are interpreted defensively. Concerns are framed as exceptions rather than indicators of change. Learning slows not because information is unavailable, but because it is filtered through expectations of stability.

Premature lock-in also constrains learning across contexts. Approaches optimised for one setting may be extended into others without sufficient recalibration. Success in one domain is taken as evidence of general suitability. The more entrenched the system becomes, the harder it is to acknowledge when those assumptions no longer hold.

Importantly, none of this implies bad faith. Overconfidence is often the by-product of pressure for certainty, accountability and reassurance. Closure feels responsible. Stability feels safe. Declaring systems "settled" simplifies governance and communication.

Yet in a field defined by evolving values and contexts, rigidity introduces fragility. Systems that cannot be questioned without reputational or operational cost become brittle. When misalignment eventually becomes visible, the adjustment required is often abrupt and disruptive.

Reversibility matters precisely because certainty does not last. The ability to revisit assumptions, reconfigure systems and reinterpret evidence is not a sign of weakness. It is a source of resilience. Futures that preserve this flexibility are better able to absorb change without crisis.

Understanding these risks does not require rejecting confidence or stability. It requires recognising that confidence should remain provisional and stability should be understood as conditional. Overconfidence arises when those conditions are forgotten.

The future of age assurance will reward arrangements that leave space for reconsideration – not because failure is expected, but because change is inevitable.

14.8 What Progress Really Looks Like in Age Assurance

If the future of age assurance will never culminate in a final settlement, it becomes necessary to ask what progress actually means in this field.

Progress, in this context, is often misunderstood. It is sometimes equated with technical sophistication, market consolidation or regulatory finality. These developments may occur, but they are poor proxies for maturity. Age assurance does not advance by eliminating complexity, but by becoming better at living with it.

One of the clearest signs of progress is improved articulation of trade-offs. Mature systems are not those that claim to optimise all objectives simultaneously, but those that are explicit about what has been prioritised and why. When trade-offs are acknowledged rather than concealed, decisions become more legible and more accountable.

This clarity changes the quality of debate. Instead of arguing about whether a system is "good" or "bad" in the abstract, stakeholders can engage with concrete questions: whose interests are being protected, whose costs are being borne and under what conditions those choices make sense. Disagreement does not disappear, but it becomes more productive.

Progress also appears in governance. As institutions gain experience, conversations about age assurance tend to become more grounded. The focus shifts from seeking definitive solutions to managing ongoing responsibility. Oversight becomes less about checking boxes and more about understanding behaviour over time. Accountability is framed as a relationship rather than a declaration.

Another marker of progress is the ability to explain decisions clearly. Mature age assurance arrangements recognise that legitimacy depends on explanation, not just performance. Being able to articulate why a particular approach was chosen, what its limits are and how challenges are handled matters as much as technical accuracy.

This explanatory capacity supports trust even when outcomes are contested. Users are more likely to accept decisions they do not like if the reasoning behind them is comprehensible and accessible. Regulators are better able to assess proportionality when assumptions are explicit. Transparency, in this sense, is not a disclosure exercise but a form of respect.

Institutional learning is another dimension of progress. Over time organisations become better at remembering. They document not only what was built, but why choices were made and what risks were anticipated. This memory allows learning to persist through personnel changes and system updates. It reduces the likelihood that known issues reappear as surprises.

More responsible use of standards is part of this maturation. Rather than treating standards as shields against accountability, experienced actors use them as tools for dialogue. They reference frameworks to clarify scope and assumptions, not to deflect scrutiny. Standards become supports for reasoning rather than substitutes for it.

Importantly, progress does not look like the disappearance of disagreement. In age assurance, disagreement is inevitable because values differ and contexts vary. Progress lies in managing that disagreement openly, without overclaim or denial.

From this perspective, the future of age assurance is not a race toward certainty. It is a gradual improvement in how complexity is handled. Systems become easier to question without becoming unstable. Governance becomes more comfortable with provisionality. Confidence becomes better calibrated to context.

This form of progress is quiet. It does not produce dramatic milestones or definitive announcements. Yet it is precisely this kind of maturity that allows age assurance to remain legitimate as conditions continue to change.

By redefining progress in these terms, the field avoids the trap of measuring success by closure. Instead, it measures success by resilience, clarity and the ability to continue learning.

14.9 Looking forward without predicting

When a field has no end state, the temptation to predict its future can become a substitute for certainty. Forecasts offer the comfort of direction, even when their accuracy is doubtful. In age assurance, this temptation is understandable – and misplaced.

Responsible engagement with the future of age assurance does not depend on foresight. It depends on readiness.

Readiness is different from prediction. It does not require knowing which approaches will dominate, which regulatory models will prevail or which configurations will endure. It requires the ability to recognise change when it occurs, to question assumptions without defensiveness and to adapt without treating revision as failure.

This orientation matters because the forces shaping age assurance do not move in straight lines. Social expectations shift unevenly. Legal frameworks respond at different speeds. Organisational incentives change with scale and context. Technical capability advances without resolving underlying value questions. No forecast can reliably integrate these dynamics into a single trajectory.

What can endure is a way of thinking.

Throughout this book, the emphasis has been on how age assurance behaves rather than what it should become. The concepts explored – context of use, trade-offs, governance, failure, learning and accountability – remain applicable regardless of how surface details change. They provide tools for interpretation rather than answers to be memorised.

This is why adaptability outperforms prediction in the long term. Systems and institutions that are comfortable with uncertainty are better able to respond to it. They do not require disruption to justify reconsideration. They do not mistake confidence for permanence. They remain open to challenge without losing coherence.

Good questions matter more than confident answers. Asking how a system behaves under changing conditions is more valuable than asserting what it will do in the future. Asking who bears the consequences of error is more important than claiming optimisation. Asking whether assumptions still hold matters more than declaring success.

Looking forward in this way is not passive. It is an active stance that resists both complacency and alarm. It accepts that age assurance will remain complex without treating complexity as a problem to be solved. It recognises that uncertainty is not a sign of failure, but a condition of responsibility.

14.10 Will we ever solve age assurance?

Age assurance does not succeed because society reaches a settled view about it. There is no moment of collective agreement after which the problem is resolved. Public attitudes toward age assurance evolve through use, resistance, accommodation and revision, shaped as much by everyday experience as by policy debate. Systems persist not because they are universally endorsed, but because they remain tolerable in practice. They are perceived as proportionate, explainable and capable of correction. When that tolerance erodes, technical correctness offers little protection.

This does not mean that age assurance is doomed to instability or perpetual controversy. It means that it must be approached as a practice of judgement rather than a problem of optimisation. Judgement is not guesswork. It is the disciplined exercise of responsibility in conditions where values conflict, evidence is partial and consequences unfold over time.

Throughout this book, the emphasis has been on understanding how age assurance behaves in design, in deployment, in governance and in lived experience. Not to arrive at a definitive answer, but to cultivate a way of thinking that remains useful as circumstances change.

Tools matter. Standards matter. Evidence matters. Certification matters. But none of these replaces responsibility. They support it. They make decisions more legible, trade-offs more visible, and accountability harder to evade. They do not absolve those who rely on them from judgement.

The temptation in complex domains is always to seek closure: to declare systems settled, questions answered, responsibilities discharged. Age assurance resists that impulse and rightly so. Systems that affect access, autonomy and inclusion demand ongoing care, not final declarations.

If this book leaves you less certain about simple answers, that is intentional. But it should also leave you more confident in your ability to engage responsibly with complexity: to ask better questions, to recognise limits and to remain attentive to how age assurance systems behave over time.

Age assurance will continue to evolve, fragment and recombine. That is not a sign that it is failing. It is a sign that it remains connected to its purpose: reducing harm to children, enabling age-appropriate participation and shaping digital systems in ways that improve outcomes for young people and society as a whole.